A SCARLET LETTER HANDBOOK

WADSWORTH GUIDES TO LITERARY STUDY
Maurice Beebe, General Editor

APPROACHES TO *MACBETH*
edited by Jay L. Halio, University of California, Davis

APPROACHES TO *WALDEN*
edited by Lauriat Lane, Jr., University of New Brunswick

A *BENITO CERENO* HANDBOOK
edited by Seymour L. Gross, University of Notre Dame

CONRAD'S *HEART OF DARKNESS* AND THE CRITICS
edited by Bruce Harkness, University of Illinois

CONRAD'S *SECRET SHARER* AND THE CRITICS
edited by Bruce Harkness, University of Illinois

STEPHEN CRANE'S *MAGGIE*: Text and Context
edited by Maurice Bassan, San Francisco State College

·*CRIME AND PUNISHMENT* AND THE CRITICS
edited by Edward Wasiolek, University of Chicago

THE *KING LEAR* PERPLEX
edited by Helmut Bonheim

LITERARY CENSORSHIP: Principles, Cases, Problems
edited by Kingsley Widmer, San Diego State College, and Eleanor Widmer

LITERARY SYMBOLISM: An Introduction to the Interpretation of Literature
edited by Maurice Beebe, Purdue University

MELVILLE'S *BILLY BUDD* AND THE CRITICS
edited by William T. Stafford, Purdue University

OEDIPUS REX: A MIRROR FOR GREEK DRAMA
edited by Albert Cook, State University of New York

THE RIME OF THE ANCIENT MARINER: A HANDBOOK
edited by Royal A. Gettmann, University of Illinois

J. D. SALINGER AND THE CRITICS
edited by William F. Belcher and James W. Lee, North Texas State University

SATIRE: THEORY AND PRACTICE
edited by Charles A. Allen and George D. Stephens, California State College at Long Beach

A *SCARLET LETTER* HANDBOOK
edited by Seymour L. Gross, University of Notre Dame

SUCCESS IN AMERICA
edited by James J. Clark and Robert H. Woodward, San Jose State College

VOLTAIRE'S *CANDIDE* AND THE CRITICS
edited by Milton P. Foster, Eastern Michigan University

ROBERT PENN WARREN'S *ALL THE KING'S MEN*: A Critical Handbook
edited by Maurice Beebe and Leslie Field, Purdue University

WHITMAN THE POET: MATERIALS FOR STUDY
edited by John C. Broderick, Wake Forest College

A
SCARLET LETTER
HANDBOOK

Edited by *Seymour L. Gross*

University of Notre Dame

WADSWORTH PUBLISHING COMPANY, INC.
Belmont, California

Sixth printing, July 1967

L.C. Cat. Card No.: 60-8658

Printed in the United States of America.

Manufactured by American Book-Stratford Press, Inc.

For Elaine

PREFACE

Before the publication of *The Scarlet Letter*, Hawthorne doubted that the novel would achieve much popularity. The extent of his error can be measured by the frequency with which the book is encountered in homes, on bookracks, and in high school and college courses. Indeed, it would be difficult to find a college graduate who has not read the novel. But unlike many other popular books, *The Scarlet Letter* has evoked a great deal of critical comment: lawyers, psychiatrists, journalists, clergymen, not to mention more professionally implicated groups, have felt the desire to record their impressions of the novel in print. The wealth of available material presents a problem to the editor who must choose selections for an anthology of *Scarlet Letter* criticism. To the inevitable objection that some favorite essay is not represented, I can only say, adapting Marvell's line to my own use, had I but time enough and space. . . .

In selecting essays, I have tried to choose the best expressions of as wide a variety of viewpoints as possible. Any approach to the novel which is not included in the anthology (such as the psychoanalytic one) can be found listed in the annotated bibliography of *Scarlet Letter* criticism and scholarship, which makes up Part Four of this volume. The preponderance of selections written in the last two decades is the result of the "close reading" of texts that characterizes much literary criticism of these years. Earlier essays, excellent as many of them are, tend to concern themselves with Hawthorne in general rather than with *The Scarlet Letter* in particular. To facilitate class discussion and to present the materials for study and research in an orderly manner, I have thought it advisable to organize the selections around "problems": theme, character, symbolism, and structure. As such, articles and sections of books have been excerpted to fit into the dominant concern of that part of the anthology in which they appear.

Because this book will presumably be used in conjunction with *The Scarlet Letter* itself, and since most modern editions of the novel have satisfactory introductions, to have written another introduction to the novel would have been to court duplication. I have, instead, used the introduction to discuss Hawthorne's fiction before *The Scarlet Letter*, confining myself for the most part to those stories which seem to me to be earlier explorations of themes found in the novel. The introduction, in brief, is designed to serve as further source material for the reader.

The questions, which comprise Part Three of this book, range from those which can be answered in relatively short papers to those which require full-dress, extended efforts. In every case, however, the questions require both a careful study of the novel and the pertinent criticism in the anthology. Wherever it seemed applicable, the reader has been directed to further readings in the library.

The book is designed to serve several purposes. The organization of questions and essays around certain critical problems makes the book appropriate for research studies, especially where there is a desire to combine research techniques with a study of literature. The wide variety of essays can serve as an introduction to the method of literary criticism in beginning literature classes. The anthology of criticism and the annotated bibliography make this a useful handbook for advanced study of Hawthorne. It is hoped, moreover, that the essays and questions will stimulate class discussion on all levels of instruction.

Since practically all of the critical selections included in the anthology are excerpts, I have taken the liberty of giving them my own titles in order to indicate the nature of their content. I have transcribed the texts as accurately as possible; I have, however, corrected obvious misprints, eliminated footnotes where feasible, and renumbered the remaining ones. The original pagination of the articles is indicated by means of raised brackets in the text. The amount of material omitted from any essay can be ascertained by checking the original pagination (indicated in the brackets) against the complete bibliographical entry at the end of each selection. Whenever a page of the text in its original form ended with a broken word, I have ignored the break and placed the page reference at the end of the complete word. Unspaced ellipses (...) are the original author's; spaced ellipses (. . .) are mine.

I would like to thank Mr. Patrick Barkey and Miss Eileen Conley of the University of Notre Dame library for their gracious efforts in behalf of this book and my colleague, Professor Joseph X. Brennan, for his perceptive reading of the introduction.

CONTENTS

HAWTHORNE'S CHARACTERS: THEIR LIVES AND MEANINGS

SYMBOLISM

STRUCTURE: ARCHITECTURAL AND SYMBOLIC

Part Three

Part Four

ACKNOWLEDGMENTS

I am indebted to the following for permission to reprint material in this handbook:

Accent and the author for permission to reprint selections from *"The Scarlet Letter:* A Reading" by Rudolphe von Abele.

American Literature for permission to reprint excerpts from "The Character of Flame: The Function of Pearl in *The Scarlet Letter"* (XXVII, Jan., 1956) by Anne Marie McNamara; and "Hawthorne's *Scarlet Letter:* 'The Dark Problem of This Life' " (XXVII, March, 1955) by Hugh N. Maclean.

Marius Bewley for permission to reprint excerpts from "Hawthorne and 'The Deeper Psychology.' "

College English and the authors for permission to reprint excerpts from "Hawthorne's Hester" (XIII, March, 1952) by Darrel Abel; "Hawthorne's Symbols *Sotto Voce"* (XX, Jan., 1959) by Sister M. Hilda Bonham; and "Pearl and the Puritan Heritage" (XII, March, 1951) by Chester E. Eisinger.

Columbia University Press for permission to reprint excerpts from *The Eccentric Design* by Marius Bewley.

ELH for permission to use excerpts from "Hawthorne's Pearl: Symbol and Character" by Darrel Abel; and " 'From the Innermost Germ,' the Organic Principle in Hawthorne's Fiction" by Roy R. Male. Reprinted from *ELH,* XVIII, 54-61, and XX, 222-228.

Harvard University Press for use of excerpts reprinted by permission of the publishers from Hyatt H. Waggoner, *Hawthorne: A Critical Study,* Cambridge, Mass.: The Belknap Press of Harvard University Press. Copyright 1955 by The President and Fellows of Harvard College.

Hendricks House for permission to reprint an extract from the Introduction to *The Scarlet Letter and Selected Prose Works* by Gordon Roper.

Henry Holt and Company, Inc., for permission to reprint an excerpt from *Four Great Novels* by Raymond W. Short, copyright 1946.

The Modern Language Association of America for permission to reprint an excerpt from "Pearl: 1850-1955" by Barbara Garlitz.

Modern Language Quarterly for use of an excerpt from "Hawthorne and the Chain of Being" by James W. Mathews, reprinted by permission of the author and the University of Washington, publisher, and Edward G. Cox, managing editor.

New England Quarterly and the author for permission to reprint excerpts from "Form and Content in *The Scarlet Letter"* (XVII, March, 1944) by John C. Gerber.

Oxford University Press, Inc., for use of excerpts from *American Renaissance* by F. O. Matthiessen. Copyright 1941 by Oxford University Press, Inc., New York. Reprinted by permission.

The Partisan Review and the author for permission to reprint a quotation from "The Seriousness of Robert Penn Warren" (Spring, 1959) by Alfred Kazin.

Philological Quarterly for permission to reprint an excerpt from "The Devil in Boston" by Darrel Abel.

Philosophical Library for permission to reprint an excerpt from *American Literature and the Dream* by F. I. Carpenter.

Charles Scribner's Sons for use of an excerpt from "God and Man in New England" by Joseph Schwartz, reprinted with the permission of Charles Scribner's Sons from *American Classics Reconsidered,* edited by Harold C. Gardiner, S.J. © 1958 Charles Scribner's Sons.

Charles Scribner's Sons for use of an excerpt reprinted with the permission of Charles Scribner's Sons from *Americans,* edited by Stuart Sherman, copyright 1922, Charles Scribner's Sons; renewal copyright 1950, Ruth Sherman.

William Sloane Associates, Inc., for permission to reprint an excerpt from *Nathaniel Hawthorne* by Mark Van Doren, copyright 1949.

University of California Press for permission to use an excerpt from "Hawthorne's Dimmesdale: Fugitive from Wrath" by Darrel Abel, reprinted from *Nineteenth-Century Fiction,* Vol. 11, No. 2, published by the University of California Press.

The University of Chicago Press for use of selections reprinted from *Symbolism and American Literature* by Charles Feidelson, Jr., copyright 1953 by the University of Chicago; and from *The American Adam* by R. W. B. Lewis, © by the University of Chicago, 1955.

University of Florida Press for use of excerpts from *Hawthorne's Faust: A Study of the Devil's Archetype* by William Bysshe Stein. Copyright 1953, University of Florida Press, publisher. Used by permission.

The University of North Carolina Press for permission to reprint an excerpt from *Hawthorne the Artist: Fine-Art Devices in Fiction* by Leland Schubert, copyright 1944 by The University of North Carolina Press, Chapel Hill, North Carolina.

University of Oklahoma Press for permission to reprint an excerpt from *Hawthorne's Fiction: The Light and the Dark* by Richard H. Fogle, copyright 1952 by the University of Oklahoma Press.

University of Texas Press and the author for permission to reprint an excerpt from *Hawthorne's Tragic Vision* by Roy R. Male, copyright 1957.

PART ONE

PROLOGUE TO *THE SCARLET LETTER:* HAWTHORNE'S FICTION TO 1850

what's past is prologue—SHAKESPEARE

PROLOGUE

One legend has it that when Hawthorne was dismissed for political reasons from his position in the Salem Custom House and went home and dejectedly told his wife the bad news, she brightly answered, "Now you can write your romance." Whether or not Sophia was such a miracle of cheerfulness, eight months later, on February 3, 1850, Hawthorne had completed *The Scarlet Letter*—America's first literary masterpiece and one of the perennial classics of the western world. In one sense, as Anthony Trollope remarked, the novel was in Hawthorne to write (the speed of composition attests to that). But in another, the dominant concerns of the novel—sin, love, isolation, to name the most prominent—had been explored in various stories among the hundred or so tales and sketches Hawthorne wrote before coming to the composition of his finest achievement.

Not all of Hawthorne's stories are valuable, however. Some reflect the need to cater to the taste for what he called stories of "evident design" in which "the moral [is] plain and manifest," the kind of story, he once told his wife, the public much preferred. Some represent a failure of the creative imagination. But it is to the early fiction that we must turn for at least a partial accounting for what one early critic called "the miracle" of *The Scarlet Letter*.

I

"No man need be perplexed . . . with theological problems of original sin, origin of evil, predestination and the like. These never ...darkened across any man's road who did not go out of his way to seek them. These are the soul's mumps and measles. . . ." So pronounced Ralph Waldo Emerson in his essay, "Spiritual Laws." The true function of the creative artist, according to Emerson's "The Poet," is to "re-attach things to nature and the Whole," in the process of which he "disposes very easily of the most disagreeable facts." In brief, nothing is really tragic if seen from the perspective of the harmonizing imagination. No doubt it was because Hawthorne's fiction explored the mysterious ambiguities and tragic possibilities that often attend the moral life that Emerson, the chief oracle of Transcendentalism, felt that it had no "inside" to it and was "not good for anything."

From one point of view much of Hawthorne's fiction can be read

2

as a commentary (whether intentional or not does not really matter) on the cosmic optimism of Transcendentalism, the dominant philosophical movement of his time and place. To the Transcendentalist, experience (in the introspective sense of that word) suggested a universe essentially benevolent and coherent. Moreover, man himself, an infinitely perfectible creature, could enter into a harmonious communion with Nature once he had freed himself of the twin coils of rationalism and dogma and learned to listen reverently to the holy music of the "Spirit of his spirit." The Transcendentalist's "pilgrimage," in the words of one of its adherents, was "from the idolatrous world of creeds and rituals to the temple of the living God in his soul."[1] Nor would this pilgrimage encounter any insuperable barriers or restricting bypaths, such as are to be found in one of Hawthorne's favorite books, Bunyan's *Pilgrim's Progress*. For evil as a root condition, an inevitably limiting factor, did not exist. Those imperfections which seemed to blemish the world were either a passing illusion—"In vain produced, all rays return; / Evil will bless and ice will burn"—as Emerson expresses it in "Uriel," or a subjective delusion: "The evils of the world are such only to the evil eye" ("The Poet"). In such a world, to quote Channing again, one need only "trust, dare, and be [and] infinite good is ready for your asking."

Insofar as Hawthorne understood Transcendentalism to place its faith in the natural virtue of man and the "optimism of nature," he felt it to be a rather risky basis for moral commitment. But another aspect of the movement—its tendency to vaporous mysticism—also disturbed Hawthorne, though not so intensely. The same impulse which led him in "The Gentle Boy" to condemn that species of religion which "violated the duties of the present life" by fixing its attention wholly on the next, led him to be extremely dubious of the "transcendentalizing" of experience, especially when the "visions" turned out to be couched in what seemed to him to be fantastically cloudy verbiage.

Hawthorne would probably have agreed with Poe that the Transcendentalists "hint everything—assert nothing." In "The Celestial Railroad" Hawthorne's description of Giant Transcendentalist, who fattens up his victims "with . . . smoke, mist, moonshine . . . and sawdust," is a kind of grotesque extension of Poe's remark:

. . . as to his form, his features, his substance, and his nature generally, it is a chief peculiarity of this huge miscreant that neither he for himself, nor anybody for him, has ever been able to describe them. . . . we caught a hasty glimpse of him, looking somewhat like an ill-proportioned figure, but

---

1 William Henry Channing, "A Participant's Definition," in Perry Miller, ed., *The American Transcendentalists* (Anchor Books, New York, 1957), p. 37.

considerably more like a heap of fog and duskiness. He shouted after us, but in so strange a phraseology that we knew not what he meant. . . .

The same kind of insubstantiality characterizes the actual Transcendentalists whom Hawthorne saw flocking to Emerson's "earthly abode" in Concord. They seem to Hawthorne, as he puts it in "The Old Manse," "visionaries" who wander lost in the hazy labyrinths "of their self-involved bewilderment"; their "system, at first air, had finally imprisoned them in an iron framework." The humor here is something less than funny: what begins as harmless theorizing ends as a life-excluding prison. (In "The Christmas Banquet" Hawthorne mentions an old clergyman who, having yielded "to the speculative tendency of the age," had renounced his ancient faith "and wandered into a cloud region, where everything was misty and deceptive, ever mocking him with a semblance of reality, but still dissolving when he flung himself upon it for support and rest.")

Even though Hawthorne admired Emerson as "a poet of deep beauty and austere tenderness," in Emerson's Transcendental impulse to leap from the thing to its essence,[2] Hawthorne thought he detected a threat to the substantial texture of experience itself, a casting away of the gifts of this world. In his *American Notebooks,* he calls Emerson "that everlasting rejector of all that is, and seeker for he knows not what," a "mystic, stretching his hand out of cloud-land, in vain search for something real." Hawthorne concedes that Emerson may be "a great searcher for facts; but they seem to melt away and become unsubstantial in his grasp." Small wonder, then, that when Hawthorne learned that some Englishmen had a taste for Transcendental literature, he mused, in his *English Notebooks,* that such a "vein of literary taste does not augur very great things." Fog, mist, clouds, vapor—these are the images that come immediately to Hawthorne's mind when he contemplates Transcendentalism, and they clearly indicate the nature of this facet of his distrust.

In his "Hawthorne and His Mosses" (1850), Herman Melville remarks "this great power of blackness" in Hawthorne, which "derives its force from its appeals to that Calvinistic sense of Innate Depravity and Original Sin, from whose visitations, in some shape or other, no deeply thinking man is always and wholly free. For, in certain moods, no man can weigh this world without throwing in something, somehow like Original Sin, to strike the uneven balance." Although this prob-

---

2 For example, in "Fate," Emerson writes that "There is no need for foolish amateurs to fetch me to admire a garden of flowers, or a sun-gilt cloud, or a waterfall, when I cannot look without seeing splendor and grace. How idle to choose a random sparkle here or there, when the indwelling necessity...discloses the central intention of Nature to be harmony and joy."

ably tells us more about Melville than about Hawthorne, it can nevertheless serve as an entrance point into that portion of Hawthorne's fiction which is informed by the concept of original sin.

Hawthorne, at least in the life of his creative imagination,[3] clearly saw life as tragic: there *was* an "uneven balance" in the world, some radical imperfection inhabiting both the will of man and nature, which the uneasy heart had to learn to endure if moral poise and the life of significance were to be achieved. So far from being merely the "mumps and measles" of the soul—passing childhood diseases—the tragic imperfections of life are the *donnée* of experience, which man can ignore only at his peril. But a qualification ought immediately to be made. Although he had a greater respect for the Calvinist tradition in religion than he did for the religious liberalism of his day, and was proud of what he chose to call the Puritan traits in his own personality, Hawthorne was no more a Calvinist, dogmatically speaking, than he was a Transcendentalist. Moreover, in such stories as "The Gentle Boy," "Endicott and the Red Cross," "The Maypole of Merry Mount," and in his personal remarks about his Puritan ancestors, such as are to be found in "Main Street" and "The Custom House," Hawthorne clearly exhibits a horror at the inhumanity that the Puritans were capable of for the "sake" of their faith. Never a church-goer after his childhood (he once described his Sundays in church as "the frozen purgatory of my childhood"), Hawthorne, despite what one takes to be a belief in a God and after-life, was actually as free of precise religious formulation as any religious liberal of his day. What attracted him to Calvinism, as Herbert Schneider has pointed out, was not its claim of divine sanction, but the truth which he discerned behind the Calvinist symbols.[4]

The moral shadows in Hawthorne's fiction are never cast in the form of theological problems; unlike Melville, Hawthorne seems never to have grappled with the nature and existence of God. In his writing, the emphasis is always on the dangers, difficulties, contradictions, and paradoxes involved in man's meeting the conditions that exist—the posited metaphysical concepts—rather than on the value, sanction, or

---

3 The distinction between man and writer is especially interesting in the case of Hawthorne. As a man—if we may trust the testimony of his wife, friends and children—he was singularly free of the dark doubts and fears that criss-cross his fiction. His marriage to Sophia Peabody, herself a sort of fellow-traveler Transcendentalist who thought Emerson "the greatest man in the world," was extremely happy, even idyllic. And when Hawthorne's son Julian read his father's fiction as a grown man, he was shocked at its sombreness, for nothing he remembered of his father would have prepared him for his father's fiction. (The student who wishes to learn more of Hawthorne's life should consult Randall Stewart, *Nathaniel Hawthorne* [New Haven, 1948], the most reliable biography of Hawthorne to date.)

4 Herbert W. Schneider, *The Puritan Mind* (New York, 1930), p. 262.

ultimate reality of these conditions. In short, Hawthorne was a moral realist rather than a moralist.

The concept of Original Sin, as R. W. B. Lewis has recently reminded us, can easily degenerate into nothing more than the image of an unredeemably depraved soul shivering "hopelessly somewhere in the void."[5] It is never so in Hawthorne's fiction. Even though he could say in his notebook that "There is evil in every human heart," and in his speculative sketch, "Fancy's Show Box," that every "heart has surely been polluted by the flitting phantoms of iniquity," there are no figures in Hawthorne who exist merely as sinners on their way into the hands of an angry God. What excites Hawthorne's imagination are the moral and psychological possibilities inherent in a character's initial confrontation of some evil within himself or in the world about him, for which his existing resources have not prepared him.

"My Kinsman, Major Molineux" (1832) is a good illustration. The story concerns a country youth who has come to the city to make his way under the influential patronage of his kinsman, Major Molineux. Although he has never been to the city before, Robin, as he is significantly called, is incredibly self-confident, utterly undaunted by the fact that he is lost in the dark of night and has no idea "whither to direct his steps." But his trek through the "strange and desolate streets" turns into a nightmare: not only will no one tell him where his kinsman lives, but he is humiliated, threatened, assaulted, and almost enticed into a harlot's house. At first he is unassailably innocent and sanguine; in time, however, he becomes disturbed enough to attempt to retreat psychologically from "this evening of ambiguity" to the safe simplicity of his Eden in the woods. But his nostalgic reverie proves unsubstantial in the face of his new, but as yet unperceived, commitment: "Then he saw them [his family] go in at the door; and when Robin would have entered also, the latch tinkled into its place, and he was excluded from his home."

It is a markedly altered Robin who calls to the next passerby. This stranger is willing to talk to him, for, symbolically speaking, Robin's fatuous self-reliance had to be discarded before adult communication could take place. The brief bit of dialogue between man and boy stands as the coda for the theme of the story. When Robin complains of the noise in the street, the man explains to him that "you must not expect all the stillness of your native woods here in our streets." To Robin's opinion that the uproar must be caused by at least a thousand persons, the man replies, "May not a man have several voices...as well as two complexions?" The climax of the story—Robin's meeting with

---

[5] R.W.B. Lewis, "Hold on Hard to the Huckleberry Bushes," *Sewanee Review,* LXVII (Summer, 1959), 464.

his kinsman—is also the climax of Robin's moral life. A nightmarish procession streams down the street, led by the ghoulish "double-faced fellow" whom Robin had met before; in its midst he sees his uncle— the symbol of all his bright dreams—tarred and feathered. Shattered, Robin clings to a post, his face pale and his eyes blank, wanting only to be shown the way home. But the kindly stranger lays a hand on the boy's shoulder and assures him that "you may rise in the world without the help of your kinsman, Major Molineux."

Robin has taken what for Hawthorne was the necessary night journey into the heart of experience, and a light has gone out of the world for him. But, as the last line of the tale indicates, this need not be the end of life: it can be the beginning. And yet this is not all; for although Hawthorne clearly insists that the life of moral poise cannot be achieved until innocence becomes experience, there is still a lingering sense of sadness that this should be so. There *is*, after all, something fetching about a robin. The same kind of ambivalence in attitude is to be found in "The Maypole of Merry Mount," where the necessity for "silken" joy to give way to "iron" moral realism is viewed with an aching heart.

The night journey may, however, take a different form, as it does in what is probably Hawthorne's most famous story, "Young Goodman Brown" (1835). Like Robin, Brown also voyages from a place of security (here Salem) to an ambiguous piece of moral geography—the forest. Just as Robin was certain he could manage the city on his own terms, so is Brown confident that he will "tarry away" but one night from his wife Faith, and then return to "cling to her skirts and follow her to heaven." But in the forest Brown encounters a vision of corruption so overpowering—he discovers that his family, the religious of Salem, and, most crushingly, his wife, all have or have had communion with evil—that in a paroxysm of despair he cries out, "There is no good on earth; and sin is but a name. Come, devil; for to thee is this world given." The deeply distrustful and desperate man that emerges from the forest has been initiated not into experience but into despair. Brown has not come to terms with the serpent in the garden of the world—he has been hypnotized by it; and in his spiritually blasted vision, sunrise is sunset, Faith is Distrust, Salem is Sodom. Because Brown refuses to believe in the reality of the Faith who skips lovingly towards him in the morning, but only in the Faith he had seen in the forest in the night, his journey into the "midnight of the moral world" stretches to the edge of eternity: "they carved no hopeful verse upon his tombstone, for his dying hour was gloom."

"The Minister's Black Veil" (1836) explores another possible consequence of the night journey. Parson Hooper has made such a voyage —though here, unlike in the two stories just discussed, we do not watch him make it—and has emerged on a sunny Sabbath morning wearing a piece of black crepe before his face. We are never to know whether the veil symbolizes an initiation into the dark mystery of life caused by an actual sin, such as is the case with Reuben Bourne in "Roger Malvin's Burial," or the sorrow that comes of having been vouchsafed an image of life's negative capabilities, as in "Young Goodman Brown." It does not matter that the veil remains always "an ambiguity of sin or sorrow," for what interests Hawthorne here is not the origin of the veil, but its effect on the community. Parson Hooper, unlike Brown, is not sin-crazed: in everything except the donning of the veil he is still the same devoted priest and loving man. But society, not wanting to face the truth about the human condition which the veil symbolizes, isolates him from the community. To accept him with the veil is to accept themselves on terms which they find repellent; to "know" Parson Hooper is to make the night journey themselves, and this they are not prepared to do.

The tragedy of the failure of love, which is implied at the end of "Young Goodman Brown," is here made more prominent. Accurately predicting the "miserable obscurity" into which his symbolic act is to consign him, Hooper pleads with Elizabeth, his betrothed, not to leave him: "It is but a mortal veil—it is not for eternity. O! You know not how lonely I am, and how frightened, to be alone behind my black veil." But she cannot accept him on these terms: her love is overwhelmed by the terrors that the veil "shadows forth," and she leaves the minister to a life that is connected to the lives of other men only in their "mortal anguish," never in their "health and joy."

Although Hawthorne posits love as the transcendent value (he once wrote his wife that only it can make us partake of reality), he never minimizes the difficulty of loving in a fallen world. After all, Brown did see his wife in the forest, and Elizabeth understandably interprets Hooper's refusal to take off the veil as a failure of his love for her. The barriers to love are even more formidable for Giovanni Gasconti in "Rappaccini's Daughter" (1844), who falls in love with a girl, Beatrice, who, through her father's scientific experiments, has become physically poisonous to other mortals. Although in love, Giovanni becomes, understandably enough, obsessed with Beatrice's lethal touch—which Hawthorne presents unequivocally and which probably constitutes the story's chief weakness. Spurred on by the scientific materialist, Baglioni, Giovanni presses an antidote on Beatrice which causes her death.

The story presents many difficulties, but its central intention is, I believe, clear. The tragedy of "Rappaccini's Daughter" is not that Beatrice should have such a terrifyingly dual nature ("though my body be nourished with poison, my spirit is God's creature"), but that Giovanni "had not a deep heart" and was, at the crucial moment, incapable of rising to the demands of love. In this sense, as the dying Beatrice tells him, there was more poison in him than in her. Had he the truly loving heart, and not merely "that semblance of love that flourishes in the imagination," then he would have seen that it was not the purely malignant purple shrub, but the shattered fountain from which gushed pure water (both of which are in Rappaccini's garden) that symbolized Beatrice. Had he understood this, then might love have transformed this "Eden of poisonous influences" into that inner sphere of happiness, which, for Hawthorne, is all of Paradise that is vouchsafed us in this world.

Like Brown, Elizabeth, and Giovanni, Aylmer in "The Birthmark" (1842) is also confronted with the problem of loving that which is made up of good and evil. But here the emphasis falls not so much on the consequences of the failure of love to respond adequately to the mysterious paradox of the beautiful and the blasted, as on the tragic waste of not accepting the limitations of the conditions of love.

Soon after his marriage, Aylmer, a famous scientist, becomes preoccupied with a tiny birthmark on his wife's cheek. The more conscious he becomes of his wife's beauty, the more distressed he is by the blemish, until it takes on the metaphysical proportions of the "visible mark of earthly imperfection"—which, of course, is what it is symbolically in the story. However misguided is Aylmer's premise that perfection is possible in this state, his desire to disengage his love from the tentacles of fallibility is at least partially noble. Even his wife, who is destroyed by Aylmer's attempt to remove the birthmark, can find it in herself to say, "Do not repent that with so high and pure a feeling, you have rejected the best the earth could offer." But Georgiana's forgiveness does not constitute absolution. Though betrayed by his finer impulses, Aylmer still stands condemned for his monstrous confusion of love and perfection. Hawthorne acknowledges the visionary grandeur of trying to transcend the "gross fatality of earth," but reminds us—perhaps ruefully—that infinity cannot be crammed into a man's head without cracking it, nor can love be refined to perfection without immolating it.

Although other Hawthorne stories address themselves to what Gerard Manley Hopkins called "the blight man was born for," the stories here briefly discussed perhaps adequately indicate something of the range of Hawthorne's imaginative investigations along these lines. Nowhere does he simplify. The night journey may be necessary to the moral life, but it is difficult and painful; and man can hardly be blamed (from the humane point of view) if he refuses the light that is darkness, or takes the darkness as the all in all. And if it is only love that can reconcile us to and transform the shattered fountain that is human nature, it is because the love is human that it wants to pierce the veil, neutralize the poison, and eradicate the birthmark.

II

Hawthorne's preoccupation with the isolated individual pervades the bulk of his work. Professor Randall Stewart is surely correct in maintaining that this theme "bears a closer relationship than any other to [Hawthorne's] own life."[6] Writing to Henry Wadsworth Longfellow in 1837, after having spent twelve relatively solitary years learning his craft in his study ("that dismal chamber" he called it somewhere else), he said:

By some witchcraft or other—for I cannot assign any reasonable why and wherefore—I have been carried apart from the main current of life, and find it impossible to get back again. . . . I have secluded myself from society; and yet I never meant any such thing, nor dreamed what sort of life I was going to lead. I have made a captive of myself and put me in a dungeon; and now I cannot find the key to let myself out. . . . there is no fate in this world so horrible as to have no share in either its joys or sorrows. For the last ten years I have not lived, but only dreamed about living.

Hawthorne did, however, manage "to get back again": the publication of *Twice-Told Tales* in 1837, his position in the Boston Custom House the following year, his brief sojourn at Brook Farm in 1841, his marriage to Sophia Peabody in 1842—all these enabled him "to open an intercourse with the world." But the spectre of the isolated heart haunted his fiction both before and after his release from "the haunted chamber."

Hawthorne's fiction is studded with figures who through some quirk, defect, or perversity find themselves doomed to exist outside "the magnetic chain of humanity." (It is true, of course, that the characters discussed in the first section of this introduction are also isolated, but their isolation is seen as a consequence of a larger issue, not as the central issue itself.) In "Wakefield" (1835), for example, Hawthorne chronicles the vagaries of Wakefield, who, for no discernible reason, suddenly leaves his family to live down the street for twenty years. The momentary whim (Wakefield had planned but a brief absence) stretches into two decades because, as Hawthorne spells it out, "by stepping aside for a moment, a man exposes himself to a fearful risk of losing his place forever." Similarly, the central figure in "The Village Uncle" (1835) "wandered out of the real world and got into its shadow, where . . . he hardly knew if he lived, or only dreamed of living." More terrible is the figure of Gervayse Hastings in "The Christmas Banquet" (1844), who, constitutionally incapable of feeling, lives and dies in the prison of his icy heart.

---

6 Nathaniel Hawthorne, *The American Notebooks*, ed. Randall Stewart (New Haven, 1932), p. lxviii.

The isolation that comes of quirk or defect appears in Hawthorne's fiction more as notations in abnormal psychology than as dramatic embodiment. If we may judge the thought by its result, then the isolation that is the result of some perversion would seem to have more fully engaged Hawthorne's imagination. The sundering of family ties, the distortion of the religious impulse, unrealistic ambition, aristocratic or intellectual pride are all not only socially destructive forces in Hawthorne's fiction, but modes of self-banishment (and hence self-destruction) as well.

In a very early tale, "The Hollow of the Three Hills" (1830), a woman comes to a witch in the hollow of three hills to learn what has befallen the family she has deserted. The three "visions" which the witch conjures up show the woman her grieving parents, her now insane husband, and the funeral of her child. More important than the melodramatic depiction of the wages of sin is the poetic evocation of the isolation in which the woman's desertion has imprisoned her. Having severed her connection with significant reality, she exists now only in the decayed and desiccated "hollow," connected to the eternal verities of love and family (symbolized by the three hills) by means of illusion; and the cold wind that whips through the hollow, as Marius Bewley has pointed out, is really the cold tremor of the hopeless heart.[7]

How the religious impulse can also lead to moral isolation Hawthorne saw quite clearly. Because Catherine in "The Gentle Boy" (1832), pursues what she conceives of as the one pure faith with "unbridled fanaticism" and without any regard for human ties, she turns herself into a moral monstrosity, mistaking monomania for martyrdom. Similarly, Richard Digby in "The Man of Adamant" (1837), leaves the salutary "sunshine" of his community to hew for himself a "tabernacle" in the sunless wilderness, where he can pray free of "the sinful supplications of the multitude." Isolated in his "tomb-like den," Digby becomes so morally perverted that he believes his situation superior to Heaven itself, for above "there would be angels to disturb him." Having removed himself from "all human...sympathies," Digby becomes physically what he already is spiritually: stone. And, finally, one must mention the Shakers, a celibate religious sect dedicated to the extinction of the human race, about whom Hawthorne wrote two stories, "The Canterbury Pilgrims" (1833), and "The Shaker Bridal" (1838). The Shakers can well stand as the *reductio ad horrendum* in Hawthorne's fiction of the religious impulse gone awry through a withdrawal from the health-giving human continuum.

Less stark but still serious is Hawthorne's concern with the isolation attendant upon ambition's search for some misty grail, symbolized

---

[7] Marius Bewley, *The Eccentric Design* (New York, 1959), p. 145.

in "The Great Carbuncle" (1837), by a fantastic gem which probably does not even exist, and which men pursue at the expense of everything significant.[8] In "The Threefold Destiny" (1838), Ralph narrowly escapes a life of cold futility when he discovers that his quest for a Great Love (he would recognize her by a carbuncle she'd be wearing), Position, and an "extensive influence . . . over his fellow creatures" is to be realized in his own home town, though in a far humbler form than he had originally projected it. The Ambitious Guest, in the story of that name (1835), does not fare as well. Driven by a nebulous desire "not to be forgotten in the grave," this significantly nameless young man wanders rootlessly over the face of the earth. Although he defines his ambition as "a beam" by which posterity will "trace the brightness of his footsteps," Hawthorne depicts it symbolically as a lifeless, cold, "abstracted reverie." His anonymous and unremarked death in an avalanche is the appropriate finish to a life that was anonymous and unremarked anyway.

Pride is clearly the most terrible form of isolation to be found in Hawthorne's fiction. Whereas there are instances of familial violation, religious distortion, and misty ambition being righted enough so that the figures in their grip are enabled to re-enter the life stream, the isolation of pride seems to have been to Hawthorne an irremediable condition. But pride, when Hawthorne comes to inspect it in his fiction, throws up some striking ambiguities in the form of human complexity that may have been hidden from his purely abstract view of the matter.

The story in which aristocratic pride is most clearly focused is "Lady Eleanore's Mantle" (1838). With a reverence for her aristocratic blood that is "hardly less than a monomania," Eleanore sets "herself above the sympathies of our common nature." When a love-crazed young commoner, Jervase Helwyse, prostrates his body for her to walk on, she hesitates, "as if doubting whether the young man were worthy of the weight of her footstep." At a ball given in her honor, she stands aloof with the "scorn of one whose spirit held itself too high to participate in the enjoyment of other souls," and draws her mantle about her as an insulation against the "mob of guests." This mantle, the symbol of aristocratic pride, it turns out, is the source of a smallpox epidemic

---

8 "The Artist of the Beautiful" (1844) would seem to be an exception. In this story the hero is forced to isolate himself from society in order to create the Ideal. It may be an exaggeration to say with Professor Von Abele that about "Warland's task clings an odor of impiety, one had almost said of blasphemy" ("Baby and Butterfly," *Kenyon Review*, 15 [Spring, 1953], 285); but there are indications in the tale that the moral risks involved in this kind of withdrawal are immense. Moreover—and here is the fundamental ambiguity—the isolated artist must have enough faith in himself to stand up to the whole world; but this is a paradoxical requisite, for the "ideal artist" must then "possess a force of character that seems hardly compatible with its delicacy."

that strikes the city; and the moral isolation of the haughty heart is physically objectified in Eleanore's sitting alone in an empty room, a heap of blasted mortality. But the story contains a modifying counter-statement. For all its social and moral deadliness, pride has its fascinations for those most apt to suffer from it, as Eleanore recognizes when she says over Jervase's body, "When men seek only to be trampled upon, it were a pity to deny them a favor so easily granted—and well deserved!" More telling still is the townspeople's reaction to the act of "hereditary pride trampling on human sympathies and kindred nature." They break out into "a simultaneous acclamation of applause [because] so essential did pride seem to the existence of such a creature." Our "common nature," which aristocratic pride violates, is seen to be implicated in an interacting guilt. As Hawthorne says through Dr. Clarke, the tale's raissoneur, whose wisdom is "a deep sense of human weakness," "Thus man doth ever to his tyrants."

Even more ambiguous is "Ethan Brand" (1850), whose central figure is the apotheosis of intellectual pride in Hawthorne's shorter fictions. Intellectual pride, which Hawthorne defined in his notebook as "a want of love and reverence for the Human Soul," which leads one to pry into the "dark depths" of the human heart, "not with a hope or purpose of making it better, but from a cold philosophical curiosity," was for Hawthorne the Unpardonable Sin—the title under which "Ethan Brand" was originally published.[9]

Although when we first meet Brand he is already self-exiled to the terrible island of his pride, he began his quest for the Unpardonable Sin (which he finally finds in himself), with a "love and sympathy" for the human heart, even when he found it to be conditioned by moral corruption. In time, however, Brand's pride in his intellectual attainments usurps the sympathetic love with which he had begun his search and renders him capable of having "wasted, absorbed, and perhaps annihilated" the soul of another human being. Although Hawthorne explicitly tells us that when Brand "lost his hold on the magnetic chain of humanity," he became a "fiend," he is also at pains to show us that not only is Brand isolated from other men by the nature of his sin, but by the vulgar littleness of the creatures who inhabit the world of "Ethan Brand" as well. In contrast to the tavern revellers with their "vulgar modes of thought and feeling" or to Bartram, that "obtuse, middle-aged clown," Brand's demonic intellectual pride takes on, almost inadvertently, a heroic cast. To be sure, Brand's final words, the

---

9 When Sophia thought about taking a spiritualist cure for her physical maladies, Hawthorne warned her against it. "The view which I take of the matter [he wrote her] is caused by no want of faith in mysteries, but from a deep reverence of the soul, and of the mysteries which it knows within itself, but never transmits to the earthly eye or ear."

index of the hopeless isolation of his pride—"Freely, were it to do again, would I incur the guilt!"—freezes the blood. But Bartram's epitaph over the marbleized remains of Brand (who has thrown himself into the lime-kiln)—"taking all the bones together, my kiln is half a bushel richer for him"—is not without its own kind of horror.

III

The foregoing discussion of the themes of sin and isolation as they manifest themselves in Hawthorne's fiction to 1850 cannot, nor is meant to, serve as a comprehensive survey of his literary production to 1850. Some of the airy, shadowless facets of his imagination have not been touched upon. The justification for concentrating on the dark half of the truth, to use Woodberry's phrase, is that these introductory remarks are meant to serve as a prologue to *The Scarlet Letter,* which is, in Hawthorne's own words "positively a hell-fired story," "and diversified no otherwise than by turning different sides of the same dark idea to the reader's eye."

PART TWO

AN ANTHOLOGY OF *SCARLET LETTER* CRITICISM

*A moral tragedy cannot be epitomized: its excitement is in its subtleties of observation, its accuracy of discrimination, its accumulated perception of issues and dilemmas.—*HERBERT READ

*Even if [the critic] is not an esthetician or philosopher, but simply a sensitive intelligence responding directly to works of art, his general point of view, though he may often forget it, serves as his formal code, his landmark—in actual practice, his way of defining his total experience to himself. This definition may not serve him in specific cases; the critic will often find himself in sympathy with writers he does not agree with. But his way of defining his life to himself can be so urgent as to become another presence in the work.—*ALFRED KAZIN

THE DARK SIDE OF THE TRUTH

George E. Woodberry

. . . .

The romance is . . . essentially a parable of the soul's life in sin; in its narrower scope it is the work of the moral intellect allegorizing its view of life; and where creative genius enters into it, in the Shakespearean sense of life in its own right, it tends to be a larger and truer story breaking[199] the bonds of its religious scheme. It has its roots in Puritanism, but it is only incidentally a New England tale; its substance is the most universal experience of human nature in religious life, taking its forms only, its local habitation and name, from the Puritan colony in America, and these in a merely allegorical, not historical manner. Certain traits, however, ally it more closely to New England Puritanism. It is a relentless tale; the characters are singularly free from self-pity, and accept their fate as righteous; they never forgave themselves, they show no sign of having forgiven one another; even God's forgiveness is left under a shadow in futurity. They have sinned against the soul, and something implacable in evil remains. The minister's dying words drop a dark curtain over all.

"Hush, Hester, hush!" said he, with tremulous solemnity. "The law we broke!—the sin here so awfully revealed!—let these alone be in thy thoughts! I fear! I fear! It may be that, when we forgot our God,—when we violated our reverence each for the other's soul,—it was thenceforth vain to hope that we could meet hereafter, in an everlasting and pure reunion."

Mercy is but a hope. There is also a singular absence of prayer in the book. Evil is presented as a thing without remedy, that cannot change its nature. The child, even, being the fruit of sin, can bring, Hester and Arthur doubt, no good for others or herself. In the scheme of Puritan[200] thought, however, the atonement of Christ is the perpetual miracle whereby salvation comes, not only hereafter but in the holier life led here by grace. There is no Christ in this book. Absolution, so

16

far as it is hinted at, lies in the direction of public confession, the efficacy of which is directly stated, but lamely nevertheless; it restores
truth, but it does not heal the past. Leave the dead past to bury its
dead, says Hawthorne, and go on to what may remain; but life once
ruined is ruined past recall. So Hester, desirous of serving in her place
the larger truth she has come to know, is stayed, says Hawthorne, because she "recognized the impossibility that any mission of divine and
mysterious truth should be confided to a woman stained with sin,
bowed down with shame, or even burdened with a life-long sorrow."
That was never the Christian gospel nor the Puritan faith. Indeed,
Hawthorne here and elsewhere anticipates those ethical views which
are the burden of George Eliot's moral genius, and contain scientific
pessimism. This stoicism, which was in Hawthorne, is a primary element in his moral nature, in him as well as in his work; it is visited
with few touches of tenderness and pity; the pity one feels is not in
him, it is in the pitiful thing, which he presents objectively, sternly,
unrelentingly. It must be confessed that as an artist he appears unsympathetic with his characters; he is a moral dissector of their souls,
minute, unflinching, thorough, a vivisector here; and he is cold[201]
because he has passed sentence on them, condemned them. There is no
sympathy with human nature in the book; it is a fallen and ruined
thing suffering just pain in its dying struggle. The romance is steeped in
gloom. Is it too much to suggest that in ignoring prayer, the atonement
of Christ, and the work of the Spirit in men's hearts, the better part of
Puritanism has been left out, and the whole life of the soul distorted?
Sin in the soul, the scarlet flower from the dark soil, we see; but, intent
on that, has not the eye, and the heart, too, forgotten the large heavens
that ensphere all—even this evil flower—and the infinite horizons that
reach off to the eternal distance from every soul as from their centre?
This romance is the record of a prison-cell, unvisited by any ray of
light save that earthly one which gives both prisoners to public ignominy; they are seen, but they do not see. These traits of the book, here
only suggested, have kinship with the repelling aspects of Puritanism,
both as it was and as Hawthorne inherited it in his blood and breeding;
so, in its transcendent spirituality, and in that democracy which is the
twin-brother of spirituality in all lands and cultures, by virtue of which
Hawthorne here humiliates and strips the minister who is the type of
the spiritual aristocrat in the community, there is the essence of New
England; but, for all that, the romance is a partial story, an imperfect
fragment of the old life, distorting, not so much the Puritan ideal—
which were a[202] little matter—but the spiritual life itself. Its truth,
intense, fascinating, terrible as it is, is a half-truth, and the darker half;
it is the shadow of which the other half is light; it is the wrath of which
the other half is love. A book from which light and love are absent may
hold us by its truth to what is dark in life; but, in the highest sense,
it is a false book. It is a chapter in the literature of moral despair, and

is most tolerated as a condemnation of the creed which, through imperfect comprehension, it travesties.[203]

. . . .

FROM *"The Scarlet Letter,"* Nathaniel Hawthorne (Boston, 1902), pp. 159-205.

SIN AND ISOLATION

Gordon Roper

. . . .

"The Scarlet Letter" is not a study of sin which is purged finally through penance and repentance in stock Christian terms; it is a study of Hawthorne's own mature interpretation of the Christian pattern of how sin is followed by isolation, and of how isolation causes a suffering which forces the individual to work towards a reunion with the force from which he has been isolated. In general, any sin will be followed by isolation, isolation from one's immediate society, or from one's substantial self, or from one's God. One effect of isolation is to cut the "electric chain of human sympathy," the great human dynamic, which naturally exists between individuals and which is one of the greatest sources of human strength. This isolation causes deep mental and spiritual suffering and is reflected in the physical nature of the individual. This suffering causes the individual to work towards a reunion with that from which he has been isolated. However, this isolation and this suffering, which may be called an inner penance, will continue until the individual can bring himself by an act of conscious self-will to accept responsibility for his sin, and then to will himself to ask forgiveness. These actions constitute a true, inner repentance, and although the individual may perform acts of outward penance and repentance, his isolation will not be reduced until he undergoes this true inner repentance.

Hawthorne, however, was more subtle than to show one central character acting out this general scheme of sin, isolation, suffering, repentance, and reunion. He was aware that sin is not an absolute, but an act only meaningful in relationship to the nature of the person who committed it. Consequently he shows three different central forces, each personifying the predominance of one of the three faculties, heart, mind, or soul, which[xxx] contemporary psychology informed him constituted the nature of man. Thus Hester is a woman in whom the heart predominates; Chillingworth a man in whom the mind predominates, and Dimmesdale a man in whom the soul, or spirit, predominates. When one of these commits an act in violation of his own nature, that act is for him a sin; the same act, if performed by another character will not be a sin, unless, for a different reason, it violates his different nature. A sin committed by any one character can be worked out only through an inner penance and inner repentance undergone in terms harmonious with his own nature; what constitutes penance and repentance for one does not necessarily constitute them for another. However, the dynamics are constant. Sin does produce isolation from whatever the sinner holds valuable; the sinner is cut off from the chain of human sympathy, and consequently loses strength, and must somehow reestablish that linkage before regaining the strength which leads to the recognition of responsibility for one's sin, and which leads to asking forgiveness. Essentially the moral is that one must be true to that variety of human nature that oneself is.[xxxi]

. . . .

FROM "Introduction," *The Scarlet Letter and Selected Prose Works* (New York, 1949), pp. vii-xlvi.

THE GREAT CHAIN OF BEING

RATHER THAN THIS, SAY "MAGNETIC CHAIN OF HUMANITY"

James W. Mathews

. . . .

Among Hawthorne's novels, *The Scarlet Letter* displays the frustration that results when each of the three principal characters fails to achieve a harmonious relationship with his environment. When the narrative begins, Roger Chillingworth, Arthur Dimmesdale, and Hester Prynne have already estranged themselves from their proper positions in the great scheme of mankind and nature. Thus the novel is a study in thwarted purposes, for as long as each remains estranged,[287] there can be no harmony in life, no success in enterprises. Following their withdrawal from the "Chain of Being,"[1] the characters commit grievous

---

1 Arthur O. Lovejoy explains the "Chain of Being" system as "the conception of the plan and structure of the world which, through the Middle Ages and down to the late eighteenth century, many philosophers, most men of science, and, in-

sins which arrest a return to the "Chain" until penance and true penitence are effected. Chillingworth is never able to make a satisfactory
readjustment; Dimmesdale only in his final moments of life meets his
fellow men honestly, thereby creating harmony for the first time; and
Hester eventually learns through years of contemplation that she must
willingly adjust her life to the requirements of nature and even society.

Roger Chillingworth admits that his was the first wrong in the
series of missteps in *The Scarlet Letter*. A brilliant English scientist
with a physical deformity, Chillingworth has married late in life and
has sent his young and vivacious bride before him to settle in Massachusetts. Finally arriving in Boston, he finds his wife receiving her
sentence as an adulteress. Immediately he recognizes Hester's sin as
the aftermath of his own erroneous judgment. He realizes that he
has transcended the bounds of the life for which his talents and his
physical appearance have fitted him. Ordinarily a wise man, he has in
his one moment of irrationality entered an unnatural union. He says
to Hester:

"It was my folly, and thy weakness. I,—a man of thought,—the book-worm
of great libraries,—a man already in decay, having given my best years to
feed the hungry dream of knowledge,—what had I to do with youth and
beauty like thine own! Misshapen from my birth-hour, how could I delude
myself with the idea that intellectual gifts might veil physical deformity in a
young girl's fantasy! Men call me wise. If sages were ever wise in their own
behoof, I might have foreseen all this."

Although Chillingworth perceives the unnaturalness of the relationships of age with youth, deformity with beauty, and a studious
mind with inhibiting social institutions, he rejects any idea of a
return to his old life. He sins: the idea of revenge possesses him until
those talents with which nature has fitted him are perverted as he
afflicts Dimmesdale with subtle punishment. Even his physical appearance is gradually transformed along with his mind. Despite the
sacrifice of his superior natural talents for powers equally unnatural,
Chillingworth is unsuccessful, and Dimmesdale eludes his grasp. The
epitome of frustration, he reluctantly acknowledges his failure when
he observes Dimmesdale upon the scaffold to confess before the townspeople. Chillingworth's soul is irretrievably estranged.

The frustration of Arthur Dimmesdale is not less intense than that

---

deed, most educated men, were to accept without question—the conception of the
universe as a 'Great Chain of Being,' composed of an immense, or—by the strict
but seldom rigorously applied logic of the principle of continuity—of an infinite
number of links ranging in hierarchical order from the meagerest kind of existents,
which barely escape nonexistence, through 'every possible' grade up to the *ens
perfectissimum*—or, in a somewhat more orthodox version, to the highest possible
kind of creature, between which and the Absolute Being the disparity was assumed
to be infinite—every one of them differing from that immediately above and that
immediately below it by the 'least possible' degree of difference." *The Great Chain
of Being* (Cambridge, Mass., 1936), p. 59.

of Chillingworth, although Dimmesdale with his last breath is able
to bring a certain peace to his own soul. The Boston minister also
comes into the narrative estranged from the "Chain of Being." Himself a great scholar from Oxford, he seems to be "at a loss in the
pathway of human existence, and could be only at ease in some seclusion of his own." Although an eloquent and influential speaker, he
in life is isolated from a truly intimate relationship with[288] his
flock; he walks alone, often in "shadowy by-paths."

Dimmesdale believes in God, he recognizes the grave consequences
of sin, and he fulfills punctiliously his external duties as a minister.
But the young scholar who is able to inspire spirituality in the souls
of others is unable to maintain the same disposition in his own heart.
Through his introversion, already a sin, he commits even a greater
one. As Paul Elmer More says, "From the cold and lonely heights
of his spiritual life he has stepped down, in a vain endeavor against
God's law, to seek the warmth of companionship in illicit love."[2]
Dimmesdale's natural course would have been marriage to one of
his many admiring parishioners, but he continues to prefer shadows.
The adultery with Hester Prynne is not the act which sets him apart
from his correct relationship to God and his fellow men: it is only
a consequence of his out-of-balance position.

Dimmesdale's aroused animal passion for a time obliterates his
spiritual nature when he considers fleeing with Hester; but in his
fitful mental state after the tryst in the forest, he is closer to revealing
himself truthfully than he has ever been. His thoughts are base as
he returns from the forest, but they are not hypocritical. Perhaps
this first honest thinking, though shocking, reveals Dimmesdale to
himself. He recognizes his own abominable spiritual state. Hawthorne
describes the revelation thus: "But he seemed to stand apart, and eye
this former self with scornful, pitying, but half-envious curiosity.
That self was gone. Another man had returned out of the forest;
a wiser one...." Aided by his superior intellect, now directed aright,
Dimmesdale begins to reason out his own salvation.

Shortly he reveals himself as Hester's secret lover and by the confession becomes at last fully compatible with the office he has sought
to fill. The importance of his confession is not that he has admitted
adultery but that he has recognized the root of his sin, for he says
to Hester: " 'we violated our reverence each for the other's soul....' "
Now Dimmesdale is restored to God, to his parishioners, and, consequently, to the "Chain of Being."

On superficial examination Hester Prynne would seem merely a
pitiable victim of circumstances, a warmhearted but naïve girl possessed by both Chillingworth and Dimmesdale in unnatural relationships. But Hawthorne does not design Hester as a character devoid

---

2 Paul Elmer More, "The Solitude of Nathaniel Hawthorne," *Shelbourne Essays*, First Series (New York, 1907), p. 45.

of responsibility for her own misery. She has at some time violated the confines in her natural category in the "procession of life"; therefore her most heinous sin in the sight of the townspeople—adultery—and her subsequent anguish follow as consequences.

What has Hester violated? Hawthorne presents her as one who transcends many of the natural bounds of womanhood. To Darrel Abel, Hester is the personification of romantic individualism, a philosophy which is distinctly counter to the "Chain of Being" idea.[289] Hester's violation of her natural position in the "Chain" occurred when she, still in England, entered a loveless marriage apparently to rise above the humble life of her family. Obviously Hester's family was not always in "poverty-stricken" circumstances, for Hester remembers "a half-obliterated shield of arms over the portal" of her home in Old England. She is described by Hawthorne as a woman of extraordinary beauty and passion, yet "lady-like" and possessing "the manner of the feminine gentility of those days."

Because of this loveless marriage with Chillingworth, Hester inhibits her own natural desires as a woman. In her forest meeting with Dimmesdale, her passion, which has smoldered underneath the scarlet letter for over seven years, bursts into flame as she removes the ignominious symbol: "Her sex, her youth, and the whole richness of her beauty came back...."

Hester's frustration, stemming from her thwarted natural impulses, is always the driving force in the illicit union with Dimmesdale. Hester has violated in the extreme what Darrel Abel recognizes as Hawthorne's idea of the distinctive feminine virtues: instinctive purity and passionate devotion as a wife and mother.[3] Rationalizing her position, Hester is mentally defiant, though physically submissive, after she receives sentence for her sin. Accordingly she strays further and further from woman's natural realm, for "the links that united her to the rest of human kind...had all been broken." Her life "turned, in a great measure, from passion and feeling, to thought....She assumed a freedom of speculation" which "would have [been] held to be a deadlier crime than that stigmatized by the scarlet letter." Hester acknowledges adultery not as a sin, but, what to her is equally sinful, as a violation of a social system. She realizes that in giving Pearl existence "a great law" has been broken, but she persists in her refusal to submit to that law.

It is evident that Hester is still at odds with her appropriate place as a woman when she suggests flight with Dimmesdale. By this proposed action she would forever estrange herself from the "Chain of Being." Even at the minister's confession she continues to think of herself as the sinned against rather than the sinner when she expresses hope that she and Dimmesdale may spend immortality together. After the death of both Dimmesdale and Chillingworth, Hester is finally

---

3 See Darrel Abel's "Hawthorne's Hester," excerpted on pp. 49-56 of this book.

free, according to society, to make for herself a new life. External circumstances have made it possible for her to be restored to the "Chain of Being," but she herself must recognize the unsoundness of her past thinking and make inner expiation. The debates between Hester's body and soul are not revealed, but ultimately—after years abroad—she resolves her conflicts and returns to New England to accept her true relationship to society. She has even rejected wealth and position which she could now enjoy through Pearl's inheritance and becomes contented with a humble life which in her youth she[290] had scorned. In her New England cottage she takes the proper place of a woman—a being of natural compassion and love for those who need her.[291]

. . . .

FROM "Hawthorne and the Chain of Being," *Modern Language Quarterly*, XVIII (Dec., 1957), 282-294. Reprinted by permission of the author and *Modern Language Quarterly*, published by the University of Washington.

THE HUMAN DILEMMA

Richard H. Fogle

Interpretations of *The Scarlet Letter* have been almost startlingly various. This is not surprising, for Hawthorne has himself pointed the way to a wide range of speculations. The concluding words of *The Scarlet Letter*, however, summarily dismiss the more cheerful readings, of which there are a number. In describing the heraldic device on the common tombstone of Hester and Dimmesdale, they describe "our now concluded legend; so sombre is it, and relieved only by one ever-glowing point of light gloomier than the shadow:—

'ON A FIELD, SABLE, THE LETTER *A*, GULES.' "

These words alone, in my opinion, are sufficient evidence for disproving the notion that *The Scarlet Letter* is "about" Hester Prynne the advanced feminist, or that the story can be satisfactorily summarized either by the moral which Hawthorne attaches to Dimmesdale, " 'Show freely to the world, if not your worst, yet some trait whereby the worst may be inferred!' " or by the doctrine of *felix culpa*, "the fortunate fall," that out of sin and evil comes good and that Hester is educated and refined by her wrongdoing. The sentiment is too darkly tragic to be appropriate to any of these conclusions, though Hawthorne at one place and another in *The Scarlet Letter* has suggested the possibility of all of them. The true conclusion of *The Scarlet Letter* is an unresolved[104] contradiction—unresolved not from indecision or lack of thought but from honesty of imagination. Hawthorne gives the only answer that his formulation of the terms permits. If we consider that the problem of *The Scarlet Letter* is primarily the problem of Hester Prynne, the verdict is at best suspension of judgment after full examination of the evidence. And, as we know, Hester emerges from trial in better condition than her codefendants Dimmesdale and Chillingworth.

This is the contradiction, and a very widely representative contradiction it is: the sin of *The Scarlet Letter* is a symbol of the original sin, by which no man is untouched. All mortals commit the sin in one form or another, which is perhaps the meaning of "your worst" in the exhortation occasioned by the death of Dimmesdale. Hester, having sinned, makes the best possible recovery; and the crime itself is of all crimes the most excusable, coming of passionate love and having "a consecration of its own." Yet the sin remains real and inescapable, and she spends her life in retribution, the death of her lover Dimmesdale having finally taught her that this is the only way. This is the dilemma: human beings by their natures must fall into error—and yet it would be better if they did not.

The letter, an "ever-glowing point of light," is gloomier than the shadow of its background. The shadow, the "Field, Sable," is roughly the atmosphere of Puritanism, the "Letter A, Gules" the atmosphere of the sin. These are at odds, and no absolute superiority is granted to either. The Puritan doctors are no fit judges of a woman's heart; nor, on the other hand, is Hester to be absolved. The letter is glowing, positive, vital, the product of genuine passion, while the sable may certainly be[105] taken as the negation of everything alive. Yet the letter is gloomier.

These shades are both of hell, and there is no hue of heaven in *The Scarlet Letter* which really offsets them. Sunlight is the nearest approach to it, and its sway is too fleeting to have any great effect. In the forest scene of chapters XVI–XIX sunshine, "as with a sudden smile of heaven," bursts over Hester and Dimmesdale, but this is merely a momentary relief. The hope which accompanies it is short-lived, delusory, and dangerous. A more steadfast light, "The sun, but little past its meridian," shines down upon Dimmesdale as he stands on the scaffold to confess his guilt. This is triumph, indeed, but little to counterbalance the continual power of the "bale fire" and "lurid gleam" of the letter. Hope and regeneration are sometimes symbolized in Hawthorne by the celestial colors of dawn, transfigured by light: blues, greens, and golds. In "Ethan Brand" the tender hues of the twilight sky are overpowered by night and the red and black of Brand's Unpardonable Sin, but they are revivified by the atmosphere of dawn. So the storm in *The House of the Seven Gables,* which accompanies the crisis and blows itself out with the death of Judge Pyncheon, gives way to a world made new and bathed in morning sunshine. There is no such scene in *The Scarlet Letter.*

The problem of *The Scarlet Letter* can be solved only by introducing the supernatural level of heaven, the sphere of absolute knowledge and justice and—hesitantly—of complete fulfillment. This may seem to be another paradox, and perhaps a disappointing one. Without doubt *The Scarlet Letter* pushes *towards* the limit of moral judgment, suggesting many possible conclusions. It is even relentless in its search in the depths of its characters.[106] There is yet, however, a point beyond which Hawthorne will not go; ultimate solutions are not appropriate in the merely human world. His sympathy with Hester and Dimmesdale is clear enough, but he allows them only to escape the irrevocable spiritual ruin which befalls Chillingworth. Figuratively his good wishes pursue them beyond life, but he does not presume himself to absolve them. Even in the carefully staged scene of Dimmesdale's death, where every impulse of both author and reader demands complete forgiveness, Hawthorne refuses to grant it. With his "bright dying eyes" Dimmesdale looks into eternity, but nothing he sees there permits him to comfort Hester. To her questions, " 'Shall we not meet again?...Shall we not spend our immortal life together?' " he can answer only, " 'The law we broke!—the sin here so awfully revealed!—let these alone be in thy thoughts! I fear! I fear!' " A grim and unflinching conclusion, considering everything. Dimmesdale is not of course Hawthorne, but the very preservation of dramatic propriety at this crucial point is significant.[107]

. . . .

FROM *"The Scarlet Letter," Hawthorne's Fiction: The Light and the Dark* (Norman, 1952), pp. 104-121. Reprinted by permission of the University of Oklahoma Press, copyright 1952.

THE CONTROLLED DIVISION OF SYMPATHIES

R. W. B. Lewis

. . . .

The opening scene of *The Scarlet Letter* is the paradigm dramatic image in American literature. With that scene and that novel, New

World fiction arrived at its first fulfillment, and Hawthorne at his. And with that scene, all that was dark and treacherous in the American situation became exposed. Hawthorne said later that the writing[111] of *The Scarlet Letter* had been oddly simple, since all he had to do was to get his "pitch" and then to let it carry him along. He found his pitch in an opening tableau fairly humming with tension— with coiled and covert relationships that contained a force perfectly calculated to propel the action thereafter in a direct line to its tragic climax.

It was the tableau of the solitary figure set over against the inimical society, in a village which hovers on the edge of the inviting and perilous wilderness; a handsome young woman standing on a raised platform, confronting in silence and pride a hostile crowd whose menace is deepened by its order and dignity; a young woman who has come alone to the New World, where circumstances have divided her from the community now gathered to oppose her; standing alone, but vitally aware of the private enemy and the private lover—one on the far verges of the crowd, one at the place of honor within it, and neither conscious of the other—who must affect her destiny and who will assist at each other's destruction. Here the situation inherent in the American scene was seized entire and without damage to it by an imagination both moral and visual of the highest quality: seized and located, not any longer on the margins of the plot, but at its very center.

The conflict is central because it is total; because Hawthorne makes us respect each element in it. Hawthorne felt, as Brown and Cooper and Bird had felt, that the stuff of narrative (in so far as it was drawn from local experience) consisted in the imaginable brushes between the deracinated and solitary individual and the society or world awaiting him. But Hawthorne had learned the lesson only fitfully apprehended by Cooper. In *The Scarlet Letter* not only do the individual and the world, the conduct and the institutions, measure each other: the measurement and its consequences are precisely and centrally what the novel is about. Hester Prynne has been wounded by an unfriendly world; but the society facing her is invested by Hawthorne with assurance and authority, its opposition is defensible and even valid. Hester's misdeed appears as a disturbance of the moral structure of the universe; and the society continues to insist in its joyless way that certain acts deserve the honor of punishment. But if Hester has sinned, she has done so as an affirmation of life, and her sin is the source of life; she incarnates those rights of personality that society is inclined to trample upon. The action of the novel springs from the enormous but improbable suggestion that the society's estimate of the moral structure of the universe may be tested and found inaccurate.

The Scarlet Letter, like all very great fiction, is the product of a controlled division of sympathies; and we must avoid the temptation to[112] read it heretically. It has always been possible to remark,

about Hawthorne, his fondness for the dusky places, his images of the
slow movement of sad, shut-in souls in the half-light. But it has also
been possible to read *The Scarlet Letter* (not to mention "The New
Adam and Eve" and "Earth's Holocaust") as an indorsement of hope-
fulness: to read it as a hopeful critic named Loring read it (writing for
Theodore Parker's forward-looking *Massachusetts Quarterly Review*)
as a party plea for self-reliance and an attack upon the sterile conventions of institutionalized society. One version of him would align
Hawthorne with the secular residue of Jonathan Edwards; the other
would bring him closer to Emerson. But Hawthorne was neither
Emersonian nor Edwardsean; or rather he was both. The characteristic
situation in his fiction is that of the Emersonian figure, the man of
hope, who by some frightful mischance has stumbled into the time-
burdened world of Jonathan Edwards. And this grim picture is given
us by a writer who was skeptically cordial toward Emerson, but for
whom the vision of Edwards, filtered through a haze of hope, remained
a wonderfully useful metaphor. The situation, in the form which
Hawthorne's ambivalence gave it, regularly led in his fiction to a
moment of crucial choice: an invitation to the lost Emersonian, the
thunder-struck Adam, to make up his mind—whether to accept the
world he had fallen into, or whether to flee it, taking his chances in the
allegedly free wilderness to the west. It is a decision about ethical
reality, and most of Hawthorne's heroes and heroines eventually have
to confront it.

That is why we have the frantic shuttling, in novel after novel, between the village and the forest, the city and the country; for these are
the symbols between which the choice must be made and the means
by which moral inference is converted into dramatic action. Unlike
Thoreau or Cooper, Hawthorne never suggested that the choice was
an easy one. Even Arthur Mervyn had been made to reflect on "the
contrariety that exists between the city and the country"; in the age
of hope the contrariety was taken more or less simply to lie between
the restraints of custom and the fresh expansiveness of freedom. Hawthorne perceived greater complexities. He acknowledged the dependence of the individual, for nourishment, upon organized society (the
city), and he believed that it was imperative "to open an intercourse
with the world." But he knew that the city could destroy as well as[113]
nourish and was apt to destroy the person most in need of nourishment. And while he was responsive to the attractions of the open air
and to the appeal of the forest, he also understood the grounds for the
Puritan distrust of the forest. He retained that distrust as a part of
the symbol. In the forest, possibility was unbounded; but just because
of that, evil inclination was unchecked, and witches could flourish
there.

For Hawthorne, the forest was neither the proper home of the admirable Adam, as with Cooper; nor was it the hideout of the malevo-

lent adversary, as with Bird. It was the ambiguous setting of moral choice, the scene of reversal and discovery in his characteristic tragic drama. The forest was the pivot in Hawthorne's grand recurring pattern of escape and return.

It is in the forest, for example, that *The Scarlet Letter* version of the pattern begins to disclose itself: in the forest meeting between Hester and Dimmesdale, their first private meeting in seven years. During those years, Hester has been living "on the outskirts of the town," attempting to cling to the community by performing small services for it, though there had been nothing "in all her intercourse with society...that made her feel as if she belonged to it." And the minister has been contemplating the death of his innocence in a house fronting the village graveyard. The two meet now to join in an exertion of the will and the passion for freedom. They very nearly persuade themselves that they can escape along the forest track, which, though in one direction it goes "backward to the settlement," in another goes onward—"deeper it goes, and deeper into the wilderness, until...the yellow leaves will show no vestiges of the white man's tread." But the energy aroused by their encounter drives them back instead, at the end, to the heart of the society, to the penitential platform which is also the heart of the book's structure.[114]

. . . .

FROM "The Return into Time: Hawthorne." *The American Adam* (Chicago, 1955), pp. 110-126. Reprinted by permission of the University of Chicago Press.

THE MYSTERY OF MORAL GROWTH

Roy R. Male

. . . .

Like many great tragedies, *The Scarlet Letter* deals with the quest for truth, the revelation of secrets. First one riddle is solved, then another, until at the close the reader has been[93] drawn up to the ultimate revelation—the secret of man's moral growth. This will remain a mystery, however, because, like the Passion of Christ, it involves an eternal paradox: the mundane wisdom of man is insanity to God, and untempered celestial wisdom is equally insane in the social world. The mature insight of Oedipus coincides with his physical blindness and banishment; Arthur Dimmesdale purifies himself at the terrible human cost of sin, physical decay, and death. The crucial moment occurs when the emotionally involved reader or spectator raises and ennobles his own perspective so that he sees not only the agony but also the purification.

In *The Scarlet Letter* the quest for truth is an effort to know Pearl. As every reader of the book recognizes, she is the scarlet letter incarnate. But as the visible embodiment of truth about the particular sin, she becomes by extension the universal truth about the Original Sin. In a notebook entry, Hawthorne had written in 1841: "Is truth a fantasy which we are to pursue forever and never grasp?" Pearl, whose inscrutable black eyes invest her with a "strange remoteness and intangibility," is a dramatization of this passage. As truth's reflector, she rejects all half-truths, including those of the Puritans. Hawthorne adroitly manipulates the archaisms of the townspeople in order to indicate Pearl's symbolic function. When Chillingworth, for instance, asks a bystander about the identity of Pearl's father, the reply is: "*Of a truth,* friend, that matter remaineth a riddle."

Though Pearl's full significance will emerge only when we see her in relation to other characters, there is another aspect of her role that deserves mention here. She possesses "a native grace." In naming her, Hester has identified the child with the pearl of great price (Matt. 13: 45-46) the *pretiosa margarita*. This pearl has often been interpreted as Christ by the theologians, but it has also been construed as everlasting[94] life or beatitude—the soul, either undefiled or redeemed in baptism. In "The Intelligence Office," Hawthorne had defined the pearl as "the soul of celestial purity." Pearl's name, her attire, and her very being thus sum up the riddle of human existence, in which man's insanity is heaven's sense. "Man had marked this woman's sin by a scarlet letter, which had such potent and disastrous efficacy that no human sympathy could reach her, save it were sinful like herself. God, as a direct consequence of the sin which man thus punished, had given her a lovely child, whose place was on that same dishonored bosom, to connect her parent for ever with the race and descent of mortals, and to be finally a blessed soul in heaven!" Pearl is a holy spirit, "worthy to have been brought forth in Eden; worthy to have been left there, to be the plaything of angels, after the world's first parents were driven out." But the temporal gap between the sin and the redemption must not be ignored; it is, in fact, at the heart of the story.

As an abstraction, Pearl is inflexible and inexorable. She has a "hard, metallic lustre" that needs grief to melt it and make her human. Both character and type, both natural and preternatural, she is in time and outside of it. She watches her reflection in the forest brook, the stream of time; a little later we are informed that "the soul beheld its features in the mirror of the passing moment." As a growing child, Pearl serves as an index to the passage of time in the narrative; as a symbol, she indicates to Hester and Arthur that truth cannot be perceived outside its temporal context.

These generalizations will derive further support when we see Pearl in relation to the two major characters. Meanwhile, having established as a working hypothesis at least that Pearl signifies truth and grace, we may turn to Roger Chillingworth. He has always been recognized as a personification,[95] but it will not suffice to see him simply as evil incarnate. "Under the appellation of Roger Chillingworth...was hidden another name," and the name is not only Prynne—it is Guilt.[1] Hawthorne's portrayal of Chillingworth illustrates how beautifully his imagination could weld the abstract to the concrete. For the physician is interesting in his own right as an alchemist-psychiatrist manqué, who tries to solve the riddle of man's existence by logical or psychological analysis. As a symbol of guilt, Chillingworth is a leech, draining his patient of nerve, will, and physical energy. But, as the whole book demonstrates, he is also the healer. Only by knowing him, confronting him face to face, is moral growth possible. Not that moral growth is guaranteed or that having this unwelcome guest is "fortunate"—it is simply inevitable in human existence. "The breach which guilt has once made into the human soul is never in this mortal state repaired. It may be watched and guarded; so that the enemy shall not force his way again *into the citadel,* and might even, in his subsequent assaults, select some other avenue, in preference to that where he had formerly succeeded. But there is still *the ruined wall.*" The italicized phrases remove all doubt of Chillingworth's identity. As guilt he invades the dwelling place, which, as we know, is customarily a symbol for the heart in Hawthorne's fiction. "My home," he tells Hester, "is where thou art and where he [the minister] is." Early in the book Chillingworth appears from nowhere to confront Hester in the prison cell of her heart; by the middle of the book he has insinuated himself into Dimmesdale's abode. "A deformed old figure, with a face that haunted men's memories longer than they liked," he gradually shrivels as[96] Hester and Dimmesdale come closer to full recognition of him.

We are now perhaps in a position to understand why Hawthorne makes Pearl "the richest heiress in her day, in the New World." Allegorically, it is clear that the death of Chillingworth would automatically bequeath a massive legacy to Pearl. But the matter is not this simple. In the final pillory scene Pearl becomes humanized. As Dimmesdale ascends, she moves down from her allegorical function and into

---

[1] This interpretation of Chillingworth's role was first suggested to me by Hillel Chodos and John L. Murphy.

fully temporal existence. She shifts, as it were, from her role as the universal principle in the spiritual realm—an intuitive or natural language, a vital hieroglyphic—to a key role in the novel, the social world, whose basic medium is money.[2] Hawthorne returns her to the Old World with the riches from the New, giving her a solid social standing.

Once we identify Pearl and Chillingworth, the structural outline of *The Scarlet Letter* is clearly revealed. The first third of the book (Chapters I to VIII) concerns Hester's limited ascension. When she ascends the platform, she stands out in sharp contrast to the flint-faced, manlike women who surround her. Every inch a woman in her dual role as sinner and saint, Hester reaches the peak of her moral development[97] in this section. She openly recognizes her guilt in Chapter III; she accepts the letter as Chillingworth's vital surrogate in Chapter IV; she grasps the truth intuitively through her art in Chapters V and VI; and she educates the leading members of the community in the meaning of that art in Chapters VII and VIII.

The middle third of the book (Chapters IX to XVI) is concerned with the burden of guilt and where it should reside. It is subdivided by the midnight pillory scene in the middle of the book. In Chapters IX to XII we see that guilt has been shifted almost completely from the woman to the man (Chillingworth now lives with Dimmesdale); and in the counterbalancing Chapters XIII to XVI we observe what has happened to the woman as a result of this shifting of responsibility.

The final third (Chapters XVII to XXIV) deals with Dimmesdale's ascension, which begins with the forest interview and ends with the revelation during the New England holiday. Where Hester's ascension was limited, his is complete; where she has been associated (though, as Hawthorne puts it, only "by contrast") with Divine Maternity, Dimmesdale attains the Word Incarnate. The book moves, therefore, from recognition through obscurity to revelation, from the light of Hester's ascension through the dark night of the soul to the final light of Dimmesdale's ascension. And the final symbol, as we shall see, sums up the whole action.

We may now pause to consider what is likely to be the major objection to this interpretation. If Chillingworth represents guilt, it

---

[2] The philosopher whose writings furnish one of the closest parallels to Hawthorne's thought is Johann Georg Hamann. Note, for instance, this passage:

"*Money* and *language* are two subjects whose investigation is as profound and abstract as their use is universal. Both stand in a closer relationship than one might presume. The theory of one explains the theory of the other; therefore they seem to flow from common sources. The wealth of all human knowledge rests on the exchange of words....On the other hand, all the goods of civil or social life have reference to money as their universal standard." (Hamann's italics.) Quoted in James C. O'Flaherty, *Unity and Language: A Study in the Philosophy of Johann Georg Hamann* (University of North Carolina Press, Chapel Hill, N.C., 1952), p. 30.

may be asked, what happens to the sin of adultery upon which the whole book is based? The question is not only relevant but of the utmost importance for a grasp of the book's archetypal meaning. The reader may well be asked to see Chillingworth both as wronged husband and as[98] guilt, but he is quite right in insisting that the sin ought to have meaning from both perspectives. The answer is that it does; it has a literal meaning in both senses of the word *literal:* "non-figurative" and "original." All readers have noticed that the actual sin is prior to the action of the book. Of course it is prior; it is the literal, the Original Sin. Why did Hester marry Chillingworth? Why was Zenobia wedded to Westervelt? Why is Miriam linked to the "model"? Why did Eve allow herself to be seduced by Satan, thus fouling her perfect union with God? Why did all evil spring from Pandora's box? On this archetypal level, the timeless abstractions represented by Pearl and Chillingworth remain constant, but, like the man and the woman, they are stripped of their names and location. The "special reference to New England" is gone, and all that remains is the basic relation between man, woman, and Deity. *The Scarlet Letter* is seen not as romance but as myth—the story of man and woman in a fallen, that is, human, world. Like Rappaccini's garden, life in this "Eden of the present world" is an adulteration of God's original creation. The woman has broken her covenant with God in order to seek the kind of knowledge that is man's province; the man has broken his covenant with God in order to know the woman. As a result, life is such "com-mixture, and, as it were, *adultery*" that "the production" is "no longer of God's making."

Thus Hawthorne educates us once again in the given conditions of human life. Originally—that is, in his youth and before this book has begun—man's role, as we have seen, is speculation; it is a rootless gamble in space, the discovery of new particulars, the exploration of new fields, physical or intellectual. For maturity, however, man needs to leave this world of the first name and become involved through passion with the woman and her temporal burden. Originally,[99] woman's role is investment; she brings to the man a dowry from the past. Without the man she lingers, literally or figuratively, in the Old World, in the ancestral homestead, buried under the patronymic. Without him she lives in time-drenched darkness; without her he is blanked out in the glare of space. Their union depends upon man's vulnerable area, his heart, and upon woman's, her head. After the union, which is where this book begins, the man wears his hand over his heart; the woman wears a cap over her head. After their union there is an exaggerated inversion of roles: the man, like Milton's Adam, is overwhelmed by a sense of time, of all history; the woman, like Milton's Eve, is blinded by speculation, offering noble but misguided ways of thwarting time. A reassertion of their natural roles, balanced and tempered by their new knowledge, must be effected if they are to find "the oneness of their being" in Pearl and re-establish something like their original relation to God.[100]

. . . .

FROM "The Tongue of Flame: *The Scarlet Letter*," *Hawthorne's Tragic Vision* (Austin, 1957), pp. 90-118. Reprinted by permission of the University of Texas Press.

ART, NATURE, SCIENCE, AND RELIGION

Rudolphe von Abele

. . . .

Analysis of *The Scarlet Letter* leads, penultimately, toward one highly tentative hypothesis at yet another, and more obscure, level of interpretation: one at which Chillingworth assumes a certain meaning, even a certain importance. Hester, after her fall and in her exile, (which have suppressed in almost all respects the "rich, voluptuous, Oriental characteristic" that captured Dimmesdale) is more or[224] less consistently seen as like a statue, a work of art. In the first eight chapters she is spoken of six times as "pedestaled," like a statue; and elsewhere she is a "statue of ignominy," "majestic and statue-like," "of marble quietude" and of "marble passiveness of brow." Chillingworth is said to have made of her a "marble image of happiness"—before she came to Dimmesdale. The impression she gives throughout, save for the scenes in the forest, is of a "marble coldness." What the community has done to her has made her frigid and repressed. The only inklings of her true nature are the "gorgeous" and "luxuriant" and "artistically done" Letter itself, and the clothes she makes for Pearl, of a "fanciful, or, we might rather say, a fantastic ingenuity"—a substitute, as it were, for passion, and also perhaps for poetry. Her true nature, like her needlework, is impulsive, sumptuous, warm.

As for Pearl, who is a "natural child," she is dealt with throughout the book in terms of an elaborate and subtly sustained pun. Rejecting the companionship of human children, she becomes intimate with growing things. "The spell of life went forth from her ever-creative spirit," says Hawthorne, and we are shown her in the scene between Hester and Chillingworth by the sea, playing in tide-pools with horseshoe crabs, jelly fish, seaweed and sea-birds; and in the forest scenes, she is given as garlanded with wildflowers and moving among wild animals without alarming them. In the final scenes of the book, too, "She ran and looked the wild Indian in the face, and he grew conscious of a nature wilder than his own." She tells John Wilson that her mother picked her off a rosebush, and while Chillingworth and Dimmesdale look on from above, she plays among the graves in the cemetery as if she were immune to death. Most often she is figured as a bird: "of scarlet plumage," "tropical," a "sea-bird," a "humming-bird," a bird of "bright plumage"; and she has a "bird-like" voice and "flies" "like a bird," or with "bird-like motion." But also she is likened to flowers, the northern lights, the day, a brook, a deer, a butterfly, a diamond, and sea-foam: all natural objects, bright, or growing, or flowing things. She has an affinity for the Letter, and parodies it in green seaweed; is in behavior wild and untameable, and of an almost total moral innocence. Of Dimmesdale she has until the very end an instinctive suspicion.

Dimmesdale and Chillingworth are not so sharply handled from this point of view; yet provide some interesting clues. The worldly innocence and spiritual profundity of the minister are everywhere stressed: he is a "heaven-ordained apostle," an "angel" in speech and[225] action, a "miracle of holiness," and "of whitest sanctity." He is associated with whiteness, both by virtue of his own striking pallor and "white, lofty and impending brow," and by the bevies of white virgins in his "flock" (for he is a "shepherd," and so linked with white-ness that way too) who have enshrined his image in their bosoms. He is, too, a kind of lamp, whose light is the Word of God: he fasts and prays to "keep the grossness of this earthly state from clogging and obscuring his spiritual lamp." Men fear that his "dawning light would be extinguished, all untimely"; and at the end, his great sermon is spoken of as "words of flame" and a "shower of golden truths." And the physician, besides being figured as a demon, is a miner, a geome-trician and an engineer: he goes "deep" into Dimmesdale; he "delves," "probes," and "burrows" "like a treasure-seeker in a dark cavern"; he "dug into the poor clergyman's heart, like a miner searching for gold," makes "long search into the minister's dim interior"—a logical thing to do since, as he himself observes, secrets, in the popular phrase, lie "buried" in the heart. As geometrician, he sets out to study Dimmes-dale like a "geometrical problem"; and as engineer, he knows "the spring that controlled the engine" of the minister's nature; he brings a "terrible machinery to bear" upon him; and "tampers" with "the delicate springs" of his mind and conscience.

The tropes suggest that the casting of Dimmesdale as a priest and Chillingworth as a physician (i.e., as an empirical scientist) was not altogether chance or convenience: especially not if the emphasis upon Hester as an artist in her own right and a work of art by default, and upon Pearl as a child of "nature," is also adduced at this point. Hawthorne, who had himself, or suspected himself of having, a strong streak of the Peeping Tom (*vide* such sketches as "Sunday Morning," "Sights From a Steeple," "Main Street," "Footprints On the Seashore," and so on), nourished a deep antipathy against the scientist, who, he apparently felt, tended also to be a Peeping Tom, in whom the "head" had outrun the "heart," and who maintained himself at an unassailable distance from mankind not out of necessity but choice: a detached intellectual, that is to say, an undigestible lump in the hot esophagus of the body politic. This antipathy manifested itself in a tendency to equate the scientist with the necromancer, the alchemist,—in a word, with the quack, and to represent him as always engaged in doing what Chillingworth is said to have done: violating, "in cold blood, the sanctity of a human heart." So with Chillingworth, so with Ethan Brand, with Rappaccini, and with Aylmer, not to speak[226] of Holgrave and, in a different way, Peter Hovenden of "The Artist of the Beautiful." And it may be that the interplay of the personages of *The Scarlet Letter* is interpretable in terms of the relations Hawthorne conceived as existing among art, nature, religion, and science. A close relation between art and science, it might be inferred from the relation between Hester and Chillingworth, is sterile, productive of calamity, and as preposterous as the union of extreme youth and old age. A close relation between science and religion resembles that between Dimmesdale and Chillingworth in that it becomes an effort on the part of science to penetrate, expose, and reduce to its own terms the concepts of religion—a destructive, insidious relation. And a close relation between art and religion tends, as Hester tends with Dimmesdale, to secularize the latter. It is a relation essentially "adulterous," since its end-product (as figured by Pearl) is a kind of adulteration, like watered milk. Pearl's essential amorality might then be taken as an indication of the dominance of "creative" over "redemptive" power—since she has almost nothing that is recognizably Dimmesdale's in her, and is explicity drawn as "wild" and "natural" *and* dressed up by Hester's *art*. Apparently, too, she becomes in time a "great lady" of society— than which it is difficult to imagine anything more contrived, and therefore the produce of art. Art is lifegiving, careless of ordinary law, and young; but science is life-destroying, hypocritical and impotent as age. Yet both are dangerous, being hostile to the religious impulse which, itself feeble and insecure in an increasingly secular age, becomes their combined victim and saves itself only by an heroic effort of integrity at the last moment.[227]

   . . . .

FROM *"The Scarlet Letter:* A Reading," *Accent,* XI (Autumn, 1951), 211-227. Reprinted by permission of the author and *Accent*.

HAWTHORNE'S CHARACTERS: Method and Emphasis

UNEARTHLY SIGNIFICANCE AND HUMAN PLAUSIBILITY

Raymond W. Short

. . . .

The psychological result upon the reader, his persuasion that [the characters in *The Scarlet Letter*] are indeed in the hands of the implacable mystery they worship, that their words and acts do reflect some supra-human order, constitutes the chief power of the novel.

Yet the impression succeeds, in the last analysis, because this blaze of symbolism and unearthly significance never essentially damages the human plausibility of the characters. Attenuated though[xxvi] they may be by Hawthorne's abstractionism, their hopes and fears of another world are felt as by real persons living in this one.

The novelist has powerfully imaged a very solid world for them to inhabit here below. The forest, the town, the market-place, the buildings, the rabble, and the officials exist for us as materially as the stone Dr. Johnson kicked out of his path in refutation of Berkeley's supersensuous universe. The people are equally firmly footed in time; they do not drift in historical anonymity, but belong to specific classes of a specified period. We know where Hester came from, and when, and why, as well as the identifying details of Dimmesdale's background and education. In a word, the moral allegory takes place in a setting that is singularly substantial and precise, and is conditioned by the actual world, as of a given point in time.

But the magical immediacy of the story depends upon more than exactitude of background. Though not conceived in the style of realism, the characters have a special kind of reality. The pure allegorist, such as Spenser or Bunyan, cares nothing at all for the strictly human aspects of his people; Hawthorne, like Melville and also like Dostoevski, *seems* to have begun with a fully realized human in mind, then to have shuffled off layers of mortal coil until only a few significant characteristics remained. Whether or not this was the method, it is the effect we get from his characters. The important thing is that the remaining characteristics are not synthetic or artificial, but genuine and human. Thus isolated, they can be made to burn with concentrated intensity. This partly explains why characters so conceived often seem more richly endowed with *élan vital* than many characters of broader development.

Characteristics brought into high relief by this method of narrowed focusing naturally fall under the keenest scrutiny, both by writer and reader. So it is common to think of characters of this order as "psychological" creations. They have a special interest for our time, perhaps because we have grown familiar with the somewhat similar separative and analytical techniques of the science of psychology. Our attention to these characters has a marked diagnostic quality, and we feel that we are closing with the mysteries of human personality.

Little Pearl, with Mistress Hibbins the least real of *The Scarlet Letter's* characters, is still far from wholly fantastic. To symbolize the reckless amorality of nature, Hawthorne wanted to use a child. He wished this child also to stand for all children and for all the[xxvii] child-like, in so far as they possess incorrigible naturalness. For these purposes, it would not do to make Pearl a "whole" child, in the sense that Tom Sawyer might be called a "whole" boy; thus far, his intentions were those of an allegorist. In working them out, however, Hawthorne abided by the conditions of life, firmly welding his allegory to psychological reality. Pearl's human characteristics are molded by her specific, though unnatural, environment, in accordance with Hawthorne's delicate observations of childhood. Her intuitive flashes and silences, as well as her compensatory volubility and irresponsibility, obey the laws of personality no less than those of allegory.

This is far more evident in the case of the greater characters, Chillingworth, Dimmesdale, and especially Hester Prynne. They are deeply, if not broadly, real. In contrast with the figures in many older allegories, they are people of inner motivation. They possess the human complement of mixed feelings and uncertain aims. They do not reveal their emotions and thoughts over a wide range of affairs, as do the major people in Proust, Joyce, and Mann, but neither are they oversimplified. Hester brings to her ordeal tensions derived from parents, old country, creative instincts, pride, and injured youth. These must be painfully sorted out into right and wrong, and without manipulation by the author. Patiently Hawthorne lets her err and backtrack in her course to salvation, unwilling that the moral issues surrounding her should infringe upon her psychological integrity.

Taking the novel as a whole, the emphasis falls upon the moral issues, rather than upon the humanness of the characters. But without the humanness, the issues, especially today, would seem arbitrary. As it is, these issues, carried by the marvelously serried symbolism, are cogent and enthralling for the indicated reason: they spring so strictly from the novel's humanity that they become indistinguishable from it.[xxviii]

. . . .

FROM "Introduction," *Four Great Novels* (New York, 1946), pp. xxi-xxviii. Reprinted by permission of Henry Holt and Company, Inc.

PSYCHOLOGY AND THE MORAL IMAGINATION

Marius Bewley

Henry James wrote of Hawthorne that 'the fine thing...is that he cared for the deeper psychology, and that, in his way, he tried to become familiar with it.' The statement says so much that, in the end, it really leaves us with very little. Whatever James himself may have meant by it (and the statement is not as clear as it looks), the remark has proved insidiously misleading to some among the later critics who have quoted it with enthusiasm. The phrase itself immediately precipitates the reader of modern fiction into the shadowy subconscious world of the uniquely private, where hidden motivations and all the 'secrets' of the inmost self swim fortuitously about. But this is not the world of Hawthorne's interest, and it has nothing to do with the gifts and realities that he bestows on his characters. There is a level at which the psychological becomes an important facet of moral reality—or to put it another way, the psychological is an avenue which, if we pursue it far enough, is bound to issue on a moral field. In reading Hawthorne it is important to remember that if there is a psychological interest, it is a facet, and only a facet, of his moral interest, and that it is this which provides the ultimate reality of his art. The presence of the psychological in Hawthorne's work, as apart from the moral, is deceptive—there is so much less of it than one might suppose. . . .

Hawthorne was interested in the psychology of his characters only insofar as he could use it as a stage on which certain complex moral problems could be dramatically enacted. The final effect of that enactment is that the individual characters themselves dissolve in the transcendent interest of the problem they dramatize. Such a practice of art can have little use for 'the deeper psychology' if this is defined as the field in which personality is individuated, and the ultimate source of private motivation. What Hawthorne leaves us with is not a sense of living characters whom he has endowed with deep psychological complexities, but a set of exploratory symbols which vibrate with a peculiar intensity in a moral ambience that is objectively grounded in Hawthorne's society. Hawthorne's characters have no[366] margin of interest in themselves when they have performed their function in the over-all pattern of the given story. The interest we feel in Hester Prynne is of an essentially different kind from the interest we feel in Isabel Archer. In the last analysis Hawthorne is not interested in Hester's private drama. She exists magnificently in the art as the focus of tangled moral forces, but she is herself as much of a symbol as the Scarlet Letter which she wears on her breast. Her role in the novel is to endow that Letter and all it stands for with the life of art, but her own life in our imagination is restricted to those boundaries. James has otherwise focused our interest in Isabel. Both the foolishness and the fineness of her moral nature is uniquely hers, the product of her own experience and her own will. Her ordeal reaches towards the universal, but in the end it remains a very particular and individual modification of it. And one dares say that it is the particularity of it which so compels our interest. It is in this area of the private and the particular, as it impinges on the universal, that we might most reasonably look for satisfactory artistic treatment of 'the deeper psychology.' But it is precisely this area that is missing from Hawthorne's characters. This is not a defect, but a condition of the kind of art he was creating, and we shall not get very far towards understanding that art until we either drop James's misleading phrase, or learn to interpret it correctly.

But if Hawthorne is not dealing with 'the deeper psychology,' just where is his area of operation? To answer this question it will be necessary not only to determine the level of his interest in man's moral nature, but to demonstrate the way in which he objectifies this interest —or, in other words, projects the inner moral or psychological travail *outward* into a world of external symbols where its significance continues to exist for the imagination apart from the protagonist in whom it had its local origin. The tendency of Hawthorne's art is always outward; it shows a habit of endowing the hidden and the private with a high degree of publicity, and of revealing not the unique differences in men's souls but the hidden samenesses. And it undertakes this task with the aid of some disturbingly simplifying formulae. I suggest that the artist who is concerned with 'the deeper psychology' would set off in the opposite direction. He would seek out the differences rather than the samenesses, and he would endeavour to focus his discoveries inward rather than outward. Such an artist would not necessarily be a greater artist; perhaps the chances are that he would be smaller. But at any rate, he would be a different kind of artist, and he would offer different satisfactions to the reader. He would tell us more about men; possibly less about man. It is man in this second and somewhat portentous sense who is Hawthorne's subject.

But to return to the question I proposed earlier: if Hawthorne is[367] not dealing with the deeper psychology, where is his area of operation or interest? *The New Adam and Eve* is far from being one of Hawthorne's better stories, but it answers the question very forthrightly. It opens on the premise that all the people in the world have suddenly died or been destroyed. Life begins all over again with the creation of a second Adam and Eve who awaken in the midst of a modern but completely empty city—a fragment left over from perished civilization:

> Just when the earliest sunshine gilds the mountain tops, two beings have come into life, not in such an Eden as bloomed to welcome our first parents, but in the heart of a modern city. They find themselves in existence, and gazing into one another's eyes. Their emotion is not astonishment. Nor do they perplex themselves with efforts to discover what, and whence, and why they are. Each is satisfied to be, because the other exists likewise; and their first consciousness is of calm and mutual enjoyment, which seems not to have been the birth of that very moment, but prolonged from a past eternity. Thus content with an inner sphere which they inhabit together, it is not immediately that the outward world can obtrude itself upon their notice.

This inner sphere of reciprocal love or affection is the domain of Hawthorne's reality—the only reality that he ever admits without qualification. About everything else, the world of the senses in which man lives and the world of abstract thought from which he builds his systems, Hawthorne cherishes the profoundest doubts. Earlier in this same story he had written:

> We who are born into the world's artificial system can never adequately know how little in our present state and circumstances is natural, and how much is merely the interpolation of the perverted heart and mind of man. Art has become a second and stronger nature; she is a step-mother, whose crafty tenderness has taught us to despise the bountiful and wholesome ministrations of our true parent. It is only through the medium of the imagination that we lessen those iron fetters which we call truth and reality, and make ourselves even partially sensible of what prisoners we are.

When we return to Hawthorne's work as a whole we find that this pervading doubt runs through it all. There is only one thing in which he believes, one truth to which he returns again and again: that is his belief in the reality of reciprocal love. His sense of moral reality, his faith in the goodness of men, is grounded in that inner sphere of[368] feeling—the indispensable medium of truly human communication—which he described in the earlier quotation above. It is this inner sphere, and not any shadowy region of 'the deeper psychology,' which we must explore if we wish to understand the motives of Hawthorne's art. The succession of Hawthorne's stories and novels, pursuing this theme with a patterned repetitiveness that sometimes becomes tedious, does much to make the exploration easy for us. This inner sphere of Hawthorne's reality is not limited to love between the sexes, although Hawthorne would seem to suggest sometimes that it finds its fullest expression there. The magnetic chain of humanity that Ethan Brand violated is a current of sympathy among these inner spheres, and it binds, or ought to bind, all men together. It is this inner sphere of feeling that Hawthorne's art regularly inhabits, or deals with; and if it often vibrates to psychological overtones, it is, in its essence, moral.[369]

. . . .

FROM "Hawthorne and 'The Deeper Psychology,'" *Mandrake,* II (1956), 366-373. Reprinted by permission of the author.

HAWTHORNE'S CHARACTERS: Their Lives and Meanings

HESTER PRYNNE

SAINTLY HESTER

Theodore T. Munger

. . . .

Grave criticism is sometimes heard,—as that [Hawthorne] has no sympathy with his characters in their suffering. . . .

The criticism is oftenest urged in connection with Hester, who is both the centre of interest and of the problem. Hawthorne takes utmost pains to make it clear how she lived. Whether she was happy or not he did not undertake to say; he would not raise so useless a question. The tragedy is pitched at too high a key for happiness. Possibly there may be victory after slow-healing wounds, but there can be no amelioration by circumstance or by deadening of sensibility. Study the thirteenth chapter—Another View of Hester—if you would seek an answer to the question whether in her case the book gravitates toward despair or points to recovery and life.

This exquisite rehearsal of Christian service and temper might well win for her canonization. It is the picture of a saint. The very things that Christ made the condition of acceptance at the last judgment she fulfilled; and the graces that St. Paul declared to be the fruit of the Spirit were exemplified in her daily life. Plainly, this is not a picture of despair, nor even of suffering, except that which necessarily haunts a true soul that has done evil. God forbid that it should be different with any of us! Forgiveness is not lethean. To forget[534] our past would defraud the soul of its heritage in life. The Scarlet Letter faded out and even acquired another meaning. Her life came to blessed uses, with rewards of love and gratitude from others that reached even unto death. The logic of this tender picture of a saintly life—a gospel in itself—must not be overlooked. Hawthorne certainly did not mean that the reader should miss the point. How could recovery from sin be better told, or be more complete? When Peter had denied his Lord

42

and wept bitterly over it, all he was told to do was to feed his Master's sheep. Hester's forgiveness did not shape itself in the form of ecstatic visions, but of service in the spirit of Him who bore witness to the truth; and by herself bearing witness to it she won the reward of its freedom. . . .

Strangers in Boston still search the burial ground of King's Chapel for the grave of Hester Prynne: so true a story, they think, must be true in fact. If it had been found they might have asked, What does the armorial device mean?

"ON A FIELD, SABLE, THE LETTER *A*, GULES."

Does the scarlet letter stand for sin or for cleansing? Is the epitaph a word of despair or of hope? In what direction did Hawthorne intend to lead our thought? If asked, he would have said, Read out of your own heart.[535]

> From "Notes on *The Scarlet Letter*," *Atlantic Monthly*, XCIII (April, 1904), 521-535.

HESTER THE TRANSCENDENTALIST

Stuart P. Sherman

. . . .
In Hester . . . it is manifest that Hawthorne intended to present an individual. She is differentiated by her rich dark beauty, her voluptuous Oriental taste for the gorgeously beautiful, and by her aspect, when she is flushed with momentary joy, of a heroine of romance. But her most interesting distinction is her moral independence and originality. It is to be noted that though her punishment causes her shame and suffering, it does not appear to bring her to any clear state of contrition or repentance. She feels that society by making her an outcast has severed her obligation to it. For it, she exists only as a terrible example. For herself, she is a free spirit liberated in a moral wilderness with her own way to make and take. In these circumstances her thinking has little reference to the doctrines expounded in the meeting-house. She thinks as her heart prompts; and her heart tells her that Arthur Dimmesdale is still her supreme good, and devotion to him her highest duty. The world's frown she had endured and the frown of heaven; "but the frown of this pale, weak, sinful, and sorrow-stricken

man was what Hester could not bear and live!" To save him she had borne in silence the burden of her knowledge of Roger Chillingworth's presence. To redeem him from misery she is ready to flee with him to other lands. Though in the years of her exile she had quietly conformed to the external regulations of society, "the world's law," says her historian, "was no law for her mind." Her readiness to leave the colony with the minister, Hawthorne desires us to[148] understand, was no mere impulse of unreflecting emotion. It was due to her vision of the possibility of reconstructing their shattered lives, and this vision in turn was the consequence of her internal emancipation from the power of the Puritan system of ideas: "She assumed a freedom of speculation, then common enough on the other side of the Atlantic, but which our forefathers, had they known it, would have held to be a deadlier crime than that stigmatized by the scarlet letter. In her lonesome cottage, by the seashore, thoughts visited her, such as dared to enter no other dwelling in New England; shadowy guests, that would have been as perilous as demons to their entertainer, could they have been seen so much as knocking at her door." This free speculative impulse in Hester, her reaching out for "spiritual laws" not generally recognized by the society of her time, makes her a Transcendentalist before the appointed hour.

In the forest scene Hawthorne represents Nature as in mysterious and joyous sympathy with the bliss of the lovers in their vision of a new life together. That he does not accept Nature as moral oracle, however, he indicates by an emphatic parenthesis—"that wild, heathen Nature of the forest, never subjugated by human law, nor illumined by higher truth." On the other hand, his giving the solution of the problem to Arthur Dimmesdale does not prove by any means that his sympathies were wholly on the side of the Puritans. His comment upon the[149] two possibilities of escape from the predicament in which he has placed his hero and heroine is more subtle than is ordinarily noticed. What he has made clear is, that for the minister, who at the end is as thoroughly dominated by Puritan forms of thought as at the beginning, confession was fated and inevitable. For him Hester's solution would have involved the repetition of a deadly sin. His temporary decision to flee with her is therefore consistently represented as filling his mind with perverse suggestions of evil. Arthur Dimmesdale, we may be sure, was happier dying on the scaffold than he would have been sailing to Europe.

It is to be observed, however, that the devilish persecution which afflicts him does not touch Hester. Nor is she exhibited as participating in the ecstasy of his confession. To his question, "Is not this better than what we dreamed of in the forest?" she only murmurs, "I know not! I know not!" And her last words express her quite heretical hope of union with the minister in another world. She believes that in her seven years of suffering she has made amends to heaven for her wrongdoing. With the lapse of time even her rigorous fellow-townsmen relent, take her again into their affections, and even turn to her for counsel "in the continually recurring trials of wounded, wasted, wronged, misplaced, or erring and sinful passion." Hawthorne, while remarking that she often thinks amiss, obviously admires the natural desire of her[150] rich warm nature to regain a place of usefulness and happiness in society. In the conclusion, furthermore, he intimates pointedly enough that the Puritans of the seventeenth century had not received the final word on the regulation of human relationships; that, when the world is ripe for it, there will be a "higher law" declared, a new revelation, "showing how sacred love should make us happy, by the truest test of a life successful to such an end!"[151]

. . . .

FROM "Hawthorne: A Puritan Critic of Puritanism," *Americans* (New York, 1922), pp. 122-152. Reprinted by permission of Charles Scribner's Sons. Copyright 1922, Charles Scribner's Sons; renewal copyright 1950, Ruth Sherman.

HESTER VERSUS HAWTHORNE

F. I. Carpenter

. . . .

According to the orthodox, Hester Prynne sinned through blind passion, and her sin caused the tragedy. According to the romantic, Hester Prynne heroically "gave all to love," and tragedy resulted from the evil of society. According to the transcendentalists, Hester Prynne sinned through deception, but tragedy resulted from the conflict of her dream of freedom with the traditional creed of her lover. Dramatically, each of these interpretations is possible: *The Scarlet Letter* is rich in suggestion. But Hawthorne the moralist sought to destroy this richness.

The Scarlet Letter achieves greatness in its dramatic, objective presentation of conflicting moralities in action: each character seems at once symbolic, yet real. But this dramatic perfection is flawed by the author's moralistic, subjective criticism of Hester Prynne. And this contradiction results from Hawthorne's apparent confusion between the romantic and the transcendental moralities. While the characters of the novel objectively act out the tragic conflict between the traditional morality and the transcendental dream, Hawthorne subjectively damns the transcendental for being romantically immoral.

Most obviously, Hawthorne imposed a moralistic "Conclusion" upon the drama which his characters had acted. But the artistic and moral falsity of this does not lie in its didacticism or in the personal intrusion of the author, for these were the literary conventions of the age. Rather it lies in the contradiction between the author's moralistic comments and the earlier words and actions of his characters. Having created living protagonists, Hawthorne sought to impose his own will and judgment upon them from the outside. Thus he described Hester as admitting her "sin" of passion and as renouncing her "selfish ends" and as seeking to "expiate" her crime. But Hester herself had never admitted to any sin other than deception and had never acted "selfishly" and had worn her scarlet letter triumphantly, rather than penitently. In his "Conclusion," therefore, Hawthorne did violence to the living character whom he had created.

His artificial and moralistic criticism is concentrated in the "Conclusion." But it also appears in other chapters of the novel. In the scene between Hester and Arthur in the forest, Hawthorne had asserted:[69]

> She had wandered, without rule or guidance, in a moral wilderness....
> Shame, Despair, Solitude! These had been her teachers,—stern and wild ones,—
> and they had made her strong, but taught her much amiss.

And again Hawthorne imputed "Shame" to Hester, and declared that her "strength" was immoral.

This scene between Hester and her lover in the forest also suggests the root of Hawthorne's confusion. To the traditional moralists, the "forest," or "wilderness," or "uncivilized Nature" was the symbol-abode of evil—the very negation of moral law. But to the romantics, wild nature had become the very symbol of freedom. In this scene, Hawthorne explicitly condemned Hester for her wildness—for "breathing the wild, free atmosphere of an unredeemed, unchristianized, lawless region." And again he damned her "sympathy" with "that wild, heathen Nature of the forest, never subjugated by human law, nor illumined by higher truth." Clearly he hated moral romanticism. And this hatred would have been harmless, if his heroine had merely been romantic, or immoral.

But Hester Prynne, as revealed in speech and in action was not romantic but transcendental. And Hawthorne failed utterly to distinguish, in his moralistic criticism, between the romantic and the transcendental. For example, he never described the "speculations" of Hester concerning "freedom" as anything but negative, "wild," "lawless," and "heathen." All "higher truth" for him seemed to reside exclusively in traditional, "civilized" morality. But Hawthorne's contemporaries, Emerson and Thoreau, had specifically described the "wilderness" (*Life in the Woods*) as the precondition of the new morality of freedom; and "Nature" as the very abode of "higher truth": all those transcendental "speculations" which Hawthorne imputed to his heroine conceived of "Nature" as offering the opportunity for the realization of the higher moral law and for the development of a "Christianized" society more perfectly illumined by the divine truth.

Therefore, Hawthorne's moralistic passages never remotely admitted the possible truth of the transcendental ideal which he had objectively described Hester Prynne as realizing. Having allowed his imagination to create an idealistic heroine, he did not allow his conscious mind to justify—or even to describe fairly—her ideal morality. Rather, he damned the transcendental character whom he had created, for being romantic and immoral. But the words and deeds by means of which he had created her contradicted his own moralistic criticisms.[70]

In the last analysis, the greatness of *The Scarlet Letter* lies in the character of Hester Prynne. Because she dared to trust herself and to believe in the possibility of a new morality in the new world, she achieved spiritual greatness in spite of her own human weakness, in spite of the prejudices of her Puritan society, and, finally, in spite of the prejudices of her creator himself. For the human weakness which made her deceive her lover in order to protect him makes her seem only the more real. The calm steadfastness with which she endures the ostracism of society makes her heroic. And the clear purpose which she follows, despite the denigrations of Hawthorne, makes her almost ideal.

Hester, almost in spite of Hawthorne, envisions the transcendental ideal of positive freedom, instead of the romantic ideal of mere escape. She urges her lover to create a new life with her in the wilderness: "Doth the universe lie within the compass of yonder town? Whither leads yonder forest track?" And she seeks to arouse him to a pragmatic idealism equal to the task: "Exchange this false life of thine for a true one!...Preach! Write! Act! Do anything save to lie down and die!"

Thus Hester Prynne embodies the authentic American dream of a new life in the wilderness of the new world, and of self-reliant action to realize that ideal. In the Puritan age in which he lived, and in Hawthorne's own nineteenth century, this ideal was actually being realized in practice. Even in our modern society with its more liberal laws, Hester Prynne might hope to live happily with her lover, after winning divorce from her cruel and vengeful husband. But in every century her tragedy would still be the same. It would result from her own deception and from the conflicting moral belief of her lover. But it would not result from her own sense of guilt or shame.[71]

.   .   .   .

FROM "Scarlet A Minus," *American Literature and the Dream* (New York, 1955), pp. 63-72. Reprinted by permission of Philosophical Library.

HESTER AS TRAGIC HEROINE

Mark Van Doren

. . . .

Above all it is Hester Prynne, whose passion and beauty[150] dominate every other person, and color each event. Hawthorne has conceived her as he has conceived his scene, in the full strength of his feeling for ancient New England. He is the Homer of that New England, as Hester is its most heroic creature. Tall, with dark and abundant hair and deep black eyes, a rich complexion that makes modern women (says Hawthorne) pale and thin by comparison, and a dignity that throws into low relief the "delicate, evanescent, and indescribable grace" by which gentility in girls has since come to be known, from the very first—and we believe it—she is said to cast a spell over those who behold her; and this is not merely because of the scarlet letter, "so fantastically embroidered and illuminated," upon the bosom of her always magnificent dress. It is because of herself, into whom Hawthorne has known how to put a unique importance. Nor is this a remote, a merely stately importance. We are close to her all of the time, and completely convinced of her flesh and blood, of her heart and mind. She is a passionate woman whom Hawthorne does not need to call passionate, for he has the evidence: her state of excitement, bordering on frenzy, in the prison after her first exposure to the crowd —her "moral agony," reflected in the convulsions that have seized the child; her pride, her daring, in after days when she makes more show than she needs to make of the letter on her bosom, the symbol she insists upon adorning with such "wild and picturesque peculiarity"; her alternations of despair and defiance; her continuing love, so unconfessed that we can only assume it to be there, for the man whose weakness seems so little to deserve it; her power of speech, so economical and so tender, when at last she is with this man;[151] her sudden revelation that through years of loneliness she has not consented to let her soul be killed.

"I pity thee," says Chillingworth near the close, "for the good that has been wasted in thy nature." These are terrible words, for they express a fear we have had, the fear that this magnificent woman has lived for nothing; for a few days of love, and then for dreary years of less indeed than nothing. Hawthorne has known how to fasten this fear upon us—it could exist in us only if we loved her too—but he also has known how to make Chillingworth's words untrue. The life of Hester increases, not diminishes, in the bleak world whose best citizen she is. Nor is this done by Hawthorne at the expense of that world. He deplores the "dismal severity" of its moral code, and for all we know he is presenting Hester as the blackest sacrifice it ever offered on its altar. But he is not doctrinaire against the code. His Puritan world is in its own way beautiful. It fully exists, as Hester fully exists. If their existences conflict, then that is the tragedy to be understood. Hester, whose solitary thought takes her far beyond the confines of the code, is nevertheless respectful of the strength in it that could kill her were she not even stronger. She is not the subject of a sermon; she is the heroine of a tragedy, and she understands the tragedy. She understands it because Hawthorne does; because at the same time that he recoils from the Puritan view of sin he honors its capacity to be a view at all. Sin for him, for Hester, and for the people who punish her is equally a solemn fact, a problem for which there is no solution in life. There was no other solution for his story, given Hester's strength, Dimmesdale's weakness, and Chillingworth's perversion, than the one he found. Rather, as we read, it finds itself. And if the conclusion[152] is not depressing, the reason is that nothing before it has been meaningless. This world has not been really bleak. It has been as beautiful as it was terrible; Hester's life has not been hollow, nor has her great nature been wasted.[153]

. . . .

FROM *"The Scarlet Letter," Nathaniel Hawthorne* (New York, 1949), pp. 114-166. Reprinted by permission of William Sloane Associates, Inc., copyright 1949.

HESTER THE ROMANTIC

Darrel Abel

Hester Prynne, the heroine of *The Scarlet Letter,* typifies romantic individualism, and in her story Hawthorne endeavored to exhibit the inadequacy of such a philosophy. The romantic individualist repudiates the doctrine of a supernatural ethical absolute. He rejects both the authority of God, which sanctions a pietistic ethic, and the authority of society, which sanctions a utilitarian ethic, to affirm the sole authority of Nature. Hester, violating piety and decorum, lived a life of nature and attempted to rationalize her romantic self-indulgence; but, although she broke the laws of God and man, she failed to secure even the natural satisfactions she sought.

Many modern critics, however, who see her as a heroine à la George Sand, accept her philosophy and regard her as the central figure of the romance—the spokesman of Hawthorne's views favoring "a larger liberty." Hawthorne's women are usually more sympathetic and impressive than his men; because Hester is more appealing than either her husband or her lover, it is easy to disregard their more central roles in the story. Furthermore, the title of the romance is commonly taken to refer mainly to the letter on Hester's dress and thus somehow to designate her as the central figure; [303] but, in fact, the ideal letter, not any particular material manifestation of it, is referred to in the title. Actually its most emphatic particular manifestation is the stigma revealed on Dimmesdale's breast in the climaxing chapter of the book, "The Revelation of the Scarlet Letter."

Hester's apologists unduly emphasize circumstances which seem to make her the engaging central figure of the romance, and they ignore or even decry the larger tendency of the book, which subordinates her and exposes her moral inadequacy. "She is a free spirit liberated in a moral wilderness."[1]

> She has sinned, but the sin leads her straightway to a larger life....Hawthorne...lets the sin elaborate itself, so far as Hester's nature is concerned, into nothing but beauty....Since her love for Dimmesdale was the one sincere passion of her life, she obeyed it utterly, though a conventional judgment would have said that she was stepping out of the moral order. There is nothing in the story to suggest condemnation of her or of the minister in their sin....The passion itself, as the two lovers still agree at the close of their hard experience, was sacred and never caused them repentance.[2]

This opinion sublimely disregards Hawthorne's elaborate exposition of the progressive moral dereliction of Hester, during which "all the light and graceful foliage of her character [was] withered up by this red-hot brand" of sinful passion. It even more remarkably ignores her paramour's seven-year-long travail of conscience for (in his own dying words) "the sin here so awfully revealed."

The most recent and immoderate advocate of Hester as the prepossessing exponent of a wider freedom in sexual relations is Professor Frederic I. Carpenter:

> In the last analysis, the greatness of The Scarlet Letter lies in the

---

[1] See Stuart P. Sherman's "Hawthorne: A Puritan Critic of Puritanism," excerpted on pp. 43-45 of this book.

[2] John Erskine, Cambridge History of American Literature, II, pp. 26-27.

character of Hester Prynne. Because she dared to trust herself to believe in the possibility of a new morality in the new world, she achieved spiritual greatness in spite of her own human weakness, in spite of the prejudices of her Puritan society,...in spite of the prejudices of her creator himself. [3]

It is a tribute to Hawthorne's art that Hester's champion believes in her so strongly that he presumes to rebuke her creator for abusing her and rejoices in his conviction that she triumphs over the author's "denigrations."

In fact, Hawthorne does feel moral compassion for Hester, but her role in the story is to demonstrate that persons who engage our moral compassion may nevertheless merit moral censure. We sympathize with Hester at first because of her personal attraction, and our sympathy deepens throughout the story because we see that she is more sinned against than sinning.

The prime offender against her is Roger Chillingworth, who married her before she was mature enough to know the needs of her nature. There is a tincture of Godwinism—even of Fourierism—in Hawthorne's treatment of Hester's breach of her marriage obligations. Godwin held that marriage was "the most odious of all monopolies" and that it was everyone's duty to love the worthiest. After her lapse, Hester told her husband, "Thou knowest I was frank with thee. I felt no love, nor feigned any." According to Godwinian principles, then, her duty to him was slight, especially if a man came along whom she could love. Chillingworth freely acknowledged that he had wronged her in marrying her before she was aware of the needs of her nature: "Mine was the first wrong, when[304] I betrayed thy budding youth into a false and unnatural relation with my decay." His second, less heinous, offense was his neglectfully absenting himself from her after their marriage. His experience understood what her innocence could not foresee, that the awakening passion in her might take a forbidden way: "If sages were ever wise in their own behoof, I might have foreseen all this." His third and culminating offense was his lack of charity toward her after her disgrace. Although he admitted his initial culpability in betraying her into "a false and unnatural relation," he refused to share the odium brought upon her in consequence of the situation he had created. True, he plotted no revenge against her, but cold forbearance was not enough. He was motivated not by love but by self-love; in his marriage and in his vengeance he cherished and pursued his private objects, to the exclusion of the claims of others, whose lives were involved with his own. He regarded his wife jealously, as a chattel,[4] not as a person with needs and rights of her own. Her error

---

[3] See F. I. Carpenter's "Scarlet A Minus," excerpted on pp. 45-47 of this book.

[4] "Woman is born for love, and it is impossible to turn her from seeking it. Men should deserve her love as an inheritance, rather than seize and guard it like a prey" (Margaret Fuller, *Woman in the Nineteenth Century* [Boston, 1893], p. 337).

touched his compassion only perfunctorily, but it gave a mortal wound to his *amour-propre*. Hester's adulterous passion was nobler, for she wished that she might bear her paramour's shame and anguish as well as her own. Thus Chillingworth triply offended against her: he drew her into a relationship which made her liable to sin, did not duly defend her from the peril in which he had placed her, and cast her off when she succumbed.

The nature of Dimmesdale's offense against Hester is too obvious to require specification, but both Hester's conduct and his own deserve whatever extenuation may be due to the passionate and impulsive errors of inexperience: "This had been a sin of passion, not of principle, nor even purpose." The minister's conduct toward Hester, then, is less blameworthy than her husband's, who had knowingly and deliberately jeopardized her happiness and moral security; Dimmesdale tells Hester: "We are not, Hester, the worst sinners in the world. There is one worse than even the polluted priest!" A distinction must be made, however, between Dimmesdale's moral responsibility and Hester's; her sin was contingent upon his, and her conduct is therefore more deserving of palliation than his. Besides, he had moral defenses and moral duties which she did not have. He had a pastoral duty toward her and a professional duty to lead an exemplary life. Also, according to Hawthorne's view of the distinctive endowments of the sexes, Hester depended upon her womanly feeling, but he had the guidance of masculine intellect and moral erudition. Above all, he was free to marry to satisfy "the strong animal nature" in him, but Hester met her happiest choice too late, when she was "already linked and wedlock bound to a fell adversary." But the minister's really abominable fault was not his fornication; it was his unwillingness to confess his error, his hypocrisy. Hester wished she might bear his shame as well as her own, but he shrank from assuming his place beside her because his perilous pride in his reputation for sanctity was dearer to him than truth. Like Chillingworth, he wronged Hester and left her to bear the punishment alone.

Society wronged Hester as grievously as, though less invidiously than, particular persons wronged her. Hawthorne distinguished between society under its instinctively[305] human aspect and society under its institutional aspect. Society as collective humanity sympathized and was charitable: "It is to the credit of human nature, that, except where its selfishness is brought into play, it loves more readily than it hates." But society under its institutional aspect pursued an abstraction, conceived as the general good, which disposed it vindictively toward errant individuals. Hawthorne remarked in "The New Adam and Eve": "[The] Judgment Seat [is] the very symbol of man's perverted state." A scheme of social justice supplants the essential law of love which is grounded in human hearts; any system of expedient regulations tends to become sacrosanct eventually, so that instead of serving humanity it becomes a tyrannical instrument for coercing non-conformists.

Harsh legalism has been remarked as a characteristic of the Puritan theocracy by social historians: "The effect of inhumane punishments on officials and the popular mind generally...[was apparently] a brutalizing effect..., rendering them more callous to human sufferings."[5] "To make the people good became the supreme task of the churches, and legalism followed as a matter of course."[6] "The theory was that Jehovah was the primary law-giver, the Bible a statute-book, the ministers and magistrates stewards of the divine will."[7] Hester, then, Hawthorne tells us, suffered "the whole dismal severity of the Puritanic code of law" in "a period when the forms of authority were felt to possess the sacredness of Divine institutions." Her punishment shows how society had set aside the humane injunction that men should love one another, to make a religion of the office of vengeance, which in the Scriptures is exclusively appropriated to God. The wild-rose bush, with "its delicate gems," which stood by the prison door, and "the burdock, pigweed, apple-peru, and other such unsightly vegetation" which grew with such appropriate luxuriance in the prison yard symbolize the mingled moral elements in "the dim, awful, mysterious, grotesque, intricate nature of man."[8] Puritan society, unfortunately, had cultivated the weeds and neglected the flowers of human nature and attached more significance to "the black flower of civilized life, a prison," than to the rose bush, "which, by a strange chance, has been kept alive in history" "to symbolize some sweet moral blossom." There is powerful irony in Hawthorne's picture of the harsh matrons who crowded around the pillory to demand that Hester be put to death: "Is there not law for it? Truly, there is, both in Scripture and the statute-book." Surely Hawthorne was here mindful of the question which the scribes and Pharisees put to Jesus concerning the woman taken in adultery: "Now Moses in the law commanded us that such

5 L. T. Merrill, "The Puritan Policeman," *American Sociological Review*, X (December, 1945), 768.

6 Joseph Haroutunian, *Piety Versus Moralism: The Passing of the New England Theology* (New York, 1932), p. 90.

7 Merrill, *op. cit.*, p. 766.

8 Hawthorne remarked, in the *American Notebooks*, that "there is an unmistakable analogy between the wicked weeds and the bad habits and sinful propensities which have overrun the moral world." There is an excellent explication of the symbolism of *The Scarlet Letter* in H. H. Waggoner's "Nathaniel Hawthorne: The Cemetery, the Prison, and the Rose," *University of Kansas City Review*, XIV (Spring, 1948), 175-90.

should be stoned: but what sayest thou?" The harshness of this tirade reflects the perversion of womanliness which has been wrought among this "people amongst whom religion and law were almost identical."[306] A man in the crowd offered timely reproof to the chider: "Is there no virtue in woman, save what springs from a wholesome fear of the gallows?"—a reminder that virtue must be voluntary, an expression of character, and that there is little worth in a virtue that is compulsory, an imposition of society.

The ostracism called too lenient a punishment by the perhaps envious matrons of the town was almost fatal to Hester's sanity and moral sense, for it almost severed "the many ties, that, so long as we breathe the common air..., unite us to our kind." "Man had marked this woman's sin by a scarlet letter, which had such potent and disastrous efficacy that no human sympathy could reach her, save it were sinful like herself." Even children "too young to comprehend wherefore this woman should be shut out from the sphere of human charities" learned to abhor the woman upon whom society had set the stigma of the moral outcast. The universal duty of "acknowledging brotherhood even with the guiltiest" was abrogated in the treatment of Hester:

> In all her intercourse with society,...there was nothing which made her feel as if she belonged to it....She was banished, and as much alone as if she inhabited another sphere, or communicated with the common nature by other organs and senses than the rest of human kind. She stood apart from moral interests, yet close beside them, like a ghost that revisits the familiar fireside, and can no longer make itself seen or felt.

The peculiar moral danger to Hester in her isolation was that it gave her too little opportunity for affectionate intercourse with other persons. Hawthorne regarded a woman's essential life as consisting in the right exercise of her emotions. His attitude toward women is that of Victorian liberalism; he looked upon them as equal to men, but differently endowed. To him, the distinctive feminine virtues were those characteristic of ideal wifehood and motherhood: instinctive purity and passionate devotion. His prescription for the happiest regulation of society was "Man's intellect, moderated by Woman's tenderness and moral sense." Dimmesdale's history shows the corruption of the masculine virtues of reason and authority in a sinner who has cut himself off from the divine source of those virtues; Hester's history shows the corruption of the feminine virtues of passion and submission in a sinner who has been thrust out from the human community on which those virtues depend for their reality and function. In this essential feminine attribute, the working of her moral sensibility through her feelings rather than her thought, she bears a strong general resemblance to Milton's Eve (who is, however, more delicately conceived). She is a pure (as Hardy used the term) or very (as Shakespeare would have said) woman: that is, a charmingly real woman whose abundant sexuality, "whatever hypocrites austerely talk," was the characteristic and valuable endowment of her sex.

In consequence of her ostracism, Hester's life turned, "in a great measure, from passion and feeling, to thought"; she "wandered without a clew in the dark labyrinth of mind." Reflecting bitterly upon her own experience, she was convinced equally of the injustice and the hopelessness of a woman's position in society:

> Was existence worth accepting, even to the happiest among them? As concerned her own[307] individual existence, she had long ago decided in the negative....[A woman who considers what reforms are desirable discerns] a hopeless task before her. As a first step, the whole system of society is to be torn down, and built up anew. Then, the very nature of the opposite sex, or its long hereditary habit, which has become like nature, is to be essentially modified, before woman can be allowed to assume what seems a fair and suitable position. Finally, all other difficulties being obviated, woman cannot take advantage of these preliminary reforms, until she herself shall have undergone a still mightier change; in which, perhaps, the ethereal essence, wherein she has her truest life, will be found to have evaporated.

Although Hawthorne to some degree sympathized with Hester's rebellious mood, he did not, as Stuart P. Sherman averred, represent her as "a free spirit liberated in a moral wilderness," but as a human derelict who "wandered, without rule or guidance, in a moral wilderness." "A woman never overcomes these problems by any exercise of thought," and Hester's teachers—"Shame, Despair, Solitude!"—had "taught her much amiss." Thus, unfitted by her intense femininity for intellectual speculations, as well as by her isolation from the common experience of mankind, which rectifies aberrant thought, she unwomaned herself and deluded herself with mistaken notions. . . .

In the last analysis, the error for which Hester suffered was her too-obstinate supposition that human beings had a right to happiness. "Hester's tragedy came upon her in consequence of excessive yielding to her own heart." Hawthorne remarked in his notebooks that "happiness in this world, if it comes at all, comes incidentally. Make it the object of pursuit, and it leads us a wild-goose chase, and is never attained." The proper pursuit of man, he thought, was not happiness but a virtuous life; he inherited the Puritan conviction that

> the good which God seeks and accomplishes is the display of infinite being, a good which[308] transcends the good of finite existence. If the misery of the sinner is conducive to such a display, which it must be because sinners are in fact miserable, then it is just and good that sinners should be punished with misery. [9]

Although we are expected to love and pity Hester, we are not invited to condone her fault or to construe it as a virtue. More a

---

[9] Haroutunian, *op. cit.*, p. 144.

victim of circumstances than a wilful wrongdoer, she is nevertheless to be held morally responsible. In her story Hawthorne intimates that, tangled as human relationships are and must be, no sin ever issues solely from the intent and deed of the individual sinner, but that it issues instead from a complicated interplay of motives of which he is the more or less willing instrument. Even so, however strong, insidious, and unforeseeable the influences and compulsions which prompted his sin, in any practicable system of ethics the sinner must be held individually accountable for it. This is harsh doctrine, but there is no escape from it short of unflinching repudiation of the moral ideas which give man his tragic and lonely dignity in a world in which all things except himself seem insensate and all actions except his own seem mechanical. The Puritans were no more illogical in coupling the assumption of moral determinism with the doctrine of individual responsibility to God than is our own age in conjoining theories of biological and economic determinism with the doctrine of individual responsibility to society. The Puritan escaped from his inconsistency by remarking that God moves in a mysterious way; we justify ours by the plea of expediency. Hawthorne, however, was content merely to pose the problem forcibly in the history of Hester Prynne.[309]

FROM "Hawthorne's Hester," *College English,* XIII (March, 1952), 303-309. Reprinted by permission of the author and *College English.*

HESTER AS A PURITAN FAUSTA

William Bysshe Stein

. . . .

Hawthorne feminizes the Faust motif in depicting the character of Hester Prynne. From the moment Hester commits her soul to the cause of the devil, she ceases to be the standard heroine of the typical romance, the shaping source of Hawthorne's inspiration. Exiled from normal society and constantly attended by the demon, she shows a remarkable development in intellect. In seven short years she changes from an emotionally passionate girl into a dynamic rebel against convention. And considering her Puritan antecedents, her radical speculations are more iconoclastic than Chillingworth's. She becomes, in other words, the feminine counterpart of Faust, a virtual Puritan Fausta. Though Hester's adultery, a sin of passion, partly links her with the devil's legions, it is not until she pledges[113] herself to silence regarding her connection with Chillingworth that she actually recognizes the authority of the evil principle. In the conspiracy of silence, she betrays an ulterior motive. She subconsciously asserts a wishful desire for earthly happiness with the man who contributed to her ruin. And unintentionally she becomes an accessory of Chillingworth in his scheme of revenge, undermining the minister's moral and physical life with her dream of illicit bliss. Hawthorne is quite explicit about her temptation:

> It might be, too,—doubtless it was so, although she hid the secret from herself, and grew pale whenever it struggled out of her heart, like a serpent from its hole,—it might be that another feeling kept her within the scene and pathway that had been so fatal. There dwelt, there trode the feet of one with whom she deemed herself connected in a union....Over and over again, the tempter of souls had thrust this idea upon Hester's contemplation, and laughed at the passionate and desperate joy with which she seized, and then strove to cast it from her. She barely looked the idea in the face, and hastened to bar it in its dungeon.

Nor does she succeed in quelling the rebellion that rages in her heart and mind. Increasingly she questions the justice of her punishment. Behind the smug countenances of her persecutors, she sees intimations of evil worse than her own. In the embarrassment of certain members of her own sex, all supposedly earthly saints, she intuits secret sin. The fiend, "whose talisman was that fatal symbol," will leave her nothing to revere. Her outward piety contradicts the general trend of her thoughts: "She assumed a freedom of speculation, then common enough on the other side of the Atlantic, but which our forefathers, had they known it, would have held to be a deadlier crime than that stigmatized by the scarlet letter." She deplores the subordinate position of women in society, and believes that the system of masculine privilege, the double standard of ethics, ought "to be torn down, and built up anew." As she gazes round her, she inwardly declares that "the world's law [is] no law for her mind." This impatience with the conventions of the culture attests the Faustian tone of her meditations. Her intellectual curiosity[114] savors of the sinful impulse that led her into adultery. She cannot "measure...ideas of right and wrong by any standard external to herself." In all her thoughts she manifests the blind pride of Lucifer and his most notorious disciple, the ill-fated Faust.

This mental outlook serves to negate the Christian quality of her numerous acts of kindness in her role of "Sister of Mercy" in the Puritan settlement. On the surface, her benevolence and charity conform to the Calvinistic conception of penance. But in her heart, wherein only the love of God is supposed to dwell, an earthlier passion holds sway. Nothing, however, that she may think or do can change the tragic course of her life. Slowly despair overwhelms her, and she contemplates suicide: "At times, a fearful doubt strove to possess her soul, whether it were not better to send Pearl at once to heaven, and go herself to such futurity as Eternal Justice should provide." Her distraught spiritual state has an analogue in Goethe's *Faust*. The hero ponders the problem of life's meaning and the futility of noble thoughts; then, melancholy and disillusioned, he discerns that suicide is the single phase of human destiny within his control. Neither his vast knowledge nor the wide range of his speculations encourages him to think that the conditions of human existence can be changed or are worth changing. He is a care-worn man who "sowed vanity to reap despair." As he reviews the disappointments of the past and the hopelessness of the future, he dolefully concludes that all his struggles are self-deception: "Everything fails me—everything—these instruments mock me...in vain I call on science; I stand before the guarded door of nature." This parallel scarcely seems a coincidence: it is another sum that rings out clearly on the register of associations spreading from Goethe's *Faust*. Only in this latter work does suicide emerge as a solution to the disquieting frustrations of thought and emotion.

When the pall shrouding Hester's spirit lifts, she resolves to take positive action. She arranges to meet the minister so as to tell him of the old physician's nefarious plan of revenge. At the same time she intends to advise him to take flight from the colony. Pearl, as if aware of her mother's desperate undertaking, demands information[115] regarding her familiarity with the devil who haunts the "forest, and carries a book with him,—a big, heavy book, with iron clasps...this ugly Black Man offers his book and an iron pen to everybody that meets him here among the trees; and they...write their names with their own blood. And then he sets his mark on their bosoms! Didst thou ever meet the Black Man, mother?" Hester thoughtfully considers the question, and then answers: "Once in my life I met the Black Man! This scarlet letter is his mark!" This utterance is in direct contrast to the evasions which she had hitherto offered Pearl explaining her infamous emblem. Hester consciously admits her alliance with the devil; she is no longer interested in resisting the temptations of the demon who haunts her unconscious. Her interview with her former lover will represent an earnest effort to defy the laws of morality to which she has to date submitted, however reluctantly.

At this point Hawthorne changes Hester's role in the story to that of a tempter, the evolution of her character, in a sense, corresponding to Chillingworth's. Hawthorne depicts the manner in which she uses her powerful sexual attraction to govern Dimmesdale's volition. The Faustian inspiration which controls Hawthorne's creative imagination stems from Lewis' *The Monk*. He takes pains to model Dimmesdale after Ambrosio, and to establish the Puritan divine's flaw of nature in his passionate animal drive. Like Ambrosio, Dimmesdale is held in high esteem by his parishioners, being thought "little less than a heaven-ordained apostle" and "a miracle of holiness." The pastor's outward piety and stern asceticism increase after his affair with Hester just as did Ambrosio's after his sexual debauches with Matilda. Dimmesdale's "devotion to study, his scrupulous fulfilment of parochial duty and...the fasts and vigils of which he made a frequent practice," become the wonder of his profession. The strong sexual predisposition of the minister is shown in his proneness to anger, and Hawthorne comments that this was "the portion of him which the Devil claimed, and through which he sought to win the rest." This is a parallel situation to *The Monk* which is almost beyond quibble.[116]

Identical motivations continue as the forest scene further develops. To lure Ambrosio into a pact with the devil, Matilda takes advantage of his sublimated lechery, and so Hester breaks down the inhibitions of Dimmesdale. When they are alone in the forest, she casts her scarlet letter aside; and when she lets her long hair flow loosely about her face, she recaptures the beauty which not too long before had made the minister forget his holy vows. As the divine responds to her devilish charms, she proposes that he seek his fortune across the seas, leaving no doubt that she will accompany him: "But thou shalt leave it all behind thee! It shall not cumber thy steps, as thou treadest along the forest-path....Leave this wreck and ruin here where it hath happened....There is happiness to be enjoyed!" What greater temptation to the weakened morale of Dimmesdale could there be? This was a hope he had never dared to express. Thus when Hester convinces him that this is the only alternative to disgrace or death, she performs the duty of a tempter. Only his confession at the election ceremony, brought on by a knowledge of imminent death more than by his tortured conscience, prevents Hester from precipitating him into irretrievable damnation. Only years later does Hester sincerely repent. The minister frustrates her as much as he does Chillingworth.[117]

. . . .

From *"The Scarlet Letter:* The New England *Faust," Hawthorne's Faust: A Study of the Devil's Archetype* (Gainesville, 1953), pp. 104-122. Reprinted by permission of the University of Florida Press, copyright 1953.

HESTER AND HER SOCIETY:
THE BALANCED GUILT

Marius Bewley

. . . .

The nature of Hester's sin is different from Dimmesdale's,[166] and it is more difficult to analyze. It differs, first of all, in not being a secret sin. As far as the adultery itself goes, it is probable that Hawthorne would have considered the public penance imposed on Hester in the opening pages of the novel a sufficient retribution. The tragedy of her life was, not that she had sexually transgressed, but that a penalty was imposed which induced alienation in her, and in the imposition of such a penalty society itself is deeply guilty. There are points at which the guilt of society almost seems to absorb the personal guilt of Hester. But such a resolution would be highly uncharacteristic of Hawthorne, and in the end we find the problem complicated by certain factors in Hester's own mind and character which suggest that inherent moral flaws have found nutriment in the social penalty under which she has had to suffer. Thus, the symbol of the scarlet letter stands for a pervasive guilt in which all have their respective shares. There is a passage from Chapter XIII, which, despite its length, it is imperative to quote here, for it gives us very clearly the two points I have made above—that the social penalty inflicted upon Hester, because it struck at the very roots of her human nature, was itself sinful; but that, among its consequences, was the development of a speculative turn of mind which Hawthorne, to a degree not often recognized today, found sinful, and imputable to Hester alone.

The effect of the symbol,—or, rather, the position in respect to society that was indicated by it—on the mind of Hester Prynne herself, was powerful and peculiar. All the light and graceful foliage of her character had been withered up by this red-hot brand, and had long ago fallen away, leaving a bare and harsh outline, which might have been repulsive, had she possessed friends or companions to be repelled by it. Even the attractiveness of her person had undergone a similar change. It might be partly owing to the studied austerity of her dress, and partly to the lack of demonstration in her manners. It was a sad transformation, too, that her rich and luxuriant hair had either been cut off, or was so completely hidden by a cap, that not a shining lock of it ever once gushed into the sunshine. It was due in part to all these causes, but still more to something else, that there seemed to be no longer anything in Hester's face for Love to dwell upon; nothing in

Hester's form, though majestic and statue-like, that Passion would ever dream of clasping in its embrace; nothing in Hester's bosom, to make it ever again, the pillow of Affection.[167] Some attribute had departed from her, the permanence of which had been essential to keep her a woman....She who has once been a woman, and ceased to be so, might at any moment become a woman again if there were only the magic touch to effect the transfiguration. We shall see whether Hester Prynne were ever afterwards to be touched, and so transfigured.

Much of the marble coldness of Hester's impression was to be attributed to the circumstance, that her life had turned, in a great measure, from passion and feeling, to thought. Standing alone in the world,—alone, as to any dependence on society, and with little Pearl to be guided and protected,— alone, and hopeless of retrieving her position, even had she not scorned to consider it desirable,—she cast away the fragments of a broken chain. The world's law was no law for her mind. It was an age in which the human intellect, newly emancipated, had taken a more active and wider range than for many centuries before....Hester Prynne imbibed this spirit. She assumed a freedom of speculation, then common enough on the other side of the Atlantic, but which our forefathers, had they known it, would have held to be a deadlier crime than that stigmatized by the scarlet letter. In her lonesome cottage, by the sea-shore, thoughts visited her, such as dared to enter no other dwelling in New England; shadowy guests, they would have been as perilous as demons to their entertainer, could they have been seen so much as knocking at her door.

In the first paragraph, Hawthorne points to the guilt of society in depriving Hester of her essential womanhood; but in the second paragraph, she complements society's guilt with her own. Speculative freedom of mind, although presumably at a more vulgar level, also characterized Zenobia in *The Blithedale Romance*: "She made no scruple of oversetting all human institutions, and scattering them as with a breeze from a fan. A female reformer, in her attacks upon society, has an instinctive sense of where the life lies, and is inclined to aim directly at that spot." This speculative freedom . . . characterized various types of the artist in Hawthorne's short stories. We get a significant clue to what this freedom of mind signified for Hawthorne at the beginning of Chapter XVIII:

Her intellect and heart had their home, as it were, in desert places, where she roamed as freely as the wild Indian in his woods. For years past she had looked from this estranged point of view at human institutions and whatever priests or legislators[168] had established; criticizing all with hardly more reverence than the Indian would feel for the clerical band, the judicial robe, the pillory, the gallows, the fireside, or the church. The tendency of her fate and fortunes had been to set her free. The scarlet letter was her passport into regions where other women dared not tread. Shame, Despair, Solitude! These had been her teachers,—stern and wild ones,—and they had made her strong, but taught her much amiss.

The modern reader may be inclined to discount Hawthorne's

criticism of Hester's speculative freedom as ironic, but Hawthorne means what he says. Her "latitude of speculation" is as disastrous in its effects on her personality as Ethan Brand's "starlit eminence" of mind was on his, and the imagery Hawthorne uses in describing the two cases is strikingly similar. Of Hester, Hawthorne says: "Standing in the world alone...she cast away the fragments of a broken chain." This is, of course, that same magnetic chain that figures so largely in the short story. If society has a hand in the breaking of that chain for Hester, Hawthorne is careful to show that Hester is ultimately guilty in her own right:

A woman never overcomes these problems by any exercise of thought. They are not to be solved or only in one way. If her heart chance to come uppermost, they vanish. Thus Hester Prynne, whose heart had lost its regular and healthy throb, wandered without a clew in the dark labyrinth of mind....

If Dimmesdale's sin moves us towards the worlds of Mr. Hooper and Gervayse Hastings, a passage like the above unmistakably relates to the Unpardonable Sin of Ethan Brand:

Then ensued that vast intellectual development, which, in its progress, disturbed the counterpoise between his mind and heart....But where was the heart? That, indeed, had withered,—had contracted,—had hardened,—had perished! It had ceased to partake of the universal throb. He had lost his hold of the magnetic chain of humanity.

Hester's exclusion from the inner sphere of reality is complete:

In all her intercourse with society, however, there was nothing that made her feel as if she belonged to it. Every word, every gesture, and even the silence of those with whom she came in contact, implied, and often expressed, that she was banished, and as [169] much alone as if she inhabited another sphere, or communicated with the common nature by other organs and senses than the rest of human kind. She stood apart from moral interests, yet close beside them, like a ghost that revisits the familiar fireside, and can no longer make itself seen or felt; no more smile with the household joy, nor mourn with the kindred sorrow; or, should it succeed in manifesting its forbidden sympathy, awakening only terror and horrible repugnance. These emotions, in fact, and its bitterest scorn besides, seemed to be the sole portion that she retained in the universal heart.

There are certain qualities in this passage that remind one of the lady's predicament in "The Hollow of the Three Hills." Because of an infidelity to her husband, that lady is also forever excluded from moral interests, and the relationship between her and her family is a communion of ghosts. Hawthorne's death-imagery is applied, in Hester's case, with a good deal of insistence: "Her face, so long familiar to the townspeople, showed the marble quietude which they were accustomed to behold there. It was like a mask; or rather, like the frozen calmness of a dead woman's features; owing this dreary resemblance to the fact that Hester was actually dead, in respect to any claim of sympathy, and had departed out of the world, in which she still seemed to mingle."

The essence of Dimmesdale's sin is concealment; Hester's is more complicated, but it is essentially a withdrawal from society on her part; for if Hester is banished, Hawthorne insists that she similarly banishes mankind from her own heart. The result is a living death. But in Chapters XVII and XVIII a rather extraordinary and un-Hawthornian thing happens. Meeting in the forest after their seven years of penitential misery, Hester persuades Dimmesdale to flee back to Europe with her: in other words, to re-establish their illicit union as a permanent thing. As a symbol of her decision, she tears the scarlet letter from her breast and throws it away:

> There played around her mouth, and beamed out of her eyes, a radiant and tender smile, that seemed gushing from the very heart of womanhood. A crimson flush was growing on her cheek, that had been long so pale. Her sex, her youth, and the whole richness of her beauty, came back from what men call the irrevocable past, and clustered themselves, with her maiden hope,[170] and a happiness before unknown, within the magic circle of this hour. And, as if the gloom of the earth and sky had been but the effluence of these two mortal hearts, it vanished with their sorrow. All at once, as with a sudden smile of heaven, forth burst the sunshine, pouring a very flood into the obscure forest, gladdening each green leaf, transmuting the yellow fallen ones to gold, and gleaming adown the grey trunks of the solemn trees. The objects that had made a shadow hitherto, embodied the brightness now. The course of the little brook might be traced by its merry gleam afar into the wood's heart of mystery, which had become a mystery of joy.
>
> Such was the sympathy of Nature—that wild, heathen Nature of the forest, never subjugated by human law, nor illumined by higher truth—with the bliss of these two spirits! Love, whether newly born, or aroused from a death-like slumber, must always create a sunshine, filling the heart so full of radiance, that it overflows upon the outward world. Had the forest still kept its gloom, it would have been bright in Hester's eyes, and bright in Arthur Dimmesdale's!

Perhaps it would be too much to maintain that the husband of Sophia Peabody was arguing a case for adultery here, and he tries to cover any tracks he may have made in that direction by a discreet reference to "higher truth." But the passage clearly established that it is *not* adultery as such that constitutes the crime of *The Scarlet Letter.* The possible renewal of the adulterous union is seen here as a resurrection into life, and as a means of once again possessing, or entering into, the inner sphere of reality.

Hawthorne was always ruthless in the way he punished those characters who broke the magnetic chain of humanity. This seems, quite literally, to have been the Unpardonable Sin as far as he was concerned. Ethan Brand and Zenobia commit suicide, Gervayse Hastings dies in despair, Goodman Brown's poisoned faith in men haunts him to the grave. One would not expect Hawthorne to let Hester off easily, then, if the essence of her sin was indeed that she had broken the magnetic chain. It is part of Hawthorne's artistic triumph in this novel, as contrasted with some of the others, that he is able to suggest (or make the reader believe that he does) the possibility of a final redemption for Hester. But the closing lines, which describe her grave, are far from the light-filled forest scene in the above quotation.[171] Hawthorne in the end emphatically rejects the possibility of escape which seemed to be offered there, and even in death Hester does not free herself from the awful symbol which shows more gloomily on her tombstone than it ever had on her breast. In the shadow of such a final paragraph all talk of redemption seems a little superfluous.[172]

. . . .

FROM "Hawthorne's Novels," *The Eccentric Design* (New York, 1959), pp. 147-186. Reprinted by permission of Columbia University Press.

ARTHUR DIMMESDALE

DIMMESDALE: EXPIATION AS SOCIAL DUTY

Rudolphe von Abele

. . . .

Expiation . . . being regarded as a social duty in such a society, the pressure upon "godly" persons who may have "fallen" is exceedingly intense indeed, far more so than upon individualists[214] whom the machinery of society leaves unintimidated. This is precisely Dimmesdale's position—the extreme possible position, of the man who is himself a judge of the qualifications of others being forced by his situation into doing what he habitually expects from them. He wants to eat his cake and have it too—to retain his position in society, a position of "holy whiteness," while simultaneously penalizing himself for his fall from grace. Legitimate ambition vies with the drive to confess: for he knows, what nobody else does, that the elite itself is poisoned by his fall. This is of course the most drastic irony of all, that the holier he becomes in all eyes but his own, Hester's and Chillingworth's, the more corrupt he is to himself. A model for the emulation of his "flock," the longer he permits them to emulate him the greater is his betrayal of their confidence. The irony is deepened when he chooses, as the moment to make confession, a moment at which his reputation can scarcely be conceived to be higher—when he is the darling of that crowd to which he confesses himself. It is a grandiose gesture, at the top of possible drama, and in that respect quite antithetical to the flagellations in his study—which fail of effect just because they are visible to no one but himself. They cannot satisfy the demands which his society has nurtured in him. Yet he cannot confess, even though the pressure to do so quite literally makes him a sick man, for reasons which may belong in the same class as those which inhibit Hamlet from killing the king: because he must maximize his drama, because he fears ostracism, because he is in love with suffering, because (even) he takes pride in the very ambiguity of his status. Whatever the precise nature of his inhibitions (Hawthorne never clarifies them for us, which may be a good thing), they sustain him for seven years, until he is at the summit of his personal prestige, and until he is offered for the first time the opportunity to escape his society in the company of the woman he has loved and the child whose father he is. At that instant, when to accept the "face of things" and escape would be to furnish his "conscience" (as Chillingworth's horror at his act indicates) with enough fuel to last it a good long time, by some curious paradox of inversion he rejects that luxury in favor of the still greater one of complying with the demands of his society. Confession, while it alienates him from his "flock" and makes escape a superfluity, in a larger sense, "brings him back" from the isolation in which he has been living, and makes death his only possible conclusion. Response to social demand at this point is a denial of selfhood, and hence a kind of suicide[215]—even, if I may push an analogy, an acceptance of castration, of which his ascetic self-discipline of the past seven years has been after all but an attenuated version, a prolonged "unmanning" of himself to placate God the Father, against whom the impiety was ultimately aimed. Of course, like suicide itself, the gesture is ambiguous: it can also be seen as the ultimate *assertion* of self.

    . . . .

FROM *"The Scarlet Letter:* A Reading," *Accent,* XI (Autumn, 1951), 211-227. Reprinted by permission of the author and *Accent.*

DIMMESDALE: FUGITIVE FROM WRATH

Darrel Abel

. . . .

How welcome should a *Death in the Lord* be unto them that belong not unto the Devil, but unto the Lord! While we are sojourning in this World, we are in what may upon too many accounts be called *The Devil's Country:* We are where the Devil may come upon us in *great wrath* continually. The day when God shall take us out of this World will be, *The Day when the Lord will deliver us from the hand of all our Enemies, and from the hand of Satan.*

—*The Wonders of the Invisible World*

The fourth and final section of *The Scarlet Letter* shows Dimmesdale,[98] apparently doomed to perdition, spectacularly saved by God's grace. God is the activating agent in this section, and is shown to have been responsible, through his "permissive" power, for the apparently pernicious but actually redemptive actions of Hester and Chillingworth. The minister's dying speech declared that God "hath proved his mercy, most of all, in my afflictions....Had either [any] of these agonies been wanting, I had been lost forever."

This section (chapters xx-xxiii) is the most artfully handled part of the book. Hawthorne carries forward the impression that evil influences on the minister must be decisive; read anticipatively, the account suggests that Dimmesdale is rapidly declining to perdition. At the same time, the narrative, retrospectively considered, affords evidence that his regeneration was in process. This section is therefore a good example of Hawthorne's famed ambiguity. Although this ambiguity makes explication difficult, it is appropriate for several reasons. It shows that God moves in a mysterious way His wonders to perform. By indicating the turbulence within the minister's mind at this critical time, it renders credible the routing of evil influences by good ones which transpires. By retarding explicit recognition of his regeneration, it effects a dramatic peripety at the end of the story.

The account of Dimmesdale's regeneration faithfully follows orthodox Puritan conceptions, in its specification of the sinner's state before regeneration, of the stages in the actual process of regeneration, and the attitudes invoked toward regeneration.

The sinner was unable to initiate and perfect his own reformation. "It was obvious that men had contrived to bring upon themselves all the anguish they suffered; it was still more obvious that neither this awareness nor the anguish itself liberated them from the trammels of perversity. A being who brought such a destiny upon himself could hardly expect to find within himself the power to master it."[1] "No man can enact regeneration by his own[99] exertion" (Miller, p. 27). God's speech in *Paradise Lost* (II, 173-182) summarizes the orthodox Puritan view:

> Man shall not quite be lost, but saved who will;
> Yet not of will in him, but grace in me
> Freely vouchsafed. Once more I will renew
> His lapséd powers, though forfeit, and enthralled
> By sin to foul exorbitant desires:
> Upheld by me, yet once more he shall stand
> On even ground against his mortal foe—
> By me upheld that he may know how frail
> His fallen condition is, and to me owe
> All his deliverance, and to none but me.

Utter moral incapability is explicitly Dimmesdale's condition at the beginning of this section. "Deadly sin" was "diffused throughout his moral system. It had stupefied all blessed impulses, and awakened into vivid life the whole brotherhood of bad ones....[His conduct] did but show his sympathy and fellowship with wicked mortals, and the world of perverted spirits."

The last and most ominous sign of the minister's moral degeneration was the pride with which he looked forward to his day of worldly exaltation, when he was to preach the Election Sermon. The conceit of his own piety was the danger most pernicious to an eminent clergyman: "The *Devil provokes* men that are eminent in Holiness unto such things as may become eminently *Pernicious;* he provokes them especially unto *Pride.*"[2] Throughout the seven past years of Dimmesdale's ministry he had felt agony because in every pastoral performance "he had spoken the very truth and transformed it into the veriest falsehood." As he told Hester, "As concerns the good which I appear to do,...it must needs be an illusion." "Puritanism...demands that the individual confront existence directly on all sides at once, that no allowance be made for circumstances or human frailty" (Miller, p. 45). So long as Dimmesdale's heart acknowledged the truth, though he could not will his tongue to utter it, he retained an essential and saving truth in his character:[100] "The only truth that continued to give Mr. Dimmesdale a real existence on this earth was the anguish in his inmost soul." But "no man, for any considerable period, can wear one face to himself, and another to the multitude, without finally getting bewildered as to which may be the true." And the minister now calls it "most fortunate" that his planned elopement with Hester will not take place until after he enacts what threatens to be his culminating

---

1 Perry Miller, *The New England Mind* (New York, 1939), p. 25.
2 Cotton Mather, *The Wonders of the Invisible World* ("Library of Old Authors," London, 1862), p. 55.

hypocrisy, the preaching of the Election Sermon. Apparently the last stage of his "eternal alienation from the Good and True" was this displacement by pride of his anguished consciousness of moral truancy; having lost his moral will, he appeared now to have lost the remorse which was its residue and the germ from which it might be revived.

The first event in a sinner's regeneration is "justification." "A change must be wrought in his status before any can be made in his nature" (Miller, p. 27). This change is of course neither conscious nor visible; it is known to have occurred only by the positive regeneration which eventuates. Following the sinner's justification, "divine grace reaches forth to the prostrate man in two ways: first it comes as a call to a new life, a summons from above—which was called 'vocation'" (Miller, p. 27). Hawthorne gives various ambiguous intimations that this call to a new life reached Dimmesdale during the three days between his meeting with Hester in the forest and the preaching of the Election Sermon. The first of these intimations is the composition of the sermon itself, on the night of his return from the forest. Before composing the sermon he still showed signs of the "unaccustomed energy" and "unwwith activity" which had so phenomenally marked the revival of his "strong animal nature." Before composing the sermon, "he ate with ravenous appetite." But "he wrote with such impulsive flow of thought and emotion that he fancied himself inspired." In this passage there are strong evidences of both animal vitality and spiritual influence; the composition of the Election Sermon apparently marks the meeting,[101] interfusion, and transference of powers in Dimmesdale. When Dimmesdale appeared in the procession, on the day of the Election Sermon, everyone remarked that he exhibited more energy than at any time since he "first set foot on the New England shore," and that he no longer held his hand over his heart. Although readers will naturally explain this phenomenal energy as a continuation of the animal vitality aroused by his meeting with Hester, "yet, if the minister were rightly viewed, his strength seemed not of the body. It might be spiritual, and imparted to him angelic administrations." To Hester and Pearl, he seemed not the same man they had so recently conversed with. To Hester, "he seemed remote from her own sphere, and utterly beyond her reach....She thought of the dim forest....How deeply they had known each other then! And was this the man? She hardly knew him now!" Pearl asked, "Mother,... was that the same minister that kissed me by the brook?...I could not be sure it was he; so strange he looked." This passage is the most crucial instance of that ambiguity I have already mentioned. Read anticipatively, with the knowledge given of the minister's moral history, he seems at this point to be a reinvigorated hypocrite; read retrospectively, he is shown to be a man inspired, who has received his "vocation."

The second way in which divine grace "reaches forth to the prostrate man" is by effecting an alteration of the sinner's nature. "It penetrates his being and there it generates—or, in view of Adam's original nature, 're-generates'—a power to respond" (Miller, p. 27). It is this power to respond which Dimmesdale becomes aware of when, passing from the church after the Election Sermon, he meets Hester Prynne at the scaffold and accosts her thus:

In the name of him, so terrible and so merciful, who gives me grace, at this last moment, to do what—for my own heavy sin and miserable agony—I withheld myself from doing seven years ago, come hither now, and entwine thy strength about me! Thy strength, Hester; but let it be guided by the will which God hath granted me.

Then, "partly supported by Hester Prynne, and holding one hand of little Pearl's," he ascended the scaffold, at midday, in the presence[102] of the multitude, and revealed the scarlet symbol of sin on his "sainted" breast. The sentence in which Hawthorne announces this act of confession is the thrilling climax of the romance: "The sun, but little past its meridian, shone down upon the clergyman, and gave a distinctness to his figure, as he stood out from all the earth, to put in his plea of guilty at the bar of eternal justice."

This "power to respond" which completes the work of regeneration "comes through the impact of a sensible species or phantasm,... some spoken word or physical experience" (Miller, p. 281). "The means ...may be any experience,...but ordinarily they are the words of a sermon and the sacraments of the church" (Miller, p. 289). Hawthorne intimates that it was the minister's own sermon that wrought this final operation of grace:

Never had man spoken in so wise, so high, and so holy a spirit, as he that spake this day; nor had inspiration ever breathed through mortal lips more evidently than it did through his. Its influence could be seen, as it were, descending upon him, and possessing him, and continually lifting him out of the written discourse that lay before him, and filling him with ideas that must have been as marvellous to himself as to his audience.

Thus, at this crisis of utmost peril to his soul, the grace of God filled the faltering minister—an interposition of God which gloriously demonstrated how the mystery of good could overcome the logic of evil. "The moment of regeneration, in which God, out of his compassion, bestows grace upon man and in which man is enabled to reply with belief, was the single goal of the Augustinian piety" (Miller, p. 25). With his last breath, Dimmesdale praised God for thus enabling him "to die this death of triumphant ignominy before the people." . . . Compared to this experience of grace, mundane happiness was of little worth. "The burden of Calvinism was that man must find his happiness in the glory and service of God, and not that man may not find happiness. The essence of sin is that man should prefer[103] lesser good ...to 'true virtue.'" "The good which God seeks and accomplishes is the display of infinite being, a good which transcends the good of finite existence."[3]

Some critics, lacking full critical sympathy with Hawthorne and preoccupied with "the good of finite existence," look upon the minister's death as a calamity, and opine that "[if] he had conscientiously been able to flee with [Hester] to a new life on the western frontier, there would have been no tragedy." But this would have been, from Hawthorne's point of view, the greatest tragedy possible for Dimmesdale, for Hawthorne did not identify physical "death and tragedy." Dimmesdale told Hester, "Were I an atheist,—a wretch with coarse and brutal instincts,—I might have found peace, long ere now. Nay, I should never have lost it." To Hawthorne, not physical but moral death was tragic and terrible: "Death is the very friend whom, in his due season, even the happiest mortal should be willing to embrace.... were man to live longer on the earth, the spiritual would die out of him." Death is always in due season when it comes at the right time to keep the spiritual from dying out in man. Even the most sanguine of Transcendentalists, Alcott, wrote, "It is not death but a bad life that destroys the soul." Dimmesdale died in that state of triumphant holiness to which every wayfaring Christian aspires; to him as to Adam, "Death becomes/His final remedy" (*Paradise Lost*, XI, 61-62).[104]

. . . .

FROM "Hawthorne's Dimmesdale: Fugitive from Wrath," *Nineteenth-Century Fiction*, XI (Sept., 1956), 81-105. Reprinted from *Nineteenth-Century Fiction*, published by the University of California Press, by permission of the publisher.

DIMMESDALE AND THE GOD OF LOVE

Joseph Schwartz

. . . .

The key to *The Scarlet Letter* is in the character of Arthur Dimmesdale, that "false and sin-stained creature of the dust." His perplexing nature provides the reader with some of the tale's most compassionate moments. His fundamental weakness is not his sin, nor

---

3 Joseph Haroutunian, *Piety Versus Moralism* (New York, 1932), pp. 263, 144.

even his hypocrisy, but his failure to recognize that God is a God of love. Hemmed in by the narrow theological system of his time, he cannot understand the nature of Him Whom he has offended. The central fact of his nature is indecision about the nature of God. This is precisely why he is the most miserable creature between Heaven and earth; and this is why Hawthorne withholds from him the natural sympathy which we would expect from so sensitive an author. His moral decline runs parallel with his confusion about God. At the very opening of the novel, Hawthorne is critical of Dimmesdale's religious sentiments. Ironically enough, as his hypocrisy corrodes his nature, his sermons become more powerful and persuasive. But his topic is always the horror of sin and the terror of hell. Hopelessness has made the topic of salvation impossible. Dimmesdale's confusion becomes indescribably tortuous.

It is down this painful road that Hawthorne takes the reader to the most compassionate scene in all of his fiction. It is the scene in the forest. Hester can no longer bear the thought of her[131] lover's torment at the hands of Chillingworth, regularly called the "fiend." She is determined to save the minister. Although she tells him that he is dying of his own weakness, Dimmesdale can find no comfort. His anguished cry, "The judgment of God is on me," admits of no comfort. Since he does not know a God of love, he has only two alternatives. He can surrender to what he regards as a terrible sin (though it had "a consecration of its own") or he can make his sin known in order to experience the arid comfort which a meaningless public confession would give him. Hester tells him that "Heaven would show mercy." His concentration on the terrible God of Calvinism has left him "powerless even to repent." Dimmesdale's only reply is that he is "irrevocably doomed." Since he cannot recognize forgiving love as one of God's attributes, he chooses to run off with Hester. The error in this choice is indicated by Hawthorne in a chapter unequaled in world fiction before 1900—"The Minister in a Maze." Only in Dostoevsky do we find such keen psychological insight. Dimmesdale's free surrender to deliberate sin stupefied his potential blessed impulses. "The wretched minister" is tempted to do "some strange, wild, wicked thing." He would corrupt the faith of an aged deacon of the church, destroy the spiritual comfort of a pious old woman, teach the little children wicked words, and, most seriously, drop a germ of evil in the bosom of a young virgin.

His other alternative is the public confession. True to the Puritanic character, he chooses this. Once again we are back at the scaffold, Hawthorne's symbol of the religious and civil law of the Calvinists, "a system of fear and vengeance, never successful, yet followed to the last." This is the most terrifying, though triumphant, moment in the minister's life. The triumph is, however, only partial. At one moment he cries out that "God is merciful!" At the next moment, he doubts.

His death scene is agonizing, because it is so incomplete. He still does not know. He is only sure that he must speak out his sin. But he does not know his destiny. The enmeshing entanglements of the human heart are revealed and laid bare; but the minister's maze still exists. The triumph of love does not belong to him. The minister, standing at the pinnacle of the religious and social order, was most confined by his narrow beliefs. Through his failure to attain to certitude, we see Hawthorne's dismay at the system he represented. But God who made us and loves us will not leave us "either to wander in infinite uncertainty, or perish by the way!"[132]

. . . .

> FROM "God and Man in New England," in Harold C. Gardiner, ed., *American Classics Reconsidered: A Christian Appraisal* (New York, 1958), pp. 121-145. Reprinted by permission of Charles Scribner's Sons, copyright 1958.

ROGER CHILLINGWORTH

CHILLINGWORTH AS MILTONIC SATAN

Darrel Abel

Roger Chillingworth, the diabolized physician in Hawthorne's *Scarlet Letter,* embodies concepts of human nature and its moral possibilities which more resemble the Calvinist humanism of the seventeenth century in England than the transcendentalist optimism of nineteenth-century New England. Puritan humanism, like all humanisms, was preoccupied with the problems of a person's progress in his earthly career. It differed from the secular, scientific humanism of post-Newtonian times, which is oriented primarily towards a sensibly-experienced, naturalistic world, in that its primary orientation was toward a supposed world of moral absolutes.[1] To Puritan humanists, a good man was a man who had in his earthly career realized his moral

---

[1] I know that so general a distinction is rashly undiscriminating, but I hope that it will be accepted as accurate on the whole.

potentialities; whereas to modern humanists (except such "humanists" as Maritain), a good man is a man who has refined his own nature and erected it above mere naturalism. This emphasis upon the self-amelioration of the individual, without the supposition of "leadings from above," accounts for the fact that, although the older humanism was always preoccupied with ethical fulfillment of the individual in his temporal existence, modern humanism is equally concerned with his esthetic refinement, and indeed often makes no clear distinction between the ethical and the esthetic.

In this paper I shall discuss Chillingworth's role in *The Scarlet Letter* as an embodiment of certain Calvinist conceptions of the development of moral personality. My quotations from other authors are not intended to show "influence,"[2] but merely to establish a correspondence of ideas.[3] My thesis about Chillingworth's role in[366] the novel is that he is a Miltonic Satan given the meaner, more realistic embodiment appropriate to the villain of an historical romance. My discussion of his role in the novel and of his embodiment of seventeenth-century conceptions will not be separated, but concurrent.

Chillingworth was an aborted spirit—not in the sense of the modern humanist, to whom human failure is failure to rise above the brute, but in the sense of the Puritan humanist, to whom human failure is a lapsing from excellence or from the possibility of excellence.

The psychology of Chillingworth's covert vengefulness toward his wife's paramour, the minister Dimmesdale, is ambiguous, but its essential traits are distinguishable. His vindictive obsession was not a fatal and inevitable opposition of the kind which Melville illustrated in the malignancy shown by John Claggart toward Billy Budd—a natural antipathy which seems to imply in the author some Zoroastrian conviction of two absolutely sundered orders of being, good and evil, implacably pitted against each other. Chillingworth and the "Black Man" whom he served stand for Goodness perverted.

Chillingworth was capable of love, and we sympathize with and approve of his desire for a life cheered by domestic affections:

My heart was a habitation large enough for many guests, but lonely and chill, and without a household fire. I longed to kindle one. It seemed not so

---

[2] This may partially justify the eclecticism of my quotations, unavoidable in a brief treatment of so comprehensive a topic.

[3] Hawthorne had read all of the authors quoted, some of them many times. The works mentioned are all recorded, as charged out to him on various occasions, in the "Charge Books" of the Salem Athenaeum Library. These have been transcribed and published: in *The Essex Institute Historical Collections*, LXVII (1932), 65-87 (no editor given); and, more recently and more accurately, by Marion L. Kesselring in "Hawthorne's Reading, 1828-1850," *Bulletin of the New York Public Library*, LIII, 55-71, 121-138, 173-194. See also Arlin Turner's "Hawthorne's Literary Borrowings," *PMLA*, LI (June, 1936), 543-562; and Austin Warren's "Hawthorne's Reading," *New England Quarterly*, VIII (December, 1935), 480-497.

wild a dream,—old as I was, and sombre as I was, and misshapen as I was,—
that the simple bliss, which is scattered far and wide, for all mankind to
gather up, might yet be mine. And so, Hester, I drew thee into my heart,
into its innermost chamber, and sought to warm thee by the warmth which
thy presence made there!

Nevertheless Chillingworth was at fault in marrying a girl a generation
younger than himself, who declared moreover that she did not love
him. In Bishop Fuller's *Holy State* (which Hawthorne read in 1834)
the expectations proper to a Christian entering[367] into holy matri-
mony are discussed:[4] Much happiness is not to be expected in marriage.
One's spouse should be loved for grace (presumably spiritual rather
than physical) and goodness. A wife should not be chosen for her
beauty. There should be no great disproportion in age. Chillingworth's
marriage to Hester violated all these prudent admonitions of the good
Bishop. From the husband's point of view, it was folly, since it prom-
ised ill for his future; from the wife's point of view, it was injustice,
since it would prevent her legitimate union with someone she could
love. (Love, of course, to Hawthorne, although hardly to Bishop Fuller,
was a more indispensable bond of marriage than any legal or sacra-
mental tie.)

   Chillingworth, disappointed in his hope of gaining his wife's affection, hated the man who had gained it unsought and even unwished.
In a sense, his malice was less a personal resentment against Dimmesdale than an expression of anger at the scheme of things which had
cheated his hopes. Like envious Satan, observing the love of Adam
and Eve in the Garden, "Imparadised in one another's arms," he was
"stirred up with envy and revenge."

   Although his anger was natural and forgivable, it became a fatal
sin when he nourished it, like Blake's Poison Tree, and made it the
settled disposition of his existence. Bishop Fuller, in "Of Anger,"
describes his case well: "Anger is one of the sinews of the soul; he that
wants it, hath a maimed mind....Nor is it good to converse with such
as cannot be angry." Anger is heavenly, or hellish, or earthly. One
should not be angry without cause, nor mortally angry for a venial
fault, nor driven by anger to an irrevocable act, nor uncontrollably
and violently angry, nor implacably angry. *"He that keeps anger long
in his bosome giveth place to the devil."* The anger of such a person
shows itself in fits of diabolical violence (Fuller, II, pp. 169-70).

   Chillingworth, implacably angry, violent even to frenzy, suffered
this diabolical possession. Never very benevolent, he easily[368] converted his injured self-love into hatred of his supplanter. He and
Hester agreed that his earlier life had been blameless:

---

   [4] Thomas Fuller, *The Holy State and the Profane State,* ed. M. G. Walten
(New York, 1938. 2 vols.), II, 212-214.

"All my life had been made up of earnest, studious, thoughtful, quiet years, bestowed faithfully for the increase of mine own knowledge, and faithfully, too, though this latter object was but casual to the other,—faithfully for the advancement of human welfare."

But Hawthorne emphasizes that the physician's benevolence had never been so innate and habitual that a lapse into malevolence would be implausible. He had been "kindly, though not of warm affections"; his efforts to advance human welfare had been admittedly "casual to" the increase of his own knowledge. His goodness had been rather a matter of deliberate choice and policy, so long as he had no motive to do ill, than of strong inclination; knowledge rather than beneficence had always been clearly his chief object; and his character had thus always retained the possibility of maleficence.

Consequently, when angry resentment gave him a motive, he chose to withdraw his name from the roll of mankind, and, as regarded his former ties and interests, to vanish out of life as completely as if he indeed lay at the bottom of the ocean, whither rumor had long ago consigned him. This purpose once effected, new interests would immediately spring up, and likewise a new purpose; dark, it is true, if not guilty, but of force enough to engage the full strength of his faculties.

The expression *chose to* in this passage is significant: to Chillingworth, righteousness had never been more than expedient conduct. Although his acts had been conformable to the "external covenant" of Calvinism, his good works had been the cool, detached, deliberated good works which are dictated more by judgment than by affection for virtue. Jonathan Edwards taught that true virtue "has its roots in an emotional rather than intellectual state of mind."[5] Of this virtue, Chillingworth had never evinced any sign. Therefore, he could say, "Evil, be thou my good," and with perfect self-possession bend his energies strenuously toward malign as he had hitherto directed them incidentally toward benign ends. He was too fatally his own master.

That Hawthorne looked upon the power of good and the power of evil as different expressions of identical capacities, rather than[369] as expressions of different capacities in man, is perfectly explicit, especially in the "Conclusion" to the romance:

Nothing was more remarkable than the change which took place, almost immediately after Mr. Dimmesdale's death, in the appearance and demeanor of the old man known as Roger Chillingworth. All his strength and energy—all his vital and intellectual force—seemed at once to desert him....This unhappy man had made the very principle of his life to consist in the pursuit and systematic exercise of revenge; and when...there was no more Devil's work on earth for him to do, it only remained for the unhumanized mortal to be-

---

5 Rufus Suter, "The Concept of Morality in the Philosophy of Jonathan Edwards," *Journal of Religion,* xiv (1934-35), 268.

take himself whither his Master would find him tasks enough, and pay him his wages duly....It is a curious subject of observation and inquiry, whether hatred and love be not the same thing at bottom. Each, in its utmost development, supposes a high degree of intimacy and heart-knowledge; each renders one individual dependent for the food of his affections and spiritual life upon another; each leaves the passionate lover, or the no less passionate hater, forlorn and desolate by the withdrawal of his subject.

Philosophically considered, therefore, the two passions seem essentially the same.

Chillingworth, then, was not badness incarnate, but goodness perverted. Like Milton's Satan, he could pity his victims; although himself "dehumanized" by his malice, he left his property to the "demon offspring" of those whom he had injured and who had injured him, "a wild infant" whose progress in humanization had paralleled his regress: and Hawthorne even suggested at the conclusion of the passage quoted above, that Chillingworth himself was perhaps not irredeemably lost: "In the spiritual world, the old physician and the minister—mutual victims as they have been—may, unawares, have found their earthly stock of hatred and antipathy transmuted into golden love." "Neither do the spirits damned lose all their virtue." In fine, we are to understand Chillingworth's sin as a tragic perversion of a force which sought its right expression in love, and, thwarted in that, turned to hate.[370]

. . . .

From "The Devil in Boston," *Philological Quarterly,* XXXII (Oct., 1953), 366-381. Reprinted by permission of the author and the editors of *Philological Quarterly.*

CHILLINGWORTH AS FAUST AND MEPHISTOPHELES

William Bysshe Stein

. . . .

In the preface to *The Snow Image* Hawthorne suggests the two interpretations possible, on the natural and the historical levels of the romance. On the natural level, "...the purposes of psychological romance" determine his intention. This approach in *The Scarlet Letter* permits him to unravel the hidden relations of the four persons whose lives have been complicated by the sin of adultery. He merges this level with the historical, "arraying some of the ordinary facts of life in a slightly idealized and artistic guise." This is a mythic technique, and in *The Scarlet Letter* the pact with the devil and the ritual archetype permit him to universalize the moral quandaries of the historical characters. Yet at no time does Hawthorne prescribe the proper mode of interpretation. Never betraying the complexity of his method of symbolization, he merely comments: "Every sentence, so far as it embodies thought or sensibility, may be understood and felt by anybody who will give himself the trouble[105] to read it, and will take up [my works] in a proper mood."

Though Hawthorne in *The Scarlet Letter* oscillates between these two levels, as skillfully enforcing one as the other, the historical interpretation is generally considered more meaningful, and the natural, with its mythic imagery, is explained away, with uneasy grace, as a kind of inexplicable technical affectation. The indifference to Hawthorne's carefully differentiated order of form has resulted in an imperfect understanding of the novel, for it is in the penumbra of the supernatural, the mirror of the universal natural world, that the novel achieves its meaning. Correlated with the historical action the dramatic symbols of the Faust myth here operate with overwhelming import. The mocking demon, the emperor in this dark realm, tempts his victims into moral defections that endanger their souls. His visible emblem in the external world is the scarlet letter. It is the banner of evil waving over the moral territory that he has partly conquered.

This technique of interpretation makes the characters most important. Their reactions to the sin of adultery, the pre-narrative motivation, are the basis of Hawthorne's speculations on the problem of evil and on its associated intellectual and spiritual values. In the case of Chillingworth, who is usually treated as a piece of machinery, a new perspective on his function is afforded, removing the blight of insane jealousy which commonly destroys his real significance. Hawthorne logically motivates all of the physician's actions, and in his plunge to doom there is something of the pathos and tragedy that marked Ethan Brand. Chillingworth, it must be remembered, during most of his life dabbles in magical experiments that fall under the jurisdiction of the devil. Yet, unlike Ethan Brand, he is not impelled by the knowledge which he accumulates to break the magnetic chain of humanity; he continually keeps the welfare of mankind in sight. When he marries Hester, he hopes that she will inspire him to greater efforts. She represents his firmest tie to humanity; she epitomizes its sympathy, tenderness, and love. She links him to the deep heart of the universe. Having a profound faith in the integrity of Hester, he sends her to the New World, intending[106] to follow her after he has arranged his affairs in Europe. Unfortunately, upon arrival he is captured and imprisoned by the Indians. After a lengthy incarceration he is ransomed, and immediately makes his way to the settlement where Hester resides. The first sight that greets his eyes is Hester on the pillory. In the terrible emotional distress that overcomes him, he sees his connection with the magnetic chain of humanity snapped. The grief which floods his heart drives him to a resolution that will, with inexorable finality, exile him from Hester's emotional world. He will, at the propitious moment, sell his soul to the devil, and proclaim his rejection of the brotherhood of man.

To emphasize Chillingworth's essentially heroic stature, Hawthorne sketches him as a Faust, whose prototype we encounter in the dramas. Hester's memories, as she stands on the scaffold, recapture one of her husband's Faustian traits. Her mind's eye dwells on "a pale, thin, scholar-like visage, with eyes dim and bleared by the lamplight that had served them to pore over many ponderous books. Yet those same bleared optics had a strange, penetrating power, when it was their owner's purpose to read the human soul." In the prison-cell scene, as Chillingworth ministers to the ailments of Pearl and Hester, Hawthorne adds another Faustian quality to the scholar's character. Like all Fausts, he has found it necessary to pursue knowledge beyond ordinary limits; and, during his captivity with the Indians, he has learned the lore of medicine. Chillingworth, talking to Hester, leaves no doubt about his talents in this study: "My old studies in alchemy...and my sojourn...among a people well versed in the kindly properties of simples, have made a better physician of me than many that claim the medical degree." Later Hawthorne imputes the old man's extraordinary skill to magic. An aged craftsman in the village declares that Chillingworth was once an associate of the notorious conjurer, Dr. Froman; and other individuals hint that he "had enlarged his medical attainments by joining in the incantations of the savage priests, who were universally acknowledged to be powerful enchanters, often performing seemingly miraculous cures by their skill in the black art." A vulgar[107] rumor prevails that Chillingworth's dark and ugly face betrays his satanic connections. It is said that "the fire in his laboratory had been brought from the lower regions, and was fed with infernal fuel; and so, as might be expected, his visage was getting sooty with the smoke."

At one point in the narrative Hawthorne makes a direct allusion to the scholar's Faustian antecedents: "...a rumor gained ground,—and, however absurd, was entertained by some very sensible people,—that Heaven had wrought an absolute miracle, by transporting an eminent Doctor of Physic, from a German university, bodily through the air, and setting him down at the door of Mr. Dimmesdale's study!" Thus Hawthorne succeeds in endowing Chillingworth with the conventional traits of the familiar Fausts. Scholar, alchemist, magician, and physician, he resembles the Faustian hero who moves across the stage in the first scene of Marlowe's and Goethe's dramas.

Nor does Hawthorne fail to give Chillingworth a glimpse of ideal beauty. The disillusioned scholar confesses that the feelings Hester aroused defied rational definition, as they went beyond the ken of magical explanation: "It was my folly....I,—a man of thought,—the bookworm of great libraries,—a man already in decay, having given my best years to feed the hungry dream of knowledge,—what had I to do with youth and beauty like thine own!" Yet he concedes that she alone was able to give him a truly human status among his fellow men: "...up to that epoch of my life, I had lived in vain. The world had been so cheerless! My heart was a habitation large enough for many guests, but lonely and chill, and without a household fire. I longed to kindle one! It seemed not so wild a dream...that the simple bliss, which is scattered far and wide, for all mankind to gather up, might yet be mine." This is the same ghost of beauty that Marlowe's Faustus invoked to ease the shock of disenchantment, the same one also that Goethe's aged Faust deemed a compensation for his failures. In the dream of perfect love they all could identify themselves with mankind.

It is this terrible sense of loss that prompts Chillingworth to[108] bargain away his soul to the devil. He will revenge himself on the criminal who stole Hester's love. And when Hester will not disclose her paramour's name, the old physician grimly asserts: "I shall seek this man, as I have sought truth in books; as I have sought gold in alchemy." In other words, he will read the secret of guilt on her betrayer's heart. But the sins that lie hidden in mortal bosoms are not, as Ethan Brand discovered, for the eyes of prying mortals. On Judgment Day they will be disclosed to God who will assign the penalty the sinner must pay. But the Puritan Faust aspires for precisely this knowledge of secret evil. He will render justice in this case. He will, as it were, usurp God's prerogative. His mind will trespass into the forbidden portals of heaven. He will make a mockery of universal morality. He will deliberately disown his brotherhood with man and his reverence for God.

In effect, without a formal contract, Chillingworth consummates a pact with Satan. Hawthorne, like Goethe, decrees the volition to evil a sufficient condition of bondage. Yet no doubt is left that the devil controls the will of the scholar-magician. After Hester refuses to reveal the identity of her lover, the husband extorts a pledge of silence from her on the legal state of their relations. But something in his cruel smile causes her to regret her promise, and she inquires in fear: "Art thou like the Black Man that haunts the forest round about us? Hast thou enticed me into a bond that will prove the ruin of my soul?" His answer is sardonically elusive: "Not thy soul! No, not thine!" Chillingworth, without as yet being sure of his method, intends to plot against the soul of her unknown lover. The Puritan Faust feels confident that his patience and diabolic art will be rewarded in due time.

In this fashion Chillingworth aligns himself with the demon. He enters into a covenant with the dark evils of his soul. He compromises the integrity of a long life dedicated to the improvement of mankind.

Just nine years before, he recalls, his life was "bestowed faithfully for the increase of [his] own knowledge, and faithfully, too,...for the advancement of human welfare. No life had been more peaceful and innocent than [his]; few lives so rich with benefits[109] conferred." As Hawthorne observes, Chillingworth at first deludes himself that he is the instrument of dispassionate justice. He attempts to rationalize his hate and jealousy as mere intellectual curiosity: "He had begun an investigation, as he imagined,...desirous only of truth,...as if the question involved no more than...a geometrical problem, instead of human passions, and wrongs inflicted on himself." But in a very short time his morbid interest in sin weakens his own resistance to it; his restrained emotions are transformed into a violent impulse of revenge: "...a terrible fascination, a kind of fierce, though still calm, necessity seized the old man within its gripe, and never set him free again until he had done all its bidding." Thus Chillingworth commits spiritual suicide. He has as little control over his moral volition as did the Faust of the chapbook or Marlowe. . . .[110]

To intensify the spiritual degeneration that accompanies the growth of the maddened scholar's monomaniacal vindictiveness, Hawthorne resorts to external diabolic symbolism. In undertaking "a devil's office" the old man acquires the emblems of that office: "Ever and anon ...there came a glare of red light out of his eyes; as if [his]...soul were on fire, and kept on smouldering duskily within his breast, until, by some casual puff of passion, it was blown into a momentary flame." A further physical evidence of his moral degradation is visible as "the former aspect of an intellectual and studious man" is gradually replaced by a look of fierce and searching ugliness. These outward alterations of his body do not go unnoted by his neighbors. They declare him to be a "diabolical agent [having] Divine permission, for a season, to burrow into the clergyman's intimacy, and plot against his soul." Even Hester's daughter, little Pearl, warns her mother against the physician: "Come away, or yonder old Black Man will catch you! He hath got hold of the minister already. Come away, mother, or he will catch you!" So far as Chillingworth himself is concerned, he admits his complete dedication to evil; he angrily tells a sympathetic Hester: "I have already told thee what I am! A fiend!"

Hawthorne has a purpose in thus exhibiting the Puritan Faust's physical and spiritual deterioration. In this manner he forcefully and vividly shows the deficiency of an intellect that renounces the mediation of the conscience to pursue a futile course of revenge. Chillingworth is not an abstraction dictated by the expediency of the plot. Hawthorne wishes to evaluate the potential of wickedness lying dormant in minds that have divorced themselves from the accepted standards of ethical behavior. When the scientist or the scholar rejects the basic spiritual values which give life meaning, he invites the catastrophe of moral anarchy. Hawthorne, generalizing from Chillingworth's conduct, remarks that the outcome of such intellectual independence is an inhuman materialism: "In their researches into the human frame, it may be that the higher and more[111] subtle faculties of such men were materialized, and that they lost the spiritual view of existence amid the intricacies of the wondrous mechanism, which seemed to involve art enough to comprise all of life within itself." Chillingworth evinces this complete absorption in the methods of philosophical inquiry. The speculation encouraged by natural philosophy is to him a means to satisfy a diseased curiosity. In the presence of the town magistrates and the clergy he inadvertently challenges the moral interdictions of Puritan religious thought: He dares suggest philosophy as a means of discovering Pearl's father: "Would it be beyond a philosopher's research, think ye, gentlemen, to analyze the child's nature, and, from its make and mould, to give a shrewd guess at the father?"

Hawthorne has still another effect to achieve in sustaining the illusion that Chillingworth is indeed a devil. Not only does the latter perform the function of fostering evil, but his external physical appearance is contrived to enhance his awesome appearance. In the supernatural shadow of *The Scarlet Letter* he is a tempter. He is so designated by Dimmesdale's parishioners, the minister himself, when he realizes his relations to the physician, brands him "tempter." Yet Chillingworth is no ordinary demon of seductive evil. His antecedents reveal his close kinship to the Satan of the Puritan fathers. Aware of the efficacy of grace, Chillingworth wishes to forestall a public confession by Dimmesdale. If the minister, giving way to self-pity and moral cowardice, flees the settlement, then he will doom himself irrevocably to everlasting hell.

But notwithstanding the Puritan acuity of the tempter, his lineage is traceable to Goethe's Mephistopheles. His assault on the spiritual defenses of Dimmesdale is designed to lure the sinner away from God. This effort closely parallels the aim of Mephistopheles in the Prologue to *Faust*. Goethe's tempter announces to God that Faust will not be able to resist the enticements standing between him and service to the divine power. Faust, however, regaining his moral perspective in the last scene of Part One of the drama, rushes to the assistance of the girl whom he has reduced to a criminal. Thereby he eludes the toils of Mephisto. Dimmesdale, in refusing to succumb[112] to the attractive temptation of flight, similarly circumvents Chillingworth. With the Puritan necromancer's failure to prevent the minister's public confession, the final phase of his characterization is attained. As in the other versions of the Faust myth, the historical background of the action determines the ultimate fate of the hero. Chillingworth's belief that he cannot pardon Dimmesdale's sin is a projection of his utter moral collapse. Therefore he stoically surrenders his soul to the devil. An unrepentant sinner, he thinks himself the victim of divine predestination: "My old faith, long forgotten, comes back to me, and explains all that we do, and all we suffer."[113]

. . . .

FROM *"The Scarlet Letter:* The New England *Faust," Hawthorne's Faust* (Gainesville, 1953), pp. 104-122. Reprinted by permission of the University of Florida Press.

PEARL

THE BEAUTIFUL BUT POISONOUS FLOWER

Julian Hawthorne

. . . .

Standing as the incarnation, instead of the victim, of a sin, Pearl affords a unique opportunity for throwing light upon the inner nature of the sin itself. In availing himself of it, Hawthorne touches ground which, perhaps, he would not have ventured on, had he not first safeguarded himself against exaggeration and impiety by making his analysis accord (so to speak) with the definition of a child's personality. Pearl, as we are frequently reminded, is the scarlet letter made alive, capable of being loved, and so endowed with a manifold power of retribution for sin. The principle[475] of her being is the freedom of a broken law; she is developed, "a lovely and immortal flower, out of the rank luxuriance of a guilty passion," yet, herself, as irresponsible and independent as if distinctions of right and wrong did not exist to her. Like nature and animals, she is anterior to moral law; but, unlike them, she is human, too. She exhibits an unfailing vigor and vivacity of spirits joined to a precocious and almost preternatural intelligence, especially with reference to her mother's shameful badge. To this her interest constantly reverts, and always with a "peculiar smile and odd expression of the eyes," they almost suggesting acquaintance on her part with "the secret spell of her existence." The wayward, mirthful mockery with which the small creature always approaches this hateful theme, as if she deemed it a species of ghastly jest, is a terribly significant touch, and would almost warrant a confirmation of the mother's fear that she had brought a fiend into the world. Yet, physically, Pearl is "worthy to have been left in Eden, to be the plaything of the angels," and her aspect—as must needs be the case with a child who symbolized a sin that finds its way into all regions of human society—"was imbued with the spell of infinite variety: in this one child there were many children, comprehending the full scope between the wild-flower prettiness of a peasant baby and the pomp, in little, of an infant princess." The plan of her nature, though possibly possessing an order of its own, was incompatible with the scheme of the rest of the universe; in other words, the child could never, apparently, come into harmony with her surroundings, unless the ruling destiny of the world should, from divine, become diabolic. "I have no Heavenly Father!" she exclaims, touching the scarlet letter on her mother's bosom with her small forefinger: and how, indeed, could the result of an evil deed be good? There is "fire in her and throughout her," as befits "the unpremeditated offshoot of a passionate moment," and it is a fire that seems to have in it at least as much of an infernal as of a heavenly ardor; and in her grim little philosophy, the scarlet emblem is the heritage of the maturity of all her sex. "Will it not come of its own accord, when I am a woman grown?" And yet she is a guiltless child, with all of a child's freshness and spontaneity.

This contrast, or, perhaps it is more correct to say, mingling, of the opposite poles of being, sin and innocence, in Pearl's nature is an extraordinary achievement; enabling us, as it does, to recognize the intrinsic ugliness of sin. Pearl is like a beautiful but poisonous flower, rejoicing in its poison, and receiving it as the vital element of life. But the beauty makes the ugliness only the more impressive, because we feel it to be a magical or phantasmal beauty, enticing like the apples of Sodom, but full of bitterness within. It is the beauty which sin wears to the tempted,—a beauty, therefore, which has no real existence. . . . Now, if Pearl were a woman, this strong external charm of hers would perplex the reader, in much the same way that the allurements of sin bewilder its votaries. . . . Pearl being a child, however, no such uncertainty can occur. She has not, as yet, what can in strictness be termed a character; she is without experience, and therefore devoid of either good or evil principles; she possesses a nature, and nothing more. The affection which she excites, consequently, is immediately perceived to be due neither to her beauty nor to her intellectual acuteness; still less to the evil effluence which exhales from these, and is characteristic of them.[476] These things all stand on one side; and the innocent, irresponsible infant soul stands on the other. Each defines and emphasizes the other: so that so far from one being led to confuse them, so far from being in danger of loving evil because we love Pearl, we love her just in proportion to our abhorrence of the evil which empoisons her manifestations. The same discrimination could not be so sharply made (if, indeed, it could be made at all) in the case of a Pearl who, under unchanged conditions had attained maturity. For her character would then be formed, and the evil which came to her by inheritance would so have tinged and molded her natural traits that we should inevitably draw in the poison and the perfume at a single breath,—ascribe to evil the charm which it derives from good, and pollute good with the lurid hues of evil. The history of the race abundantly demonstrates that a chief cause of moral perversity and false principle has been our assumption of absolute proprietorship in either the good or the evil of our actions. Pearl, still in the instinctive stage of development, shows us the way out of this labyrinth. As the pure sunlight vivifies noxious as well as beneficent forms of existence, so the evil proclivities of the child's nature are energized, though not constituted, by the divine source of her being.[477]

. . . .

FROM "Problems of *The Scarlet Letter*," *Atlantic Monthly*, LVII (April, 1886), 471-485.

PEARL AND THE PURITANS

Chester E. Eisinger

. . . .

Criticism has done so much to mark out and define the influence of puritanism upon Hawthorne that we need not dwell upon the matter here. Suffice it to say that the evidence of Hawthorne's indebtedness to the Puritans is overwhelming. The proposition that little Pearl may be understood by reference to the Puritan theories of nature and liberty, therefore, is not as far-fetched as it might appear. The claim put forward here is that Pearl is a "natural" child not only in her illegitimacy but in the natural, i.e., unfettered, condition[323] of her life. As wild and as free as nature, she owes allegiance to the domain of nature. She is, as a consequence, virtually beyond the reach of divine salvation and is completely outside human society. Now Hawthorne, believing as the Puritans did that each individual soul is precious, is under obligation to release Pearl from her bondage to nature, find her a place in human society, and make her a consciously human creature. Then she will be susceptible to God's grace should it be offered her.

He meets his problem by subjecting Pearl to a kind of psychic shock when Dimmesdale, in his expiation scene, recognizes her as his daughter and awakens through suffering all her human sympathies, thus sweeping her into the community of men. Before this she was unable to obey civil and divine law. Now she may, if she will.

It is necessary at this point to set forth the portions of Puritan thought relevant to this discussion: the view of nature and the conception of polity. No sharp distinction can be made between the two because certain basic assumptions are prevalent in all aspects of Puritan thought.

According to Puritan theory, adherence of the unregenerate man to nature and natural law will lead to a life of riot and confusion. Such a man is a creature of instincts, carrying his appetites and ambitions to excess. No one can doubt, says John Cotton, "the depravation of nature." For the regenerate man, however, nature is good. The Puritan defined nature as the art of God, but, since the Fall has invalidated the efficacy of human reason, only those men who through faith have been granted God's salvation can read aright the lessons of nature. The Puritan held that no one, whether or not in a state of grace, can live by nature alone.

Nature and the unregenerate man are factors necessary to a discussion of Puritan polity, for they are integral to a discrimination between natural and civil liberty and between natural and civil government. The natural man, according to the Puritans, enjoyed natural liberty, which was antithetical to civil liberty and led to excesses in conduct. To live by natural liberty was to deny the authority of God and the doctrine of original sin. The social covenant could be preserved only by adherence to the doctrine of civil liberty. A sound Puritan commonwealth, therefore, could not tolerate the exercise of natural liberties nor abide the presence of those who lived by them. Only those individuals who were conscientiously working toward salvation or those who had already attained it could be admitted into Puritan society. These could be trusted to honor the ends and observe the limitations of civil liberty. . . .[324]

In the opening chapter of *The Scarlet Letter* Hawthorne calls our attention to "a wild rose-bush" growing at the side of the prison door. Its flowers "might be imagined to offer their fragrance and fragile beauty to the prisoner as he went in, and to the condemned criminal as he came forth to his doom, in token that the deep heart of Nature could pity and be kind to him." What was the origin of the rosebush? With characteristic diffidence, Hawthorne suggests alternate possibilities: it has survived out of the wilderness, or perhaps "it had sprung up under the footsteps of the sainted Anne Hutchinson." Why does Hawthorne bring the rosebush into his story at this point? With a quiet cynicism he has been observing, prior to mention of the rosebush, that new colonies, utopian as they might be in intention, always establish at the outset a cemetery and a prison. These are the marks of civilization; the latter, especially, is a symbol of government and law. The rosebush, in obvious contrast, is wild. It is a throwback to the wilderness that existed before civil society in New England. Or its genesis is associated with Anne Hutchinson, who was, in the eyes of the Puritans, a criminal and who was thrust out of their society. Nature, therefore, has especial affinities with the wild or with the criminal, with that which is beyond the pale of civil society. Behind the prison door are Hester and Pearl. It seems clear that Hawthorne is seeking to identify the wildness of nature with sin against society: the first symbolized by the rosebush, the second personified by Hester and Pearl.

As the book progresses, Hawthorne seems to reinforce this identification. When Pearl and Hester visit the Governor's mansion, they walk into the garden, where the child, sighting the Governor's rose-bushes, begins to cry for a red rose. Confronted by the dignitaries of church and state, among them the good Mr. Wilson, who seeks to catechize the child, Pearl acts perversely. She refuses to say who made her and finally announces that she "had not been made at all, but had been plucked by her mother off the bush of wild roses that grew by the prison-door." Although she is well aware of the answer expected of her, she prefers in her perversity this fanciful explanation that links her with the natural wildness of the uncultivated plant. Her departure from orthodoxy shocks the Governor, who is convinced of the darkness of her soul and of its depravity.

In still other portions of the novel Hester is granted a kinship with a real and moral wilderness that carries her beyond accepted Puritan attitudes toward society and theology. Hawthorne speaks of the wildness of her nature, which awakens the sympathy of the forest and its dwellers. He points out that Hester had been outlawed from society, and so freed, in a sense, she had developed an intellectual range far greater than Dimmesdale's. Her speculation had led her, however, into a "moral wilderness; as vast...as the untamed forest.... Her intellect and heart had their home, as it were, in desert places, where she roamed as freely as the wild Indian in his woods....The tendency of her fate and fortunes has been to set her free."[325] Freedom and nature stand on one side; on the other stand the stability, security, and orderliness that are embodied in the divinely directed Puritan community.

Hester, however, is not our principal interest, although it is useful to observe how Hawthorne works out the selfsame idea with respect to her and to Pearl. Furthermore, it is clear that the moral wilderness has engulfed Hester partially as a consequence of a sin, of which Pearl is the living symbol. Pearl is heir, then, not only to a passion that transcended the moral law but to an intellect that was at once free and subject to confusion. In short, Pearl's mother, having conceived the child in sin by giving way to natural passion, brings down upon herself and the child social and religious ostracism and forces herself and the child into a sympathetic relation with nature. As Hawthorne says, "The child's own nature had something wrong in it, which continually betokened she had been born amiss,—the effluence of her mother's lawless passion."

Indeed, if the reader attends to the consistent imagery applied to Pearl, he must come to regard her as an untamed, wild, even nonhuman creature. She is of nature but not of man. She is endowed with "natural dexterity" and "natural grace." On one occasion she is a lovely flower, possessed, a page later, with a "wild-flower prettiness." On at least five occasions she is likened to a bird: "a wild tropical bird, of rich plumage," a "floating sea-bird," and so on. On innumerable occasions she is a sprite, an imp, an elf, a dryad. Hawthorne endows her with "airy charm" and "elfish intelligence"; Pearl is hardly a human child but is an airy sprite, a little elf gathering handfuls of wild flowers. She is capable of an eldritch scream, and Hawthorne, indulging the Puritan appetite for demonology, has Mistress Hibbins suggest that the child is of the "lineage of the Prince of the Air!"

Certainly it is some instinctive, hardly human portion of the child's makeup that gives Pearl her feeling of affinity to Dimmesdale. As a mere babe she stretches her arms toward him. At the Governor's mansion, when he defends Hester's right to keep the child, Pearl, "that wild and flighty little elf," steals up to the minister and caresses him in an "unwonted mood of sentiment" and display of human emotions. She reverts immediately to airy indifference. It is as though the elfish and human portions of her soul were warring for mastery. In this struggle Dimmesdale holds the key. Throughout the novel, until Dimmesdale's confession, Pearl seeks recognition from her father and, being rejected, remains the "natural" child allied to the birds and to the creatures of the nether world. Not until Dimmesdale acknowledges her publicly, as we shall see, does she become a full-fledged human being.

For her kinship with nature is the dominant fact of her existence. Whenever she is outdoors, particularly in the wilderness, there seems to be a conscious desire on her part to merge with natural objects; while on the part of natural objects there is a tendency to absorb Pearl. She plays with her reflected image in a pool of water and seeks "a passage for herself into its sphere of impalpable earth and unattainable sky," as though[326] she would become one with the elements. Again, when Pearl stands on one side of the brook, that "boundary between two worlds," and Hester and Dimmesdale summon her to the other side, Pearl seems to have melted into a natural environment, caressed by the sun, enveloped by and identified with the brook. Hester feels herself estranged from the child who seems to have "strayed out of the sphere in which she and her mother dwelt together" into the realm of Pan or the Druids. She gives up throwing pebbles at a flock of beach-birds after wounding one "because it grieved her to have done harm to a little being that was as wild as the sea-breeze, or as wild as Pearl herself." In the forest, when Hawthorne manipulates light and shade so magnificently, the sun seems deliberately to avoid Hester at first. But Pearl catches the sunshine, and "the light lingered about the lonely child, as if glad of such a playmate." Later, even the "great black forest...became the playmate of the lonely infant." Finally, Hawthorne makes explicit what has been evident for some time: "The truth seems to be...that the mother-forest, and these wild things which it nourished, all recognized a kindred wildness in the human child." Not always is she a human child, for when she decorates herself with wild violets, anemones, and columbines, she becomes a "nymph-child, or an infant dryad, or whatever else was in closest sympathy with the antique wood."

Hawthorne leaves us in no doubt as to the significance of Pearl's identification with nature. A disciple of neither the eighteenth century's belief in nature's simple plan nor the Romantic notion of living in harmony with nature, this latter-day Puritan looked askance at the uncontrolled and uncontrollable realms of nature. Pearl is wild because she is a child of nature. Nature is wild, untrammeled, because man cannot put his stamp upon it and regulate it. In the great colloquy in the forest, between Hester and Dimmesdale, the former announces firmly that the minister must escape his torture by fleeing to another land. Dimmesdale is tremendously relieved. He feels the "exhilarating effect ...of breathing the wild, free atmosphere of an unredeemed, unchristianized, lawless region." Now, while Hawthorne does not say that this area is the domain of nature, he does make it quite clear that Dimmesdale is preparing to depart, spiritually as well as bodily, from the Christian community, which is the very antithesis of that region just described. Futhermore, nature seems to approve of this decision, as well as of this region. For no sooner do the lovers begin to savor the effects of their decision than the gloom of the forest vanishes. "Such was the sympathy of Nature—that wild, heathen Nature of the forest, never subjugated by human law, nor illumined by higher truth—with the bliss of these two spirits!" If Pearl is a child of this realm, then her wildness is understandable, as is her position with respect to the organized society of her time.

The Christian community does not admit Pearl or recognize her as one of its members because she belongs to nature and not to man or to human society. Nature finds a kindred wildness in Pearl; society demands that she be submissive. The ideals of the two areas are irreconcilable, and Pearl must become a part of one or of the other.

As a matter of fact, she has no choice in the matter. Society thrusts her out, while nature, as we have seen, takes her in. Her character and her origin determine in part the direction of her allegiance. Hawthorne tells us that, while[327] Pearl's character possessed depth and variety, "it lacked reference and adaptation to the world into which she was born. The child could not be made amenable to rules. In giving her existence, a great law had been broken; and the result was a being whose elements were perhaps beautiful and brilliant, but all in disorder." Pearl is passionate and ungovernable. Her mother is forced to "permit the child to be swayed by her own impulses." Chillingworth remarks that " 'there is no law nor reverence for authority, no regard for human ordinances or opinions, right or wrong, mixed up with that child's composition.' " The only " 'discoverable principle of being' " governing her is " 'the freedom of a broken law,' " as Dimmesdale, so eminently qualified to make the judgment, says. The result is that Pearl is cut off from society and even from mankind. She was born an "outcast of the infantile world" who "had no right among christened infants." Puritan children of the community sensed something "outlandish, unearthly" in both Pearl and Hester, who "stood together in the same circle of seclusion from human society." No wonder, then, that Pearl looks upon the world as adverse. No wonder that she is likened to a "creature that had nothing in common with a bygone and buried generation, nor owned herself akin to it. It was as if she had been made afresh, out of new elements, and must perforce be permitted to live her own life, and be a law unto herself." The continuity of life that links most of us to society and to humanity is denied Pearl.

Yet, all the time, Hawthorne means to reclaim Pearl from nature and to restore her to the jurisdiction of God and man. He clings to the notion that a child of God can return to God. The Puritans held, after all, that God created both man and nature. While Pearl seems to be allied almost completely with nature, Hawthorne never allows us to forget that she has an immortal soul that God will eventually judge: God granted Hester a lovely child who could finally be a "blessed soul in heaven." Illegitimate though she may be, the authorities of the colony are concerned for her spiritual well-being in the interest, again, of her immortal soul. It is this concern that impels the Governor to propose that Pearl be taken from Hester. In the debate over this matter, Dimmesdale, who is defending Hester's interest in the child, argues that Pearl has " 'come from the hand of God' " to act on Hester as a blessing and a retribution and to teach her that if " 'she bring the child to heaven, the child also will bring its parent thither!' " These passages demonstrate conclusively that Hawthorne never abandons the child.

It is through Dimmesdale's expiation that Pearl becomes a human being. Her ultimate salvation rests with God, but her fate as a woman in this life lies in her father's hands. When he confesses his sin, Pearl is reclaimed from the realm of nature, and her wildness and perversity wither away. Or perhaps one could say that they are blown away by the kiss of love and recognition that Dimmesdale exchanges with Pearl when they come together on the scaffold in the revelation scene. "Pearl kissed his lips. A spell was broken. The great scene of grief, in which the wild infant bore a part, had developed all her sympathies; and as her tears fell upon her father's cheek, they were the pledge that she would grow up amid human joy and sorrow, nor forever do battle with the world, but be a woman in it." Into these sentences Hawthorne has packed virtually the complete significance of Pearl. Once the sin of her birth has been acknowledged, a psychic transformation overtakes her. When Dimmesdale[328] reveals himself, the long search for the father is ended. A sense of certainty, even of social status, in a way, is now possible for Pearl. All the latent human emotions rise up in this crisis to overwhelm that wildness that had linked her to nature. Thus the expiation of the sin gives every expectation that Pearl will grow into a woman at one with the world, partaking of its good and of its bad as do all human beings. Mankind and society have claimed their own.

As the book trails off, Hawthorne gives us adequate assurance that Pearl has at last adapted herself to society. She becomes the richest heiress of her day in the New World. Probably "her wild, rich nature had been softened and subdued, and made capable of a woman's gentle happiness." We may safely surmise that, equipped with money and a receptive feminine disposition, Pearl makes a good marriage and bears children. She treats her mother with love and consideration. Pearl stands at the end as an apotheosis of Puritan morality.[329]

. . . .

FROM "Pearl and the Puritan Heritage," *College English*, XII (March, 1951), 323-329. Reprinted by permission of the author and *College English*.

PEARL AS REGENERATIVE SYMBOL

Darrel Abel

. . . .

The processes of nature are not mere successions of events, but sequences in which one event "springs" from another and partakes of a common nature. Flowers and fruits are not spontaneous, external appendages of branches, but grow out of them and possess characters peculiar to themselves. A man born of a given pair of parents "inherits" their traits. Such continuities in nature are evidences of a "constitution or established order." [1]

In this "constitution or established order" children play the same part in the human world that new growth plays in the natural world. Hawthorne remarked: "It is a marvel whence [the white pond lily] derives its loveliness and perfume, sprouting as it does from the black mud over which the river sleeps...." Analogously, he said of Pearl that "her innocent life had sprung, by the inscrutable decree of Providence, out of the rank luxuriance of a guilty passion." Pearl thus stands as a regenerative symbol—a phenomenal resurgence among the sullied members of adult society of the power of goodness which men can obscure but not extinguish in themselves.

In the person of Pearl this regenerative symbolism is manifest in two ways, which may be called reincarnative and talismanic. She is a reincarnation of the best human possibility of her ancestors—of potentialities which, imperfectly realized in past generations, are once more offered opportunity for a better realization in this "germ and blossom of womanhood." The pathos of Pearl's situation arises from our awareness that such realization is contingent upon her sinful parents' giving her a connection with the moral order of the universe by resuming their "lapséd powers." The dramatic effect of thus defining Pearl's moral dependency is to enlarge the notion of moral consequence attaching to her parents' behavior; through it, we are made aware that, as Hawthorne said, "Every crime destroys more Edens than our own." Not merely Pearl's personal fulfilment, but all the upward-yearning generations of humanity behind her which are awaiting a better realization in her life, may be defeated. [54]

Pearl's talismanic symbolism is at once less significant intrinsically and more important dramatically than is her reincarnative symbolism. The former is acted out more fully, and has more apparent effect on the plot of the novel than does the latter. As a talismanic symbol, Pearl offers instinctive affiance to whatever is good in the persons around her—a trait which vividly reminds adults of the power of goodness still present in themselves, however obscured by the debasing practices of the world: "As the pure breath of children revives the life of aged men, so is our moral nature revived by their free and simple thoughts" ("Little Annie's Ramble"). Pearl makes repeated instinctive appeals to her parents to prefer spiritual goods to animal satisfactions; and the changes in her moods, her conduct, and her character during the progress of the story are an index to the varying moral condition of Hester and Dimmesdale. Old Mistress Hibbins serves a complementary talismanic function in the story, except that she is a touchstone of experienced and conscious evil rather than of innocent and unconscious

---

1 Joseph Haroutunian, *Piety Versus Moralism: The Passing of the New England Theology* (New York, 1932), pp. 16-17.

goodness: whenever Mistress Hibbins appears in the story, it is to accost someone in whom she detects an access of evil impulses, and to urge him to declare himself irrevocably for the devil's party.

These things Pearl, although a Child of Nature, symbolizes by virtue of being also (a more important consideration to Hawthorne) a Child of Man. What she was as "germ and blossom" of human stock was her most significant mode of being.

Since the conditions of Pearl's human geniture were of immense importance, her nurture, natural and humane, must be effectual in the degree to which it realizes the best possibilities latent in those conditions. Whereas Lucy,[2] from the beginning of her development, is shown to be (fortunately, from her author's point of view) removed from human associations, Pearl is established in a human relationship which strongly influences her. She does not enjoy full and normal relationship with society: "Mother and daughter stood together in the same circle of seclusion from human society." But the most indispensable influence upon the child is the maternal one, and so long as this operated Pearl could not become a pure Child of[55] Nature. In fact, the maternal connection was strengthened, even to morbidity, by the ostracism of Pearl and Hester. To Lucy, human associations are not essential but rather trammeling to growth; to Pearl, they are so essential that defective ones are better than none at all.

Human associations being for Hawthorne a *sine qua non* of full human development, it is evident that Nature could not have such an entire and effectual influence upon Pearl as she had upon Lucy. But it is necessary to define the mode and value of the influence which Nature did have upon her Child Pearl; for as I have asserted Pearl is in her most fundamental character a Child of Nature. She is of course a "natural child" in the euphemistic sense of the phrase. But a Child of Nature is properly speaking one who discovers conscious and valuable affinities with the natural world and enjoys an active and formative relationship with that world.

Hawthorne did not regard human nature and physical nature as distinct orders of being, but rather as the subjective and objective—sentient and material—aspects of a single order of being which included and transcended them both. Both participated in the grand scheme of existence which his Puritan ancestors were wont to call "God's Sovereign Constitution." Therefore, there is in Hawthorne's work no emphatic opposition between personal and natural life; he did not see man as a creature separate from the rest of creation, inhabiting a visible world irrational and dead. Like Emerson, he believed in a "relation between mind and matter" which "stands in the will of God." Coleridge uttered this transcendentalist doctrine in similar

---

[2] Wordsworth's Child of Nature described in his Lucy poems. Mr. Abel's article begins with a discussion of "Lucy, The Child of Nature as Ideal."

terms, remarking "an inherent relationship between nature and the human soul, a relationship apprehended by a vision at once emotional and intellectual." Little Pearl manifests this relationship between man and nature; her life and the life of nature are contiguous and sympathetic modes of being. Therefore, Hawthorne observed: "The mother-forest, and these wild things which it nourished, all recognized a kindred wildness in the human child." This "wildness," however, is[56] not the wildness of savagery but the wildness of innocence, like that state of prelapsarian innocence in which Adam and Eve, as well as "all Beasts of th' Earth, since wild," were instinctively gentle and sportive. So Hawthorne said of Pearl, "The infant was worthy to have been brought forth in Eden," and recorded (with characteristic deprecation) the rumor that even a wolf in the forest, responsive to her primitive innocence, "came up, and smelt of Pearl's robe, and offered his savage head to be patted by her hand." It was Pearl's conscious kinship with Nature which prompted her to respond perversely, when the Reverend Mr. Wilson asked her who had made her, "that she had not been made at all, but had been plucked by her mother off the bush of wild roses that grew by the prison door"—an answer which, like other parts of her conduct and speech, expresses her symbolism rather than her character. To express Pearl's fundamental Naturalness, Hawthorne as inevitably chose a flower metaphor as did Wordsworth to express Lucy's.

Pearl's relationship with Nature was intensified, like her relationship with her mother, by her ostracism. Hester's dwelling on the verge of the forest, at the outskirts of the town, symbolized her retreat from Man to Nature; this situation encouraged the Child's easy association with Nature, the human person's "true parent" ("The New Adam and Eve").

Although Pearl thus enjoyed an unusually rich life in Nature, the point of crucial if obvious importance in interpreting her character is that Hawthorne represents the Child of Nature as being infrahuman. Wordsworth looks upon Lucy as a consummate creature; Hawthorne shows Pearl to be *une fille manquée*, lacking a character—an immense defect in the opinion of Hawthorne, who declared himself to be "a man who felt it to be the best definition of happiness to live throughout the whole range of his faculties and sensibilities" ("The Custom House"). Pearl's Nature was not a blemish—it was indeed an indispensable and valuable part of her reality; but it was not a fulfilment, for she had only a nascent spiritual life. The Nature which she participated in was "that wild heathen Nature,...never subjugated by human law, nor illumined by higher truth" which put on a brighter[57] aspect for her adulterous parents when they decided to turn their backs on moral duty to satisfy their carnal desires.

Although Hawthorne regarded the Child of Nature as an imperfect being, he did not regard her as a corrupted or depraved being, as the Calvinists regarded all infants. Pearl was not one of those "infants flagitious" the justice of whose damnation Wigglesworth vindicated in "The Day of Doom." Unlike Hawthorne, the Puritans did not conceive of child-nature as a distinct developmental phase of human character. They looked upon the infant as a person with a moral character already formed—and that character was the sinful one settled upon all mankind in the decree of damnation. Therefore children were taught that "in Adam's fall we sinnéd all," and their parents were exhorted to

Consider them as creatures, whom you (as instruments) have brought into being, tainted with innate corruption.

....

Your children are born with a corrupted nature, perverted by sinful examples, ignorant of God, in a state of growing enmity to him, and, in consequence of all, exposed to his wrath and curse, and in the way of everlasting ruin.

Hawthorne thought, as did the Puritans, that the only distinctively human reality was moral reality; but unlike the Puritans, he regarded infant humanity as being in a pre-moral or infra-moral condition. Pearl, therefore, as a Child of Nature was not a perverted or damned creature. She was an Undine—a beautiful half-human child who instinctively aspired to possession of a soul. Coleridge, who thought that "Undine's character, before she receives a soul, is marvellously beautiful," remarked in another connection that "all lower natures find their highest good in semblances and seekings of that which is[58] higher and better. All things strive to ascend, and ascend in their striving." The striking variability of Pearl's temper resulted from her insistent yearning toward spiritual realization, at times baffled by the evil in lives involved with her own, but springing up again irrepressibly, in her chidings of Hester whenever Hester gave signs of ignoring her moral obligations, and in her repeated mute intimations to Dimmesdale that he should abandon the falsehood which was eating away the moral truth in his existence.

Pearl's aspiration toward moral life could not be assisted by the Nature in her. Hawthorne's view of the relation of the Child to Nature differed significantly from the early Wordsworthian view in this respect. He did not think that Nature can teach more of "moral evil and of good than all the sages can," but held views nearer to those which Wordsworth expressed more than forty-five years after the Lucy poems in "The Westmoreland Girl." Hawthorne apparently thought that Nature quickened the Child's sensibilities, so that moral truths might more readily find entrance, but that the actual moral character of the Child would be determined by the quality of the human influences which worked through these awakened sensibilities. Intimacy with Nature, which, in Wordsworthian phrase, exercised "the essential passions of the heart," would prepare the Child for human and spiritual affections. Many of Hawthorne's comments on the value of Nature to the developing Child echo Wordsworth: "Is not Nature better than a book?" he asks, in "Earth's Holocaust," adopting the theme of "Expostulation and Reply" and "The Tables Turned." He created a whole company of children (among them the dream-children in "The Village Uncle," the mountain-children[59] in "The Ambitious Guest," and Ernest in "The Great Stone Face"), who like Lucy, were moulded by "silent sympathy" with Nature. . . .

Nature could thus quicken the Child's sensibilities, so that she might be receptive to moral truths, yet nature alone was incapable of doing more to assist moral development. The latent spirituality of the Child of Nature could be unfolded only by the attractions toward moral life proffered by those persons with whom her budding character was connected. Her instinct toward goodness, as spontaneous as a seedling's leaning to the sun, had to be met by a shower of benign influence. Although in a certain basic sense Nature is man's "true parent," his human parents have the responsibility of imparting his moral reality to him. "Marriage," Coleridge wrote, "simply as marriage, is not the means 'for the procreation of children,' but for the humanization of the offspring created." Pearl's prospect of becoming[60] humanized by such means was grievously beclouded by the irregularity of her birth and the persistent error of her adulterous parents.[61]

. . . .

FROM "Hawthorne's Pearl: Symbol and Character," *ELH, A Journal of English Literary History,* XVIII (March, 1951), 50-66. Reprinted by permission of the author and the editors of *ELH.*

THE CHARACTER OF FLAME

Anne Marie McNamara

. . . .

The double nature of little Pearl functions...on two distinct levels (the natural and the preternatural), in two directions (towards a known and an unknown parent), through two sets of actions (the explicit and the implicit) translatable upon two planes of meaning (the literal and the figurative). She approaches and affects Hester and Dimmesdale in appropriately different ways suited to the capacity of each to receive and understand her meaning. On the natural level she acts on Hester as a real child; on the preternatural level she acts on Dimmesdale as a "more-than-child," an elf-dryad-nymph, a spirit child. In each case, her method of approach is determined by the nature of the desired effect. In Hester the need is for the restoration of the discarded public acknowledgment of adultery, the embroidered scarlet letter. In Dimmesdale the desideratum is the revelation of the private, hidden stigma of the same sin. As a real child, Pearl causes a visible change in Hester by audibly, imperiously, and petulantly demanding that her mother pin the discarded A in its customary place on her breast. Hester understands and obeys, and the estrangement between[540] the mother and child is immediately mended: Pearl leaps the brook and embraces her mother.

But the estrangement between Pearl and Dimmesdale is not a temporary condition, induced by one overt act and dissipated by another. The offense of her father against her is the deliberate and guilty concealment of parenthood during her whole lifetime. The healing of this serious breach (divined by the elf-nature but not by the child-nature in Pearl) cannot be effected as was the other, immediately, visibly, audibly, objectively. The spirit child communicates her disapproval in another way, one exquisitely appropriate to Dimmesdale's sensibility—through a silent, indirect, subjective language. In the entire scene at the brookside she does not speak to him with her human voice at all. She addresses him indirectly through her persistent rejection of his advances and through actions ostensibly directed towards her mother. When Hester, restored to Pearl's favor, entreats the child to greet the minister and assures her that he loves her, Pearl phrases in two succinct questions the only terms on which the alienation may be terminated: "Doth he love us? Will he go back with us, hand in hand, we three together, into the town?" Public revelation of the real relationship among the three is to Pearl the only means of reconciliation. She ignores her mother's request that she love the minister. She is not cajoled by the promise of a future home in which the three will be together and in which Dimmesdale will love her dearly. Her only reply is again a question: "And will he always keep his hand over his heart?" She clearly implies that guilt will plague Dimmesdale even if he succeeds in the plans for escape which he and Hester are now formulating. Her mother, not sensing the profound implications of her questions, lightly evades them. Consequently, stubbornly refusing to show any friendliness towards the minister and grimacing with disapproval, Pearl receives his embrace only at her mother's insistence and immediately bathes her forehead in the brook to wash away all vestiges of his "unwelcome kiss."

Pearl's actions at the brookside nettle her mother and produce immediate and tangible results. They work differently on Dimmesdale. For him they have more than their superficial meaning. His fancy that the brook flowing between Pearl and her parents is a boundary between two worlds may suggest his awareness of the double level of Pearl's action. His comment is eloquent: he says[541] that the brook separates Pearl from Hester; he does not say that it separates Pearl from him. On the other hand, when Hester is about to call to Pearl to join her and the minister, the child's distance from them is judged differently by the two. To Hester, Pearl is "not far off," but to Dimmesdale she is "a good way off." Does he mean that she seems to be in another world from which she is reaching out to him? Do his observation and insight suggest knowledge of the commencement of the "otherworldly" influence of his child upon his spirit? Does his incipient realization prepare him for an extraordinary meeting of their extraordinary minds? He is nervous and anxious as she mistrustingly delays her approach. He is afraid as the child's penetrating glances apparently at once seek and divine the relationship between Hester and himself: his hand involuntarily steals over his heart—and over the mark of that relationship. He is deeply disturbed as Pearl bursts into passionate cries and gesticulations of protest and demand. Her insistent designation of the cause of her displeasure—the absence of the scarlet letter from her mother's breast—unnerves him. He seems aware that her agitation is more than a childish tantrum, for he uses the word *preternatural* to describe it.

Although Pearl's outburst at the brookside is directed towards her mother, it affects Dimmesdale traumatically. This hypersensitive man experiences almost simultaneously the extremes of exaltation and depression—Hester's plan for the resumption of their love affair and Pearl's adamant rejection of his affection. His unacknowledged daughter tells him in her wordless language that his acquiescence to Hester's will to escape is a false answer to his problem and is distasteful to her. She will not enter into arrangements which involve a continuance of his concealment of sin. No wonder that the minister who leaves the elf at the brookside is a minister in a maze.

The narrator's final comment on the forest meeting characterizes it as "fateful." This statement is valid and acceptable on both the natural and the supranatural levels: the interview is fateful as the time of Hester's and Dimmesdale's decision to enter deliberately upon a life of sin; it is fateful as the silent impetus to the agitated minister's subsequent action on the day of the Governor's[542] inauguration.

Three passages in a previous chapter entitled "The Interior of a Heart" lend credibility to the perspicuity which I have imputed to the minister at this forest meeting. The first prefigures the major action of Pearl at the brookside, her insistent pointing at her mother's breast; the second illustrates Dimmesdale's power of perception—however dim at first—of a subtle influence unperceived by others; the third foreshadows the peculiar ability of Dimmesdale to interpret Pearl's meaning.

The first of these significant foreshadowings occurs in the detailing of Dimmesdale's relationship with Chillingworth after the latter's discovery of the secret stigma. Diabolically playing upon his victim, Chillingworth seeks to overpower him through the agony of fear. In the figure of speech chosen by the narrator to describe the physician's evil plan, the elements of unearthly power and of finger-pointing are adumbrations of the incriminating knowledge and the accusing gesture of Pearl at the brookside. The importance of this association grows as one recalls the triple pattern in which these two elements are found in the forest scene. Three times the narrator repeats the pattern: the child stands on the farther side of the brook, authoritatively pointing her finger at her mother's breast, while beneath, mirrored in the brook, is her image, imperious and beautiful, pointing in the same accusing way. If Dimmesdale had been startled with sudden fear by a "grisly phantom..., a thousand phantoms...all flocking round [him] and pointing with their fingers at his breast," may he not react similarly to see "the bright-apparelled vision" of Pearl, "now like a child, now like a child's spirit," using the same condemnatory gesture? True, the gesture is not made directly at him by Pearl—since her method of approach to him is indirect—but its repetitive pattern commences immediately after a passage which shows Pearl's uncanny divination of the lovers' relationship and the minister's involuntary, guilty reaction to the suspicious knowledge in her "wild, bright eyes": "his hand...stole over his heart." May not the thrice-repeated pattern of her direct communication with Hester and her indirect communication with Dimmesdale suggest a real child-Hester relationship but a spirit child-Dimmesdale relationship? The image of the child in the pool, the narrator says, is "more refined and spiritualized than the reality." Moreover, the finger-pointing of Pearl may recall to Dimmesdale[543] his agonizing vigil on the pillory at midnight when, his eyes fixed on the blazing A in the night sky, "he was, nevertheless, perfectly aware that little Pearl was pointing her finger towards old Roger Chillingworth, who stood at no great distance from the scaffold. The minister appeared to see him, with the same glance that discerned the miraculous letter." As the real child on the edge of the pool points accusingly at her mother's breast, silently reproaching her for discarding her A, Dimmesdale is aware of the image-child in the pool, pointing reproachfully in the same way. If the meteor which Dimmesdale saw in the first instance "kindled up the sky...with an awfulness that admonished Hester Prynne and the clergyman of the day of judgment," as the narrator points out, may not the same fear of doom be generated in Dimmesdale's sensitive mind by his association of the A and the finger-pointing of the one instance with the same phenomena in the other?

The second of these foreshadowing references not only offers ground for Dimmesdale's receptivity to subtle influences but also obviates the objection that the lack of *immediate* perceptible evidence of Dimmesdale's understanding of Pearl's meaning at the brookside renders suspect the assumption that she is the cause of his ultimate confession. In the narrator's explanation of Chillingworth's method in his plot to break the resistance of his patient, he says that the evil work "was accomplished with a subtlety so perfect that the minister, though he had constantly a dim perception of some evil influence watching over him, could never gain a knowledge of its actual nature." May not Dimmesdale, then, be said to have at the brookside the first "dim perception" of the redemptive influence of Pearl?

The final foreshadowing concerns the metaphor of the Tongue of Flame. Ascribing Dimmesdale's prestige among the townspeople to his heavenly gift of sympathy for human nature, the narrator uses the Pentecostal Tongues of Flame to symbolize the supernatural penetration and love which distinguished the clergyman in his understanding and expressing the feelings of the human heart. The juxtaposition of this passage with that which describes Pearl as the enigmatic symbol of the lovers' secret—the "living hieroglyphic"—shows that the same figure has been used again. "She had been offered to the world...as the living hieroglyphic, in which was revealed the secret they so darkly sought to hide,—all written in[544] this symbol,—all plainly manifest, —had there been a prophet or a magician skilled to read the character of flame!" In the Bible narrative, tongues of flame were the symbols of the power of eloquence given by Heaven to men who were chosen to understand and reveal truth in order to effect the salvation of others. In the imaginative narrative with which we are concerned, the narrator interprets them as symbols "not of the power of speech in foreign and unknown languages, but that of addressing the whole human brotherhood in the heart's native language." The scarlet-garbed child —"The character of flame"—addresses an unspoken truth to a man capable in mind and heart of comprehending it. Dimmesdale is the only one of the clergymen of the town marked with "Heaven's last and rarest attestation of their office, the Tongue of Flame." His burden of hidden sorrow gave him sympathetic understanding and the gift of expressing "highest truths through the humblest medium of familiar words and images." The first use of the figure, therefore, is a foreshadowing of and a preparation for the second, and the second recalls the context of the first and lends credibility to the silent communication at the brookside.[545]

· · · ·

From "The Character of Flame: The Function of Pearl in *The Scarlet Letter*," *American Literature*, XXVII (Jan., 1956), 537-553. Reprinted by permission of the author and the editors of *American Literature*.

THE MICROCOSM OF CHAOS

Barbara Garlitz

. . . .

Do Pearl's affinities with nature indicate her innocence, her lawlessness, or her amorality? Whatever may have been Hawthorne's view of nature, in *The Scarlet Letter* it is neither beneficent nor amoral. The forest is a place of immorality—the home of the savage Indian, the place of the witches' Sabbaths, the symbol of Hester's "moral wilderness." The sun in the forest shines on Hester only when she gives in to a lawless passion. That the sun immediately envelops Pearl, that the forest accepts her as one of its own, can only signify, as Winters and Eisinger have said, Pearl's intrinsic lawlessness. However, some would say that since Pearl is a child and not yet a moral agent, her identification with nature only signifies the natural lawlessness or amorality of children. But, as we shall see, this is a modern attitude, not Hawthorne's. It seems unwise, however, to call Pearl simply a lawless child of nature, for at the end of the forest episode she rejects nature. When Pearl stands at the brookside, dressed like "an infant dryad," she is "in closest sympathy with the antique wood." Hawthorne lingers over the description of Pearl and her image in the water. Eisinger says that she is "enveloped by and identified with the brook," that she merges with untamed nature (p. 327).[1] But the opposite happens. We know that Hawthorne liked to believe "that the reflection is indeed the reality...that the disembodied shadow is nearest to the soul." Pearl's image, "more refined and spiritualized then the reality," represents the better part of her nature, for, after contemplating it, she assumes "a singular air of authority," that is, her mission of retribution, and forces Hester to reassume the scarlet letter. However, lawless Pearl may be, we cannot disregard her mission which, for Hawthorne, was a remnant of her original innocence.

At present most critics, whether or not they identify Pearl with nature, consider her amoral. Although as early as the 1880's Pearl was called a creature "of moral indifference" and "anterior to moral law," so far as I know, the first one to call Pearl unequivocally amoral was Walter Blair in 1942. As Chillingworth's "blackness" becomes a sym-

---

[1] See Chester E. Eisinger's "Pearl and the Puritan Heritage," excerpted on pp. 84-90 of this book.

bol of his evil, so Pearl's association with radiant light betokens "the unmorality of a child." But the radiance which surrounds Pearl is not the white light of amorality, it is the reflected fire of Hester's passion: "There[694] was fire in her and throughout her: she seemed the unpremeditated offshoot of a passionate moment." However, the present majority opinion that Pearl is amoral is not entirely a reflection of the current view of childhood; Hawthorne once says of Pearl that perhaps she might be "a law unto herself, without her eccentricities being reckoned to her for a crime." Nevertheless, it is doubtful if Hawthorne thought of Pearl's general perversity and lawlessness as the natural characteristics of amoral childhood. In the 1850's, when people did not think children innately good, they thought their evil traits proof of the inheritance of the sin of Adam, or (a popular physiological counterpart) of the evil of their parents. It was not until the last third of the century, as a result of the theory of evolution, anthropological studies, and psychological studies of child behavior, that the physico-theological explanation of sin was seriously challenged. It came to be felt that children's selfishness or aggression was not original sin or bad heredity but original animality, the persistence in man of the brute elements which were his necessary tools in the struggle for survival. Until the child acquires morality through education, he can only be called amoral, not sinful.[2] As we shall see, Hawthorne, in accounting for Pearl's character, writes in terms of the physical inheritance of sin.

Nevertheless, Pearl seems to many modern readers a realistically described amoral child. And others have called her an exact picture of a "capricious, roguish, untamed child," "a living child," and similar things.[3] Many, among them the Van Dorens, Julian Hawthorne, and Randall Stewart, have shown how her character is based on Hawthorne's daughter Una. On the other hand, some have complained that Pearl is entirely "miraculous—speaking, acting, and thinking, like an elf," that she "is no more than an animated symbol."[4] In detail Pearl is a realistically observed child; for example, delivering a message to Hester she "zigzags" across the square. Even when she seems most a symbol, when she performs her mission of retribution, none of her ac-

---

2 See, e.g., Gabriel Compayré, *L'Evolution intellectuelle et morale de l'enfant* (Paris, 1893) and James M. Baldwin, *Mental Development in the Child and the Race* (New York, 1895). For a general discussion of the origin of the concept of the amorality of children see F. R. Tennant, *The Origin and Propagation of Sin* (Cambridge, Eng., 1902), pp. 93-112 or his "The Child and Sin" in *Religion and the Child*, ed. Thomas Stephens (New York, 1905), pp. 154-184.

3 Anne Wales Abbot, rev. of *The Scarlet Letter, North Amer. Rev.,* LXXI (July 1850), 142; Spiller, Thorp, et al., *Literary History of the United States* (New York, 1953; 1st ed., 1946), p. 424.

4 Anthony Trollope, "The Genius of Nathaniel Hawthorne," *North Amer. Rev.,* CXXIX (Sept. 1879), 211; Herbert Gorman, *Hawthorne, A study in Solitude* (New York, 1927), p. 88.

tions is "inconsistent[695] with the conceivable actions of any child under the same conditions."[5] When Pearl forces Hester to reassume the scarlet letter, she may be an infant Fury or only an ordinary child unable to abide "the slightest change in the accustomed aspect of things." We find her mission incredible, but for Hawthorne it had a basis in innocent child nature. Pearl, however, has another symbolic function: she is "the scarlet letter in another form; the scarlet letter endowed with life!"[6] Critics have felt that here the union of real child and symbol was not completely successful, that "there is an essential conflict between childish innocence and the signification of the letter." And even those who think that she concentrates in her nature "all the wild irrepressible freedom that springs from a broken law," still feel that she is alternately real child and symbol, or that the "symbolism is achieved only by a decided loss of realistic effect." But this is not the case; Hawthorne brilliantly transmuted reality into symbol by giving Pearl the general characteristics of children, but in so exaggerated a form that they become the symbol, not of the scarlet letter but of what produced it—Hester's diseased moral state.

We have already seen that the circle of radiance which surrounds Pearl is not the ordinary brightness of childhood. Pearl is not a little ray of sunshine, as the nineteenth century was fond of calling children; her radiance has the intensity of a flame and becomes a symbol of Hester's wild passion. Again, Pearl has the vivacity and energy of children, but in such an extreme degree that it transcends the limits of childhood joy and becomes a "disease...the reflex of the wild energy with which" Hester "fought against her sorrows before Pearl's birth." Every child is somewhat lawless, but Pearl "could not be made amenable to rules"; she is "the effluence of a lawless passion." All children are occasionally perverse, but "Pearl had a tenfold portion" of childish perversity. All children hate, but Pearl was capable of "the bitterest hatred that can be supposed to rankle in a childish bosom." This intense perversity and hate are the perpetuation of "the warfare of Hester's spirit" before Pearl's birth. Pearl's difficulty in feeling sympathy is much more than a manifestation of the "fitful sympathies of childhood," it is her main fault,[696] the root cause of her wildness. And this defect may also be due to Hester, for there is a fundamental parallel between Hester's chief sin, which is not lust but a radical defiance of society ("The world's law was no law for her mind"), and Pearl's almost complete lack of what in a Humeian ethic is the basis of society and its moral laws—sympathy.

---

[5] Richard H. Fogle, *Hawthorne's Fiction: The Light and The Dark* (Norman, 1952), p. 114.

[6] Even in her mission Pearl might be called the scarlet letter, which signifies not only Hester's sin but the retribution of society.

In making Pearl a microcosm of Hester's moral chaos, Hawthorne was not merely creating an elaborate symbol for the scarlet letter; he was also describing a real child in terms of the current physiological psychology, which offered him a means of natural symbolism. According to this psychology, in part derived from the phrenologists Gall and Spurzheim, children inherit "moral propensities" from their parents. The moral "faculties" which predominate in the parents, either in general or at the time the child is conceived, will be transmitted to the child.[7] Evil in children was explained physiologically. For example, the theologian Horace Bushnell, in *Views of Christian Nurture* (Hartford, 1847) p. 192, felt it impossible that a person "who has fallen out of the harmony of his mold by sin, should yet communicate no trace of evil from himself...no moral discolor to the generations that derive their existence from him. To make that possible, every law of physiology must be adjourned." Andrew Combe expressed the common belief that "the temper and turn of mind in the child are often a legible transcript of the mother's condition and feelings during pregnancy."[8] And in *The Principles of Physiology* (New York, 1841), in the same chapter which furnished the source for Hawthorne's *The Birthmark*, he gives case histories of how "the temporary state of the mother during gestation may influence the whole future life of the child" (p. 242).

Hawthorne believed in the physiological inheritance of moral character. *The House of The Seven Gables* deals with "the bad passions, the mean tendencies, and the moral diseases which...are handed down from one generation to another." In "Glimpses of English Poverty" Hawthorne speaks of the foundlings' "patrimony of disease and vice," of their inheritance of the "evil habits of their parents." In *The Blithedale Romance* the difference between Zenobia and Priscilla is attributed to heredity; proud Zenobia is the true offspring of[697] Fauntleroy and his wife in their pride, and the shadowy, shrinking Priscilla of the disgraced Fauntleroy and his second meek-spirited wife. Pearl, like Zenobia and Priscilla, shows "the modifying influences...of parental character." Hester once lists Pearl's chief characteristics as "unflinching courage," "uncontrollable will," "sturdy pride," "bitter scorn," and "acrid and disagreeable affections." Except, perhaps, for the last item, they are precisely the attributes which predominated in Hester and which, according to the laws of physiological psychology, would have to predominate in Pearl. Hester calls them "sterling attributes," but they are a dubious inheritance. However, Hawthorne makes

---

[7] On these points see Johann C. Lavater, *Essays on Physiognomy*, trans. Rev. C. Moore (London, 1797), I, 137, and George Combe, *The Constitution of Man* (Boston, 1829), pp. 148-149. Hawthorne read both.

[8] *A Treatise on the Physiological and Moral Management of Infancy* (Edinburgh, 1846), p. 81.

Hester's disturbed mental state during pregnancy the chief cause of "the little moral chaos" of Pearl's character. In utero the originally white rays of her moral life are stained and, as we have seen, she absorbs "the warfare of Hester's spirit," "her wild, desperate, defiant mood, the flightiness of her temper," her "gloom and despondency." Throughout the book Hawthorne refers to Pearl's character as an inheritance ("All this enmity and passion had Pearl inherited, by inalienable right, out of Hester's heart"), and occasionally compares this inheritance to a disease (Pearl's excessive hate is like an "infant pestilence—the scarlet fever"). Pearl, like other characters in Hawthorne, acquires a moral disease, but in her case it is physiologically predetermined.

It has been said that in *The Scarlet Letter* Hawthorne made a study of three types of sin—"the revealed sin of Hester, the concealed sin of Dimmesdale, and the unpardonable sin of Chillingworth." But he also dealt with a fourth type—the inherited sin of Pearl. This inherited sin is not original sin, for Hawthorne is careful to say that Pearl is originally innocent and he has her retain, to an extraordinary degree, the sinless child's insight into truth. It is interesting that the Hawthorne who scorned the Unitarian and Transcendentalist belief in innate goodness, that the Hawthorne who [according to Melville] was pervaded by the "black conceit" of "Innate Depravity and Original Sin" did this. But when he wrote of children, Hawthorne was never consistently able to rise above the contemporary belief in the sinless child. Early stories—*The Gentle Boy* (Ilbrahim) (1832), *Little Annie's Ramble* (1835)—give us the stock sinless child of the period. The child in *The Artist of the Beautiful* (1844), however, struggles unsuccessfully between "childish faith" and "the hard skepticism" he inherited[698] from his grandfather. But there is no steady progress towards realism. Joe in *Ethan Brand* (1850) and the child in *Feathertop* (1852) have the sinless child's insight into truth. On the other hand, the notebook accounts of his children are coolly deductive; Hawthorne is more willing to ascribe a selfish motive to their actions than a pure one. But amidst this realism we find Hawthorne wondering if Julian, aged two, sitting on the floor and placidly staring into space, is not having "recollections of a pre-existence." And shortly before Hawthorne gave us *The Scarlet Letter* in which not only Pearl but children in general are described as perverse, unsympathetic, and capable of hate, he wrote *The Snow Image,* an extraordinary plea for the belief in the heaven that lies about us in our infancy. Pearl is a mixture of Hawthorne's sober observation of childhood and of his continuing belief in the sinless child. In accounting for Pearl's character, the physiological psychology of the period must have appealed to Hawthorne; for it enabled him to shift the responsibility for her evil to Hester, to make her originally innocent but the victim of an unusually faulty moral inheritance. If Pearl had not been regenerated at the end, she might well have said with later nineteenth-century characters, "I was born bad, and I have lived bad, and I shall die bad in all probability." "Is it my fault that I became what I am?"[699]

. . . .

FROM "Pearl: 1850-1955," *PMLA*, LXXII (Sept., 1957), 689-699. Reprinted by permission of the author and *PMLA*.

SYMBOLISM

THE EXCESSES OF SYMBOLISM

Henry James

. . . .

In *The Scarlet Letter* there is a great deal of symbolism; there is, I think, too much. It is overdone at times, and becomes mechanical; it ceases to be impressive, and grazes triviality. The idea of the mystic *A* which the young minister finds imprinted upon his breast and eating into his flesh, in sympathy with the embroidered badge that Hester is condemned to wear, appears to me to be a case[113] in point. This suggestion should, I think, have been just made and dropped; to insist upon it and return to it is to exaggerate the weak side of the subject. Hawthorne returns to it constantly, plays with it, and seems charmed by it; until at last the reader feels tempted to declare that his enjoyment of it is puerile. In the admirable scene, so superbly conceived and beautifully executed, in which Mr. Dimmesdale, in the stillness of the night, in the middle of the sleeping town, feels impelled to go and stand upon the scaffold where his mistress had formerly enacted her dreadful penance, and then, seeing Hester pass along the street, from watching at a sick-bed, with little Pearl at her side, calls them both to come and stand there beside him—in this masterly episode the effect is almost spoiled by the introduction of one of these superficial conceits. What leads up to it is very fine—so fine that I cannot do better than quote it as a specimen of one of the striking pages of the book.

But before Mr. Dimmesdale had done speaking, a light gleamed far and wide over all the muffled sky. It was doubtless caused by one of those meteors which the night watcher may so often observe burning out to waste in the vacant regions of the atmosphere. So powerful was its radiance that it thoroughly illuminated the dense medium of cloud, betwixt the sky and earth. The great vault brightened, like the dome of an immense lamp. It showed the familiar scene of the street with the distinctness of midday, but also with the awfulness that is always imparted to familiar objects by an unaccustomed light. The wooden houses, with their jutting stories and quaint gable-peaks; the doorsteps and thresholds, with the early grass springing up about them; the garden-plots, black with freshly-turned earth; the wheel track, little worn, and, even in the market place, margined with green on either side,—all were visible, but[114] with a singularity of aspect that seemed to give another moral interpretation to the things of this world than they had ever borne before. And there stood the minister, with his hand over his heart; and Hester Prynne, with the embroidered letter glimmering on her bosom; and little Pearl, herself a symbol, and the connecting-link between these two. They stood in the noon of that strange and solemn splendor, as if it were the light that is to reveal all secrets, and the daybreak that shall unite all that belong to one another.

That is imaginative, impressive, poetic; but when, almost immediately afterwards, the author goes on to say that "the minister looking upward to the zenith, beheld there the appearance of an immense letter—the letter A—marked out in lines of dull red light," we feel that he goes too far and is in danger of crossing the line that separates the sublime from its intimate neighbor. We are tempted to say that this is not moral tragedy, but physical comedy. In the same way, too much is made of the intimation that Hester's badge had a scorching property, and that if one touched it one would immediately withdraw one's hand. Hawthorne is perpetually looking for images which shall place themselves in picturesque correspondence with the spiritual facts with which he is concerned, and of course the search is of the very essence of poetry. But in such a process discretion is everything, and when the image becomes importunate it is in danger of seeming to stand for nothing more serious than itself. When Hester meets the minister by appointment in the forest, and sits talking with him while little Pearl wanders away and plays by the edge of the brook, the child is represented as at last making her way over to the other side of the woodland stream, and disporting herself there in a manner which makes her mother feel herself, "in some indistinct[115] and tantalizing manner, estranged from Pearl; as if the child, in her lonely ramble through the forest, had strayed out of the sphere in which she and her mother dwelt together, and was now vainly seeking to return to it." And Hawthorne devotes a chapter to this idea of the child's having, by putting the brook between Hester and herself, established a kind of spiritual gulf, on the verge of which her little fantastic person innocently mocks at her mother's sense of bereavement. This conception belongs, one would say, quite to the lighter order of a story-teller's devices, and the reader hardly goes with Hawthorne in the large development he gives to it. He hardly goes with him either, I think, in his extreme predilection for a small number of vague ideas which are represented by such terms as "sphere" and "sympathies." Hawthorne makes too liberal a use of these two substantives; it is the solitary defect of his style, and it counts as a defect partly because the words in question are a sort of specialty with certain writers immeasurably inferior to himself.[116]

. . . .

FROM *Hawthorne* (New York, 1879).

THE SYMBOLIC DEVICE OF MULTIPLE CHOICE

F. O. Matthiessen

. . . .

But beyond any interest in ordering of plot or in lucid discrimination between characters, Hawthorne's imaginative energy seems to have been called out to the full . . . by the continual correspondences that his theme allowed him to make between external events and inner significances. Once again his version of the transcendental habit took it straight back to the seventeenth century, and made it something more complex than the harmony between sunrise and a young poet's soul. In the realm of natural phenomena, Hawthorne examined the older world's common belief that great events were foreboded by supernatural omens, and remarked how "it was, indeed, a majestic idea, that the destiny of nations should be revealed in these awful hieroglyphics, on the cope of heaven." But when Dimmesdale, in his vigil on the scaffold, beholds an immense dull red letter in the zenith, Hawthorne attributes it solely to his diseased imagination, which sees in everything his own morbid concerns. Hawthorne remarks that the strange light was "doubtless caused" by a meteor "burning out to waste"; and yet he also allows the sexton to ask the minister the next morning if he had heard of the portent, which had been interpreted to stand for Angel, since Governor Winthrop had died during the night.

Out of such variety of symbolical reference Hawthorne developed one of his most fertile resources, the device of multiple choice, which James was to carry so much further in his desire to present a sense of the intricacy of any situation for perceptive being. One main source of Hawthorne's method lay in these remarkable providences, which his imagination felt challenged to search for the amount of emblematic[276] truth that might lie hidden among their superstitions. He spoke at point in [*The Scarlet Letter*] of how "individuals of wiser faith" in the colony, while recognizing God's Providence in human affairs, knew that it "promotes its purposes without aiming at the stage-effect of what is called miraculous interposition." But he could not resist experimenting with this dramatic value, and his imagination had become so accustomed to the weirdly lighted world of Cotton Mather that even the fanciful possibilities of the growth of the stigma on Dimmesdale did not strike him as grotesque. But when the minister "unbreasts" his guilt at last, the literal correspondence of that metaphor to a scarlet letter in his flesh, in strict accord with medieval and Spenserian personifications, is apt to strike us as a mechanical delimitation of what would otherwise have freer symbolical range.

For Hawthorne its value consisted in the variety of explanations to which it gave rise. Some affirmed that the minister had begun a course of self-mortification on the very day Hester Prynne had first been compelled to wear her ignominious badge, and had thus inflicted this hideous scar. Others held that Roger Chillingworth, "being a potent necromancer, had caused it to appear, through the agency of magic and poisonous drugs." Still others, "those best able to appreciate the minister's peculiar sensibility, and the wonderful operation of his spirit upon the body," whispered that "the awful symbol was the effect of the ever-active tooth of remorse," gnawing from his inmost heart outward. With that Hawthorne leaves his reader to choose among these theories. He does not literally accept his own allegory, and yet he finds it symbolically valid because of its psychological exactitude. His most telling stroke comes when he adds that certain spectators of the whole scene denied that there was any mark whatever on Dimmesdale's breast. These witnesses were among the most respectable in the community, including his fellow-ministers who were determined to defend his spotless character. These maintained also that his dying confession was to be taken only in its general significance, that he "had desired by yielding up his breath in the arms of that fallen woman, to express to the world how utterly nugatory is the choicest of man's own righteousness." But for this interpretation, so revelatory of its influential proponents, Hawthorne leaves not one shred of evidence.[277]

. . . .

FROM "The Scarlet Letter," *American Renaissance* (New York, 1941), pp. 275-282. Reprinted by permission of Oxford University Press, New York; copyright, 1941.

THE NATURE OF SYMBOLIC PERCEPTION

Charles Feidelson, Jr.

. . . .

The "Custom House" essay, introductory to *The Scarlet Letter,* is a portrait of the artist as symbolist in spite of himself. Of course Hawthorne indulges in his usual peccavi: "It was a folly, with the materiality of this daily life pressing so intrusively upon me, to attempt to fling myself back into another age; or to insist on creating the semblance of a world out of airy matter....The fault was mine." But this reverence for the material present and trivial view of the imagination do not obscure the central theme of the sketch—the theme implicit in the vignette of Hawthorne poring over the scarlet letter. That self portrait—which, be it noted, is a self-projection, since Hawthorne in point of fact came upon his subject quite otherwise—amounts to a dramatic definition of the following "romance" and of the author's relation to it. The author's *donnée,* as James would call it, is neither Imagination nor Actuality per se but a symbol whose inherent meaning is *The Scarlet Letter.* The world that the writer seeks is generated by contemplation of the symbol, not by the external yoking-together of two realms which by definition are different in kind. This integral act of perception effectually "opens" an imaginative reality. That it is not the material reality of nineteenth-century Salem becomes wholly irrelevant, since the meaning of the symbol, accreted by generations who have lived with it and in it, is continuous in time.

Such would seem to be the implication of the essay as a whole. The Custom House itself, with Hawthorne as Surveyor of the Customs, is the stage for potential commerce or "intercourse with the world." The Custom House is at once the Surveyor's ally and his enemy. As enemy, it destroys his creative power by involving him in material commerce, in weighing and gauging, in all the mechanistic ways of thinking which, as Melville said, made "the round world itself but an empty cipher, except to sell by the cartload." On the other hand, business at the Salem wharf is virtually at a standstill, and the Custom House actually imposes very few practical duties on the Surveyor. As his ally, it embodies, like its aged inhabitants,[9] the residue of past experience; it is the analogue of the Surveyor's own consciousness, in which, though a mere "writer of storybooks," he feels a continuity with his Puritan and seafaring ancestors. Thus the Custom House makes possible another kind of commerce and another kind of revenue: a traffic with the world by means of the significance vested in a traditional symbol. The discovery of the scarlet letter amid the old documents of the Customs-lists of wrecked or rotten ships and dead merchants— signalizes not a retreat into the past but a penetration into persistent meaning.

In this way "The Custom House" throws light on a theme in *The Scarlet Letter* which is easily overlooked amid the ethical concerns of the book. Every character, in effect, re-enacts the "Custom House" scene in which Hawthorne himself contemplated the letter, so that the entire "romance" becomes a kind of exposition of the nature of symbolic perception. Hawthorne's subject is not only the meaning of adultery but also meaning in general; not only *what* the focal symbol means but also *how* it gains significance. This aspect of the book is emphasized by Hawthorne's pointed use of the most problematic kind of symbol, a letter, and by his method of circling interpretation through the minds of various characters. In the opening chapters the scarlet "A" is the object of hundreds of eyes; Hester is not the only one who wears the symbol, if "wearing" it is synonymous with discovery and absorption of its meaning. As Mr. Wilson delivers his "discourse on sin...with continual reference to the ignominious letter," the minds of the populace are confirmed in the mold of Puritan thought, and the real Hester for them is the Adulteress. Hester, standing before them, is caught in their vision of the world. Looking down at the letter on her bosom and touching it with her finger, she feels that this hostile society and its judgment upon her are "her realities." Yet, at the same time, "the scaffold of the pillory was a point of view," and one wholly different from that of her judges. Although the pageant of her past life which presents itself before her cannot withstand the pressure of the surrounding Puritan vision, the independent view that she will later attain is foreshadowed by this "mass of imperfectly shaped and[10] spectral images." As the years pass, the symbol has a "powerful and peculiar" effect upon her being; Hester escapes the Puritan world by taking the letter to herself, extending the "lawlessness" of adultery into all her habits of thought, and reshaping conventional values into her own reality. "The world's law was no law for her mind...She assumed a freedom of speculation...which our forefathers, had they known it, would have held to be a deadlier crime that that stigmatized by the scarlet letter." For all her seeming compliance with the doctrines of the Puritans, the symbol has rendered to her, and she inhabits, a realm quite different from theirs.

More important than this divergence, however, is the fundamentally similar process by which Hester and the Puritan populace come to terms with the symbol of adultery. In both cases the "A" is psychophysical, entering into and shaping the perceiving mind and the objective scene. This notion is applied with variations to the other principal characters. Pearl, as Hawthorne reiterates at tiresome length, *is* the scarlet letter both physically and mentally. Her function in the book is more than to symbolize the union of Hester and Dimmesdale; she is actually a kind of commentary on the symbol itself. As "the scarlet letter in another form" she reveals what the letter is—the psychophysical presence of "adultery," whatever meaning that word may take. In Dimmesdale the symbol is diverted from its normal course and emerges obliquely as the psychosomatic mark on his breast. Dimmesdale is constrained from accepting either the popular version of adultery or Hester's. He cannot believe for long that what they did "had a consecration of its own," but he cannot repent and thereby take his destined place in the world projected by the Puritans. Thus his agony is not only moral but intellectual. As he tells Hester, he is cut off from any reality, conventional or otherwise. The "strange sympathy betwixt soul and body" which characterizes his disease is the indirect satisfaction of his frustrated yearning for "substance."

Chillingworth, who discovers the psychosomatic malady of Dimmesdale, is himself afflicted in the same way: his aspect changes, just as his mind is transformed, from the scholar to the[11] devil. But in his case the effect of the symbol on body and mind is complete, because Chillingworth has totally submerged himself in a symbolic role. His interpretation of the letter is a heterodox Calvinism: embarking on his obsessive quest for the "A" in Dimmesdale, he is unconsciously throwing himself into the character of Satan in the Puritan myth of the Fall. Naturally enough, after he becomes aware of what has happened to him, he turns to Calvinism for comfort, asserting that "a dark necessity" beyond the human will has determined the whole action: "Ye that have wronged me are not sinful, save in a kind of typical illusion; neither am I fiend-like, who have snatched a fiend's office from his hands. It is our fate." Again, however, his view is heretical, since it denies moral responsibility, and his statement actually has a rather aesthetic turn. Chillingworth holds that he and the others are committed to roles in a symbolic drama, the "typical illusion" of which he speaks; in effect, their lives, both mental and physical, are a function of the meaning of the scarlet letter, which alone remains real amid the appearances that it generates. While Hawthorne obviously regards this speech as the misguided speculation of a lost soul, the unusual vigor of the language indicates the appeal which he found in these ideas. With the reservation that human lives do not become illusory, but gain reality, through the operation of the symbol, he himself could have subscribed to the sweeping theory of Chillingworth. Something like it is implicit in the tableau of Hester, Dimmesdale, and Pearl on the scaffold, with the immense letter "A" shining above them in the sky. The celestial letter transmutes the everyday objects of the scene: "All were visible, but with a singularity of aspect that seemed to give another moral interpretation to the things of this world than they had ever borne before." The world thus illuminated is at once physical and ideal. At its center are human beings who perceive the world by wearing the symbol in mind and body:

> And there stood the minister, with his hand over his heart; and Hester Prynne, with the embroidered letter glimmering on her bosom; and little Pearl, herself a symbol, and the connecting link between those two. [12]

. . . .

FROM "Four American Symbolists—Hawthorne," *Symbolism and American Literature* (Chicago, 1953), pp. 6-16. Reprinted by permission of the University of Chicago Press.

THE ORGANIC AND THE MECHANICAL

Roy R. Male

. . . .

The functioning of . . . images of the organic and the mechanical may best be observed in *The Scarlet Letter,* Hawthorne's masterly, concentrated vision of early American cultural history. For the chief conflict of the book, introduced in the opening chapter, "The Prison Door," is the organic-mechanical antithesis, the struggle between individual development and restrictive society. The spike-studded prison-door with its ponderous iron work, its "beetle-browed and gloomy front," is contrasted with a wild rose-bush which calls up reminiscences of the wilderness before the advent of the settlers as well as of the "heterodox religionist" Anne Hutchinson. Assembled before the "iron-clamped" door are the Puritan inhabitants of Boston, whose faces are "petrified" in a "grim rigidity." Hester bears the "heavy weight," the "leaden infliction" of eyes lowering upon her beneath the brims of *"steeple-crowned"* hats. With one exception—a sensitive young mother who later perishes in this mechanical society—the women are "iron-visaged" *bel*dams who urged at the very least "the brand of a hot iron" on Hester Prynne's forehead. The scaffold,[223] appropriately placed very near the market-place, constitutes "a portion of a penal machine." Above it is the pillory, an "ugly engine" which aptly symbolizes the crushing grip of repressive society upon the individual.

Outside the limits of this society are Pearl, the Indians, and the sailors. As Hawthorne elsewhere observes of Indian artifacts, these creatures are endowed with a "rudeness" and an "individuality . . . , so different from the productions of civilized machinery, which shapes everything on one pattern." Pearl is not amenable to rules: organic like the wild rose, she is a being "whose elements were perhaps beautiful and brilliant, but all in disorder; *or with an order peculiar to themselves,* amidst which the point of variety and arrangement was difficult or impossible to be discovered." The sailors, "wild men of the ocean, as the Indians were of the land," gaze admiringly at Pearl, recognizing a kindred being, "gifted with a soul of the *sea-fire.*"

These extremes, portrayed by image and symbol, point up the predicament of Hester Prynne and Arthur Dimmesdale. Hester is torn between Dimmesdale the conformist who in the final analysis will always need "the pressure of a faith about him, supporting, while it confined him within its iron framework," and Pearl, whose source, as she perversely informs John Wilson, is the wild rosebush. Almost every detail of Hester's visit with the governor is illumined by the organic-mechanical antithesis. Governor Bellingham's mansion is described as Coleridge had described the mechanical form: it is stucco, in which fragments of broken glass are plentifully intermixed and is "further decorated with strange and seemingly cabalistic figures and diagrams, suitable to the quaint taste of the age, which had been drawn in the stucco when newly laid on, and had now grown hard and durable, for the admiration of after times." The mechanical superficiality of the exterior is matched by the iron hammer hanging on the door and by the heterogeneous furnishings within—the gilded volumes and the artificial *oaken* flowers carved on the furniture. Hanging[224] on the walls are stiff portraits of departed worthies with ruffs separating head and heart.[1] As a mechanical society distorts and exaggerates individual aberration, so the suit of mail "of most modern date" magnifies the scarlet letter and makes an imp of Pearl. Small wonder that Hester should turn away in despair and seek some sign of organic life in the garden and that Pearl should cry for a red rose. Small wonder, too, that, as suffering inhabitants of such a society, Hester and Arthur should later greet each other in the forest with the questions: "Art thou *in life?*...dost thou yet *live?*"

In this forest interview, amid the fallen leaves which suggest Dimmesdale's predicament, Hester makes clear the ethical aspects of the organic principle. In all things she has retained her integrity as an individual except when she failed to reveal the identity of her husband; the act for which she was branded as sinful by the community "had a consecration of its own." Pointing to the organic freedom of the forest and the sea, she exhorts Arthur to action in terms reminiscent

---

[1] This reading is supported by the fact that Hester's humane father had a beard which "flowed over the old-fashioned Elizabethan ruff"; Mistress Hibbins on the other hand, is arrayed in a triple ruff.

of Emerson's "Self-Reliance": "Exchange this false life of thine for a true one. Be, if thy spirit summon thee to such a mission, the teacher and apostle of the red men. Or,—as is more thy nature,—be a scholar and a sage among the wisest and most renowned of the cultivated world. Preach! Write! Act! Do anything, save to lie down and die!" And as Hester offers to accompany Arthur, the rekindling of their love is matched by the sympathy of nature: each green leaf is gladdened, and the yellow fallen leaves are transmuted to gold.

But the sins of the past, like the scarlet letter, cannot be thrown off, nor does Hawthorne ever indicate that uncivilized individualism can ultimately be regarded as the good life ("The Old Manse is better than a thousand wigwams"). Hester, in her isolation, has become critical not only of the judicial robe, the pillory, and the gallows but also of the fireside[225] and the church. And the forest, though it is untrammeled by convention and conformity may also be a "moral wilderness." The complexity of Hawthorne's symbolism is apparent as we follow Dimmesdale back to Boston. The pathway in the woods "seemed wilder, more uncouth with its rude natural obstacles, and less trodden by the foot of man, than he remembered it on his outward journey." On the one hand, he is closer to the freedom of individual growth, less hampered by the principles and prejudices of the social system; on the other, he is, as the chapter title indicates, "the minister in a maze"— more deeply involved in a moral wilderness with its "plashy places" and its "clinging underbrush." Upon his return to the town he is stirred by the desire to kick over the traces, to affront the public opinion which has enslaved him, to acknowledge his companionship with the independent (and drunken) sailor. But the darker side of this revolution in his moral code appears with Mistress Hibbins, the ruff-adorned embodiment of evil, who recognizes "a secret intimacy of connection" with Dimmesdale. Yet, as a result of his forest experience, he writes an Election sermon which seems to be divinely inspired—a sermon which has "special reference" to the New England which communities of mankind were "planting in the wilderness." Thus the theme of the sermon is closely related to the main problem of the book: how to make the proper adjustment between organic individual development and necessarily restrictive social control without destroying the integrity of the individual. Though the sermon ends with a hopeful prophecy of a "high and glorious destiny," it has an undertone of pathos because it is being preached by one crushed through his failure to make this adjustment.

The contrast between the wild rose and the prison-door, the organic and the mechanical, also illumines the concluding chapters. The Puritans' holiday has a "sable tinge," though "the blackest shade of Puritanism" was to come with the next generation. No entertainment appealing to the imagination is[226] permitted: "no rude shows of the theatrical kind; no minstrel, with his harp and legendary ballad,

nor glee-man with an ape dancing to his music." Demonstrations of
physical force are more in keeping with this community: wrestling
matches and "what attracted most interest of all—on the platform of
the pillory...two masters of defence were commencing an exhibition
with the buckler and the broadsword. But, much to the disappointment
of the crowd, this latter business was broken off by the interposition
of the town beadle, who had no idea of permitting the majesty of the
law to be violated by such an abuse of one of its consecrated places."
The ponderous sobriety of the community is further emphasized by a
procession of the "men of rank and dignity." First after the martial
music comes the military, "clad in burnished steel"; next are the men
of civil eminence, distinguished by their "square cast of countenance";
and next in order comes Dimmesdale, whose mind is busy marshalling
its own procession of stately thoughts.

This sombre holiday scene is "enlivened" by the diversity of hue
which the few untrammeled individuals provide. Pearl, decked out in
airy gayety, the Indians in their savage finery, the sailors with their
palm-leaf hats, and above all, the sea-captain, whose showy attire nevertheless has an organic unity of its own—these are the representatives
of individual freedom. Their colors, like those of Pearl's costume and
the embroidered letter on Hester's bosom are crimson and gold.[2] Hester,
appropriately dressed as usual in gray, belongs to neither world and
stands in "a small vacant area."

It is only after Dimmesdale has delivered the Election Sermon
that he at last finds courage enough to break away from the mechanical
procession, thus freeing himself from both Chillingworth and Bellingham. He joins Hester on the scaffold—a weak individual crushed into
an unnatural conformity by the iron fetters of a Puritan society, escap-
ing only through confession and death. Hawthorne's failure to resolve
the conflict between individual and society and his hurried disposal
of Pearl emphasize the complexity which we have already observed[227]
in the crucial forest scene. He saw that if society is considered atom-
istically as a collection of self-centered individuals the antagonism
between legal restraints and individual liberty is irreconcilable. Only
in a civilized organization of socially-inclined individuals—the Christian
brotherhood of man—is self-realization of the highest kind possible.
But since for Hawthorne full self-realization involves both good and
evil, this sociological implication rests upon his deeper moral conviction that the evil in the world stems from man's own nature, upon
"that Calvinistic sense of Innate Depravity and Original Sin" which
so forcibly impressed Melville. In *The Scarlet Letter* the organic idea

---

2 Cf. "Main Street": "These scenes, you think, are all too sombre. So, indeed,
they are; but the blame must rest on the sombre spirit of our forefathers, who
wove their web of life with hardly a single thread of rose-color or gold..."

serves to complement and intensify Hawthorne's tragic perception of the entangled good and evil in human life.[228]

. . . .

FROM " 'From The Innermost Germ,' the Organic Principle in Hawthorne's Fiction," *ELH, A Journal of English Literary History,* XX (Sept., 1953), 218-236. Reprinted by permission of the author and the editors of *ELH.*

THE CEMETERY, THE PRISON, AND THE ROSE

Hyatt H. Waggoner

. . . .

In the three paragraphs of his opening chapter Hawthorne introduces the three chief symbols that will serve to give structure to the story on the thematic level, hints at the fourth, and starts two of the chief lines of imagery. The opening sentence suggests the darkness ("sad-colored," "gray"), the rigidity ("oak," "iron"), and the aspiration ("steeple-crowned") of the people "amongst whom religion and law were almost identical." Later sentences add "weatherstains," "a yet darker aspect," and "gloomy" to the suggestions already begun through color imagery. The closing words of the chapter make the metaphorical use of color explicit: Hawthorne hopes that a wild rose beside the prison door may serve "to symbolize some sweet moral blossom, that may be found along the track, or relieve the darkening close of a tale of human frailty and sorrow."

A large part of the opening chapter is allotted to this rosebush and to some weeds that also grow beside the prison. Having learned to respect the economy with which Hawthorne worked in his tales, we should guess, even if we had not read beyond this first chapter, that these will turn out not to be merely "realistic" or "atmospheric" details. We should expect to meet them again, with expanded connotations. Actually, the flower and weed imagery is second in importance only to the color imagery in the novel. The more than thirty occasions on which it is subsequently found are not, like the even more frequent heart images, casual, or partly to be accounted for as stylistic mannerisms, the reflexes[119] as it were of Hawthorne's style, but chief keys to the symbolic structure and intention of this work.

Finally, in addition to the Puritans themselves, the jail before which they stand, and the weeds and the rose, one other object, and only one, is mentioned in this first chapter. In the only generalized comment in a chapter otherwise devoted to objective description, Hawthorne tells us that "The founders of a new colony, whatever Utopia of human virtue and happiness they might originally project, have invariably recognized it among their earliest practical necessities to allot a portion of the virgin soil as a cemetery, and another as the site of a prison." The three climactic scenes of the novel take place before the scaffold in front of the prison. The cemetery, by contrast, remains in the background. We are not allowed to forget it, we learn that Chillingworth has a special interest in it, but we are not encouraged to make it the center of our attention until the end, when it moves into the foreground as the site of the tombstone with the strange inscription.

The cemetery, the prison, and the rose, with their associated values and the extensions of suggestion given them by the image patterns that intersect them, as the ugliest weeds are later discovered growing out of graves, suggest a symbolic pattern within which nearly everything that is most important in the novel may be placed. The cemetery and the prison are negative values, in some sense evils. The rose is a positive value, beautiful, in some sense a good. But the cemetery and the prison are not negative in the same sense: death, "the last great enemy," is a natural evil, resulting as some theologies would have it from moral evil but distinguished by coming to saint and sinner alike; the prison is a reminder of the present actuality of moral evil. Natural and moral evil, then, death and sin, are here suggested. The rose is "good" in the same sense in which the cemetery is an "evil": its beauty is neither moral nor immoral but is certainly[120] a positive value. Like the beauty of a healthy child or an animal, it is the product not of choice but of necessity, of the laws of its being, so that it can be admired but not judged. Pearl, later in the story, is similarly immune from judgment. There is no strong suggestion of moral goodness in this first chapter, nor will there be in what is to follow. The cemetery and the weeds contrast with the rose, but only the suggestions of worship in the shape of the hats of the Puritans contrast with the prison, and those steeple-crowned hats are gray, a color which later takes on strongly negative associations.

Among the ideas implicit in the opening chapter, then, are, first, that the novel is to be concerned with the relationships of good and evil; second, that it will distinguish between two types of good and evil; and, third, that moral good will be less strongly felt than moral and natural evil. A symmetrical pattern is theoretically suggested here, and as we shall see, in the rest of the novel. But what is actually felt is an asymmetrical pattern, an imbalance, in which the shapes of moral and natural evil loom so large as to make it difficult to discern, or to "believe in" once we have discerned, the reality of moral goodness or redemption. The rose, in short, is finally not sufficient to relieve "the darkening close of a tale of human frailty and sorrow." The celestial radiance later seen gleaming from the white hair of Mr. Wilson is not sufficient either, nor the snowy innocence said to exist in the bosoms of certain maidens. In writing *The Scarlet Letter* Hawthorne let his genius take its course, and death and sin turned out to be more convincing than life and goodness.[121]

The "burdock, pigweed, apple-peru, and such unsightly vegetation" growing beside the prison, that "black flower of civilized society," where grass should have been, begin the flower and weed imagery, which, in some thirty images and extended analogies, reinforces and extends the implications of the imagery of color and light. . . .

First, and most clearly, the unnatural flowers and unsightly vegetation are aligned with moral evil, and with Chillingworth in particular. He too with his deformity is "unsightly." Low, dark, and ugly, he suggests to some people the notion that his step must wither the grass wherever he walks. The sun seems not to fall on him but to create "a circle of ominous shadow moving along with his deformity." It is natural enough then to find him explicitly associated with "deadly nightshade" and other types of "vegetable wickedness," to see him displaying a "dark, flabby leaf" found growing out of a grave, and to hear that prominent among the herbs he has gathered are some "black weeds" that have "sprung up out of a buried heart." When his evil work was[131] done "he positively withered up, shriveled away...like an uprooted weed that lies wilting in the sun." Flower and weed imagery unites with light and color imagery to define Chillingworth's position as that of the chief sinner.

But Chillingworth is not the only one so aligned. Less emphatically, the Puritans themselves are associated with weeds and black flowers. The implications of color imagery first set up the association: as their "Puritanic gloom" increases in the second generation to "the blackest shade of Puritanism," we begin to see them as cousins to the "nightshade" and so are prepared for Pearl's pretense that the weeds she attacks in her solitary games are Puritan children. Accustomed to her apparently infallible instinct for the truth, we see in her game something more than childish imagination.

The second relationship deserving of note also starts in the first chapter. We recall Hawthorne's saying of the wild rose-bush in bloom beside the prison that he hoped it might "relieve the darkening close" of his tale. No "sweet moral blossom" plays any significant part in the main story, but the happy fortune of Pearl, related in the concluding chapter, does offer a contrast with the "frailty and sorrow" of the tale proper. Thus Pearl's final role is foreshadowed in the first chapter. But Hawthorne does not wait until the end to make this apparent. He constantly associates her not only with the scarlet letter on her mother's dress but with the red rose. The rose bears "delicate gems" and Pearl is the red-clad "gem" of her mother's bosom. Her flowerlike beauty is frequently underscored. And naturally so, for we are told that she had sprung, "a lovely and immortal flower," out of the "rank luxuriance" of a guilty passion.

The position thus defined is repeatedly emphasized. Pearl cries for a red rose in the governor's garden. She answers the catechetical question who made her by declaring that she had not been made at all but "had been plucked by her[132] mother off the bush of wild roses that grew by the prison door." She decorates her hair with flowers, which are said to become her perfectly. She is reflected in the pool in "all the brilliant picturesqueness of her beauty, in its adornment of flowers." Her "flower-girdled and sunny image" has all the glory of a "bright flower." Pearl is a difficult child, capricious, unintentionally cruel, unfeeling in her demand for truth, but she has both the "naturalness" and the beauty of the rose, and like the rose she is a symbol of love and promise.

These are the associations Hawthorne most carefully elaborates, but there are two others worth noting briefly. Weeds or "black flowers" are on several occasions associated with Hester. The most striking instance of this occurs when Pearl pauses in the graveyard to pick "burrs" and arrange them "along the lines of the scarlet letter that decorated the maternal bosom, to which the burrs, as their nature was, tenaciously adhered." The burrs are like Pearl in acting according to nature, and what they suggest in their clinging cannot be wholly false. Hester implicitly acknowledges the truth of what the burrs have revealed when she suggests to Dimmesdale that they let the "black flower" of their love "blossom as it may."

But a more frequent and impressive association is set up between Hester and normal flowers. Even the badge of her shame, the token of her "guilty" love, is thus associated with natural beauty. The scarlet letter is related to the red rose from the very beginning. As Hester stands before her judges in the opening scenes, the sun shines on just two spots of vivid color in all that massed black, brown, and gray: on the rose and the letter, both red. The embroidery with which she decorates the letter further emphasizes the likeness, so that when Pearl throws flowers at her mother's badge and they hit the mark, we share her sense that this is appropriate. Burrs and flowers seem to have an affinity for Hester's letter. Hawthorne was too much of a Protestant to share the Catholic[133] attitude toward "natural law": the imagery here suggests that moral law and nature's ways do not perfectly coincide, or run parallel on different levels; they cross, perhaps at something less than a right angle. At the point of their crossing the lovers' fate is determined. No reversal of the implied moral judgment is suggested when nature seems to rejoice at the reaffirmed love of the pair in the forest: "Such was the sympathy of Nature—that wild, heathen Nature of the forest, never subjugated to human law, nor illumined by higher truth—with the bliss of these two spirits! Love, whether newly born, or aroused from a death-like slumber, must always create a sunshine."

Hester's emblem, then, points to a love both good and bad. The ambiguity of her gray robes and dark glistening hair, her black eyes and bright complexion, is thus emphasized by the flower and weed imagery. As Chillingworth is associated with weeds, Pearl with flowers, and Dimmesdale with no natural growing thing at all, so Hester walks her ambiguous way between burdock and rose, neither of which is alone sufficient to define her nature and her position.[134]

. . . .

FROM "The Scarlet Letter," *Hawthorne: A Critical Study* (Cambridge, Mass., 1955), pp. 118-150. Reprinted by permission of The Belknap Press of Harvard University Press. Copyright 1955 by the President and Fellows of Harvard College.

HESTER'S NEEDLEWORK: SYMBOLISM SOTTO VOCE

Sister M. Hilda Bonham

Much has been written about Hawthorne's use of symbols, especially about those in *The Scarlet Letter*. Conspicuous symbols such as the letter itself, the scaffold, mirrors, light and shadow, and Pearl have attracted the comments of critics down the years, until it would seem that there is little more to be said on the subject—that, as one editor protested, the quota is filled. If these more prominent examples represented Hawthorne's art of the symbol in its entirety or even at its perfection, it might be admitted, at least tentatively, that the wealth of studies devoted to them has come close to exhausting the subject. Serious students of Hawthorne, however, know that he was no mere verbal sleight-of-hand performer, pulling symbols out of his inkwell and sprinkling them like so many asterisks on the pages of his narratives. They have more than adequately recognized that symbolization

—called by William Van O'Connor *"the* characteristic of the human mind"—was at the marrow of Hawthorne's creative genius. So fundamental was this tendency in Hawthorne that under the magic of his pen any sensible object in the story might from time to time slip into the symbol role, pointing up an incident, a character, an atmosphere with little or no awareness on the part of the average reader of its fulfillment of this second function. It seems possible that this type of symbolization makes a contribution to the narrative greater than that of the symbols which have been investigated so exhaustively and that tracing the part such a symbol plays in the novel may enrich to some degree our knowledge of Hawthorne's art.

Hester's needlework—obviously integral to the story and yet not merely an element of plot—lends itself readily to such an analysis. It is easy to show that with each reference to her skill Hawthorne adds another deft stroke to his portrait of a strong-willed, passionate, sensitive, speculative, large-hearted woman, at the same time indicating the severe limits placed on her contacts with the community.

It is Hester's exceptional proficiency in the art of the needle that first directs the reader's attention to one of her character traits. Revealed at its apogee, with no indication as to how the art was acquired and with every implication that improvement in it would be inconceivable, it points to an independence noticeable in her from the moment when "on the threshold of the prison-door, she repelled...by an action marked with natural dignity and force of character" the town beadle, who in ushering her forth had dared to lay his hand upon her shoulder (ch. 2), to the forest meeting where she revealed to the supine Dimmesdale the boldly conceived plans which were to enable them to escape from the colony. The defiant spirit that impelled Hester to use her needle to ornament with gold embroidery her mark of shame and to make an animated scarlet letter of Pearl (ch. 7) is likewise evident in her "haughty smile," her "glance that would not be abashed" (ch. 2), and her desperate "recklessness" (ch. 2) on the scaffold; in her "Nevertheless, I will enter," to the servant of the Governor (ch. 7), and in her fierce "You shall not take her!" to the authorities who would deprive her of her child (ch. 8). More subtle, and yet no less real, is the parallel between what she achieved by means of her needlework—a livelihood sufficient for herself and Pearl with something over for the poor and even a certain part in the community's celebrations of birth, life, and death—and the steadfast[184] endurance, without being crushed, of seven years of almost unbearable ignominy.

Even more close is the relation between the fantastic quality found in many of the products of Hester's needle and her passionate nature. The "rich voluptuous, Oriental characteristic," the "taste for the gorgeously beautiful" (ch. 5), found expression in the "gorgeous robes" in which she dressed Pearl—robes which made Mr. Wilson fear that Hester had no better "thought than to make a mountebank of her child" (ch. 8) and the "fantasies and flourishes" of which made Pearl seem "the unpremeditated offshoot of a passionate moment" (ch. 7). On the other hand, it is significant that this woman, in whose "tomb-like heart" passion was "even yet neither dead nor asleep, but only imprisoned" (ch. 15), clothed herself in coarse material of a sombre hue, her needle thus pointing up the suppression as well as the expression of her passion.

Along with strength and passion there was in Hester a noticeable sensitiveness—a refinement. She was "lady-like...characterized by a certain state and dignity" (ch. 2). Likewise, the garments worked by Hester's needle, though elaborate and luxuriant, were never gaudy. Far from implying a lack of control, they exhibited so sure a grasp of the principles of design that an accurate description of them necessarily involved the words "delicate" and "exquisite" as the only appropriate terms.

Hester Prynne, it would seem then, was not merely a seamstress; she was an artist. Her "creations" showed ingenuity, originality, and daring—in keeping with her tendency to intellectual activity, stronger than that, at least Hawthorne thought, ordinarily possessed and exercised by the normal female. The same capacity that made her in her solitude assume a "freedom of speculation" (ch. 13) found expression in the dress in which she appeared on the scaffold "wrought for the occasion, in prison, and modelled much after her own fancy" (ch. 2), in the stitch, probably original and now a lost art, used to embroider the scarlet letter, and in the "peculiar cut" of Pearl's "crimson velvet tunic" (ch. 7).

Any sketch of Hester's character would be incomplete were it to omit her grandeur. That she was drawn on a large scale, not only in body but also in heart, is evident in the generosity she showed in her dealings with Dimmesdale, with the poor, even with Chillingworth. It is not a quality of her needlework that suggests this large-heartedness —although it is implicit in the richness of the materials she used when she was free to choose and the splendor of the effects she achieved; it is rather the variety in the uses to which her art was put and in the people who wore the garments she made. Her work was seen in "the ruff of the Governor; military men wore it on their scarfs, and the minister on his band; it decked the baby's little cap; it was shut up to be mildewed and moulder away, in the coffin of the dead" (ch. 5). The one exception to the universality of the recipients of her service—the bride—while it "indicated the ever-relentless rigor with which society frowned upon her sin" (ch. 5), at the same time emphasized the extent of those to whom her service did reach. Male and female; the infant, the growing child, the middle-aged, the elderly; those who could afford to pay generously, those of moderate means, the poor who could not pay at all; magistrates and the humblest of citizens; the living and the dead; the few who, like the young wife, in the marketplace, sympathized with her plight and the many who treated her with scorn—none of these was excluded by Hester from the circle of those whom she served.

But Hester was excluded by them—cut off by her offense from all normal social contacts; and here too her needlework functions as a symbol, pointing up the attitude of the Puritan community toward sin, guilt, and penitence. The fact that "it is not recorded that in a single instance, her skill was called in aid to embroider the white veil which was to cover the pure blushes of a bride" (ch. 5), has already been alluded to. Professor Frederic I. Carpenter once stated (*CE*, Jan. 1944) that according to traditional Puritanism Hester's sin "shut her off forever from paradise." The flatness of his statement might be questioned, since in the scene of the minister's confession Hawthorne emphasizes the potential mercy of God as a part of Dimmesdale's belief; yet it cannot be disputed that the attitude of the magistrates, ministers, and townspeople was certainly not one that would have encouraged any[185] hope, even remote, of social reinstatement in the future or any assurance that even in the sight of God sins that were "scarlet, shall be made as white as snow" (Isaiah, 1:18). Therefore, although not imputing to Puritan theology the denial of the doctrine of forgiveness of sins, Hawthorne does censure the severity of the Puritanic code of law and the harshness that made Hester's social ostracism so painfully complete. The exclusion from this one branch of needlework symbolizes this harshness and the resulting atmosphere of hopelessness which came close to driving Hester to despair.

This searching out and spotlighting the way in which one of Hawthorne's unobtrusive symbols functions could be misleading, since their effectiveness lies principally in working without calling attention to themselves. When one returns to the novel, however, even though fresh from the search, one finds that the symbol slips back into its place in the story. And it continues to place in relief a trait, a mood, an action so inconspicuously that the reader is unmindful that this emphasis results from Hawthorne's continual awareness of the correspondences between external events and internal significances and his tendency to express these correspondences in symbols.[186]

. . . .

From "Hawthorne's Symbols *Sotto Voce*," *College English*, XX (Jan., 1959), 184-186. Reprinted by permission of the author and *College English*.

STRUCTURE: Architectural and Symbolic

THE SCAFFOLD

Leland Schubert

. . . .

The structural plan of *The Scarlet Letter* is one of its most beautiful and artistic qualities. No really great work of art is absolutely geometric in its composition. Even the "Last Supper" of Leonardo—so neat in its mathematics—is not flawless in this respect. The good artist avoids absolute balance, absolute repetition, absolute rhythm. Hawthorne has come as close to the absolute in *The Scarlet Letter* as he safely could. The novel's introduction, "The Custom House," is at once a part of the story and separate from it. It is joined to the story by its reference to the letter and by its title which sounds and looks like the titles of the chapters in the novel. (This is the only instance in which the introduction to a Hawthorne novel has a specific and descriptive title.) "The Custom House" is separate from the story in that it is not a first chapter; it is frankly introductory. The last chapter of the book is called "Conclusion." It has a chapter number, twenty-four, and is thus structurally tied into the story. But[137] it, too, is separate from the main flow. It is a summary which ties the various threads together; and it leaps ahead in time, it explains what becomes of the characters. It is related to "The Custom House" by a reference to the "manuscript of old date," described in the introduction, and by a mention of Mr. Surveyor Pue who figures in "The Custom House." Thus the introduction and the conclusion constitute a kind of frame around the story of Hester Prynne. It is true that this frame is not built in quite the same way as many of Hawthorne's frames are, and that it is not perfectly balanced. But its two sections are as much separated from the main story as they are related to it; and I think we may treat them either as a structural part of the story or as a frame. For the sake of simplifying the analysis of the novel's structure, I have chosen to think of "The Custom House" and "Conclusion" as a frame, apart from the story itself.

125

When we make this separation, the pattern of the story becomes clear and beautiful. It is built around the scaffold. At the beginning, in the middle, and at the end of the story the scaffold is the dominating point. Just as it literally rises above the market-place, so does it structurally rise out of the novel's plan and attribute pattern to it. In chapter two, after the very short first chapter, Hester is taken up on the scaffold. In chapter twelve, the middle chapter (when we omit the concluding chapter), Dimmesdale mounts the scaffold. In chapter twenty-three, the last (omitting the conclusion), Dimmesdale takes Hester and Pearl up there with him. These three incidents are, in every sense, the high points of the novel. The middle chapter, number twelve, tends to divide the story into two parts (or three parts, counting this middle chapter). This division is logical when we realize that up to chapter twelve neither the reader nor Chillingworth is certain that Dimmesdale is the father of little Pearl; after chapter twelve, there can be nó doubt.

There is more to the pattern than this two-fold division. The scaffold, in Boston, stands in the market-place. The[138] setting of the first three and the last three chapters is the market-place. In the first three chapters, Hester's ignominy is established. The last three chapters build up to and include Dimmesdale's victory over Chillingworth. Thus these two groups of chapters are set-off from the remainder of the story by locale as well as by function. The chapters between the first three and the middle one fall nicely into two groups of five and three chapters each. The group of five—chapters four through eight—deal chiefly with Pearl and Hester and describe Hester's struggles in the community. The group of three—chapters nine, ten, and eleven—deal with Chillingworth and Dimmesdale and show Chillingworth gaining the minister's confidence and digging out his secret. There are also eight chapters between chapter twelve and the last three, and they, too, fall into two groups of three and five chapters each. The group of three—chapters thirteen, fourteen, and fifteen—deal with Hester and Pearl again and indicate Hester's improved condition both in the community and within herself. The group of five—chapters sixteen through twenty—show the partial reunion of Hester and Dimmesdale and their growing resistance to Chillingworth's power.[139]

. . . .

From "The Scarlet Letter," *Hawthorne the Artist: Fine-Art Devices in Fiction* (Chapel Hill, 1944), pp. 131-161. Reprinted by permission of the University of North Carolina Press, Chapel Hill, North Carolina, copyright 1944.

THE FOUR-PART FORM

John C. Gerber

. . . . Form in *The Scarlet Letter* rises out of a basic division of the whole into four parts, each of which gains its distinctiveness from the character that precipitates or is responsible for the action that takes place within its limits. Furthermore, the order of the parts is determined by the desires and capabilities of the characters. Thus the community, aside from the four main characters, is responsible for the action in the first part (Chapters I-VIII); Chillingworth for that in the second (IX-XII); Hester for that in the third (XIII-XX); and Dimmesdale for that in the fourth (XXI-XXIV). Within each part, moreover, there is a noticeable division[25] between cause and effect, between material dealing primarily with the activating agent and material dealing primarily with the person or persons acted upon. . . .[26]

It is not surprising that Hawthorne should have the community directing events as the story opens. Indeed, once he has selected his main characters he can do little else, since none of them can logically create the social situation which is the necessary antecedent to the spiritual complication. Hester is indifferent to what the people think of her baby, Dimmesdale is afraid of what they think, and Chillingworth is too recent a newcomer to affect their thought. Hence, in no case can a social situation be forced unless the community[28] forces it. When the story opens, therefore, the people of the town of Boston are the logical and necessary activators, and they remain such throughout the first eight chapters of the book.

It is not entirely proper, however, to conceive of the community during this time as directly forcing the main characters into further sin. It does force isolation upon Hester. Otherwise, its function is to place the characters into such juxtaposition that new choices between good and evil must be made by each of them. If in every case the character chooses evil, the town can hardly be blamed except as an accessory before the fact. The rich irony of the situation is that the community while in the very act of abetting the spread of sin is complacently certain that it is stemming it.

Specifically, Boston places Hester upon the scaffold where she is seen and recognized by Chillingworth; it compels Dimmesdale to speak about Hester before the entire town, thereby forcing the issue of confession; it throws Hester and Chillingworth together in prison, where Chillingworth, because of his wife's distraught condition, is able to extract a vow to conceal his identity; it requires Hester to wear the scarlet letter; and through a threat against Pearl it brings the main characters together in a scene at the Governor's hall in which Dimmesdale unwittingly betrays his feelings to Chillingworth. . . .[29]

The transition from the first to the second part of *The Scarlet Letter* is so sound in motivation and so subtle in presentation that the reader is likely to be unaware until pages later that a fundamental break in the book has been passed. It occurs in this way. At the conclusion of Chapter VIII, the Reverend Mr. Wilson, as spokesman for the community, closes the case of Boston *versus* the unknown lover of Hester Prynne. In turning down Chillingworth's request for further investigation he says:

"Nay; it would be sinful, in such a question, to follow the clew of profane philosophy. Better to fast and pray upon it; and still[34] better, it may be, to leave the mystery as we find it, unless Providence reveal it of its own accord. Thereby, every good Christian man hath a title to show a father's kindness towards the poor, deserted babe."

It is abundantly clear, however, that so charitable a disposition of the case is not acceptable to Chillingworth. Not only has he vowed to discover the identity of Hester's lover, but already his mind has been kindled by the possibilities of "a philosopher's research" into the mystery. Confronted with this double urge to investigation on the one hand and the community's withdrawal from the case on the other, the old doctor is placed in a position where he must force the action or give up all but the slenderest hope of revenge. By this time, however, the reader knows enough about Chillingworth to realize that the second alternative is for him not really an alternative at all. The reader, therefore, is not at all surprised that in Chapter IX the responsibility for the main action of the story shifts from the community to him.

The happenings which Chillingworth precipitates in this second part of the book can be quickly summarized. At first by frequent consultations and then by effecting an arrangement whereby he can live in the same house with Dimmesdale, the physician succeeds in becoming a daily and often hourly irritant to Dimmesdale's already sensitive conscience. Cautiously but surely, he succeeds in wearing down the young minister's defenses until in desperation Dimmesdale resorts to flagellation, fasts, and long vigils to ease the increasing torture. Generally, this section is a study of psychological cause and effect, with the victim frantically but ineffectively trying to deal with the effects rather than eliminating the cause. More particularly, it is a rich study in guilt and isolation. Before it is over, Chillingworth forces

Dimmesdale into so deep a consciousness of sin that to the distracted minister it seems as if all the bonds which have held him to the forces for right have frayed beyond repair. But in so doing, Chillingworth[35] breaks all his own connections with what Mr. Arvin calls "the redemptive force of normal human relations," and substitutes for them an ineluctable union with evil.[36]. . .

The depths into which Dimmesdale has been thrust by Chillingworth are best demonstrated in the final chapter of this section, the midnight vigil scene on the scaffold. Here, Hawthorne makes it plain that the minister is not only incapable of changing his sinful course by the action of his own will but has been so weakened that he is incapable of right action even when assistance is offered by outside agents. The vigil itself is another of Dimmesdale's attempts at penance. There might, he feels, be a moment's peace in it. Once on the scaffold, the realization of his isolation sweeps across him, and he involuntarily shrieks aloud. In the moments that follow, three persons appear: Governor Bellingham, Mistress Hibbins, and the venerable Father Wilson. Here are three opportunities for him to break his loneliness and to establish connection with one of the great societies—earthly, hellish, or heavenly. But an involuntary shriek is not enough; before Dimmesdale can be admitted to one of these great companies, a voluntary confession or commitment must be made. One of these three persons must be hailed. For a man of average moral strength, the problem would be to choose among the three. For him the problem is whether he shall choose any. In the end, he cowers silent upon the scaffold and the figures disappear. Thus does Arthur Dimmesdale reach the extreme of his isolation. For the time being, seemingly, earth, hell, and heaven are all closed to him. Had he chosen hell, his eventual fate would have been more terrible, but his immediate suffering could not have been greater.[40]

When his mind begins to give way under the impact of this new sense of alienation, he again reacts involuntarily, this time to burst into a peal of insane laughter. What follows is a series of four rapid occurrences, each of which serves to remind the distracted minister of a source of power which is denied him only because of his failure to expiate his guilt. But in each case, Dimmesdale fails to grasp the opportunity and succeeds only in sinning further. Hester and Pearl, first of all, bring a rush of new life to the collapsing man. Here, presumably, is the perfect reminder of that bond of human affection which strengthens the human heart and enables it to find the path to truth. But when Pearl reminds her father of the expiation which is necessary before the bond can be strong and lasting, he dodges her question by giving it an impersonal and stereotyped answer. Secondly, the meteoric flash across the sky should remind him of strength through union with the tremendous yet wholesome forces of nature. Instead, his diseased mind, extending its "egotism over the whole expanse of nature," sees only a large A, symbol of his guilt. In the third place, the appearance of Chillingworth should remind him of the horror of union with evil and, by contrast, the glory of a courageous stand before God. But though his "soul shivers" at the old physician, he obediently follows him home. Finally, the following morning, his own rich and powerful discourse to his congregation should by its own "heavenly influences" catapult him into giving expression to the truth, that quality which by his nature he loves most of all. Yet when the sexton asks him so simple a question as whether he has heard of the A in the sky the preceding night, Dimmesdale answers, "No, I had not heard of it."

Four decisions are thus forced upon Dimmesdale: he must assert his position in relation to man, to nature, to God, and to his own original and better self. In each case, from sheer weakness and despair of spirit he only adds new falsity to that[41] which already exists. Chillingworth has worked better than he knows. If Dimmesdale is to be saved, aid must come from some outside source.

In the transition from part two to part three of *The Scarlet Letter,* content has again created form. Hawthorne once more has brought his story to a point where only one character is in a position to force the action. The community has been provided no reason for reentering the story as an activating force; Chillingworth has rather obviously run his course; and Dimmesdale is clearly lacking in both physical and moral vigor. Only Hester is capable of action. It is Hester, moreover, who wants action. For the first time she has fully comprehended the result of her vow to Chillingworth, and her sense of responsibility for Dimmesdale's condition has thrust all thoughts of her own temporarily from her mind. It is not surprising, therefore, that Chapter XIII should begin with a summary of Hester's activities during the seven years since the scaffold scene and that the following pages should reveal her as the source of whatever action takes place.

The third part of *The Scarlet Letter* extends from Chapter XIII to Chapter XX. In form, it is almost an exact duplicate of the second part. Each sketches the immediate past of the main character, details the present action initiated by that character, and describes the results of that action upon another character. In each case, the other character is Dimmesdale.

Hester is sketched as independent and disillusioned. In some ways her isolation has been almost as complete as Dimmesdale's. For seven years now, heaven and earth "have frowned on her." Even though society has grown more benignant, it has never really accepted her save in time of sickness or death; God, never really a great influence in her life,[42] seems to have become less real; nature's sunlight vanishes on her approach; and her own personality has lost its womanly charm. In brief, shame, despair, and solitude have been her teachers just as they have for Dimmesdale.

Two elements, however, have strengthened her while Dimmesdale weakened: her intellectual speculation and her daughter Pearl. The former has been possible only because her sin has been public and her mind hence not cramped by fears of exposure. It has resulted in a latitude of thought which allows her to picture herself as the prophetess of a new order and which causes her to scorn the institutions of the old: "the clerical band, the judicial robe, the pillory, the gallows, the fireside, or the church." In the second place, Pearl has kept a sense of moral direction in Hester, even though Hester has never fully acted upon it. Once, Pearl saved her mother from the devil in the guise of Mistress Hibbins; constantly, she has saved her from complete surrender to her own cynicism. In a loose sense, Pearl performs the same service for Hester that Chillingworth does for Dimmesdale, since both serve as pricks to the conscience. When their functions are examined more closely, however, it can be observed that these services have opposite effects. For Dimmesdale, if let alone, might eventually get his spiritual house in order. His natural gravitation is heavenward, and he continues to move toward evil simply because Chillingworth keeps nudging him in that direction. But Hester's inclination is not so dominantly heavenward, and she is kept from an alliance with the Devil largely because Pearl keeps hold of her. Intellectual speculation, stimulating as it has been, has led Hester into moral confusion. It is Pearl who has kept this confusion from collapsing into surrender. This she has done by keeping alive the spark of human affection and by standing rigidly against falsity wherever in her precocious way she has sensed it. Given these complementary sources of power, Hester is easily the strongest character in the book at this point.[43] Even Chillingworth can recognize a quality "almost majestic" which shines through her despair. . . .[44]

That Hester is able to win release from her vow to Chillingworth is due primarily to his admiration for his wife's cynical independence and to his own surrender to the course of events. The latter is the more important and represents the difference between the second and third parts of the book. In the second part the vow of secrecy was necessary so that he could direct events; now he is content merely to "let the black flower blossom as it may."

Hester's actions from this point break loosely into two lines, that directed toward expiation of her sin of hypocrisy and that directed toward escape from the consequences of her act of adultery. The two lines form an illuminating contrast between the proper and improper methods of dealing with guilt, the one leading to moral triumph and the other to moral failure. Fundamentally, the success of the first line is due to the fact that it arises out of a keen sense of responsibility for wrongdoing. To Hester this sense comes first when she sees Dimmesdale's emaciated figure upon the scaffold at midnight. Her later self-analysis is cuttingly honest. In all[46] things else she has striven to be true. Truth has been the one virtue to which she might have held fast, and did hold fast "in all extremity" save in that one moment of weakness when she consented to deception. But now she finds that "a lie is never good, even though death threatens on the other side." In short, she has been false to her own nature, with the result that Dimmesdale has suffered possibly beyond repair. Realizing all this and recognizing at last the obligation which she owes Dimmesdale because of her love and her share in his crime, Hester becomes deeply and earnestly repentant.

Sincere repentance brings proper action. First, Hester obtains her release from Chillingworth, for any other procedure would merely have substituted one dishonesty for another. Then she waylays Dimmesdale in the forest in order to confess and implore his forgiveness. Confession can rectify the false relation which her silence has created, but only forgiveness from the one who has suffered can bring her peace. "Wilt thou yet forgive me!" she repeats over and over again until her lover at length replies, "I do forgive you, Hester." . . .[47]

Hester's second line of action is related to her sin of adultery and her attempt to overcome the isolation imposed by it. Ironically, the very element which led her to repent for her sin of hypocrisy—truth to her own nature—now provides her with a justification for her act of adultery. When Dimmesdale observes sadly that Chillingworth's sin has been blacker than theirs, Hester is quick to whisper, "What we did had a consecration of its own! We felt it so! We said so to each other!" Confident in this belief, she proposes that they dispel their sense of moral isolation by translating it into physical terms. She and Dimmesdale and Pearl must flee to Europe. And her insistence that Dimmesdale agree represents the highest point in her activities as a directing force in the story. . . .[48]

When Hester suggests a solution involving an easier means and an alternative end—temporal happiness—the solution appears so simple and so breathtaking to Dimmesdale that he wonders why they had never thought of it before. It offers a whole new realm of action, unchristianized and lawless but free and exciting. So exciting is it, in fact, that he is quick to put down any temporary misgivings. Reunion with God? He is irrevocably doomed anyway. Reunion with his people? Hester is all that he needs to sustain him. Union with his own[49] spirit? Already he can feel life coursing through his veins without it. And so for the first time he consents with purpose and deliberation to something that basically he knows to be wrong. The immediate result is a sudden plunge into moral confusion. Like Hester before him, he has sinned against his own better nature. . . .[50]

The fourth part of *The Scarlet Letter* offers an interesting variation from the other three parts. Whereas each of these gives immediate attention to the character which is to direct its action, the fourth part withholds such attention for almost two chapters. Indeed, these chapters, "The New England Holiday" and "The Procession," might with some justice be considered a final section of the third part inasmuch as they deal chiefly with the results of Hester's activities as they operate upon Hester herself. There are other and more cogent reasons, however, for considering them as belonging to the fourth part of the book and as a kind of introduction for[51] Dimmesdale's final act. The most obvious is that the background ties these chapters with Chapter XXIII, in which he takes control. Hawthorne is carefully setting the stage for his climax. In terms of content there are other elements to be considered. Dimmesdale's final action must not appear as something opposing Hester's desires but as something evolving from them and sublimating them. Hence, it must be made clear to the reader that Hester has lost confidence in her own scheme and will ultimately be favorably affected by Dimmesdale's expiation rather than antagonized by his seeming disregard for her plans and wishes. Another element is the character of his action. Whereas the community, Chillingworth, and Hester needed days, months, and even years to accomplish their purposes, Dimmesdale needs only moments. Theirs was a series of actions, each carefully plotted and integrated with every other; his is one bold stroke. Their actions created complexities; his removes them. Hence, his can be encompassed and should be encompassed in a much smaller space. But it is equally true that the setting must be carefully prepared, or the action will pass before the reader is prepared to comprehend its full significance. It seems useful and understandable, therefore, that Hawthorne should devote Chapters XXI and XXII to introductory material, Chapter XXIII to Dimmesdale's expiatory action, and Chapter XXIV to the consequences of that action.

By contrast with her previous aggressiveness, Hester's mood in the market place sinks from one of loneliness to one of almost complete despair. Seldom has she seemed so completely isolated. Her frozen calmness, we are told, is due to the fact that she is "actually dead, in respect to any claim of sympathy" and has "departed out of the world, with which she still seems to mingle." The good people of the town sidle away from her and strangers openly gawk. Nor has she come any closer to Pearl. When Pearl keeps asking about the minister, Hester shuts her off with "Be quiet, Pearl! thou understandest not these things." Even Dimmesdale she sees moodily as existing[52] in a sphere remote and "utterly beyond her reach." Indeed, she can hardly find it in her heart to forgive him for "being able so completely to withdraw himself from their mutual world; while she groped darkly, and stretched forth her cold hands, and found him not." Finally, the news that Chillingworth is to take passage on the same ship transforms her loneliness into consternation and despair. "Hester's strong, calm, steadfastly enduring spirit almost sank, at last, on beholding this dark and grim countenance of an inevitable doom, which...showed itself, with an unrelenting smile, right in the midst of their path."

Once Dimmesdale begins to direct the action, however, any effort of either Hester or Chillingworth becomes incidental. With a fine sense for dramatic contrast, Hawthorne has Dimmesdale reach his greatest success as a minister a few short minutes before he confesses his crime. Never has he been more uplifting and never more spiritually inclined. Already we know the Election Sermon as something born of new awareness and a sudden stiffening of the spirit. Since the world is no longer illusory or his own heart confused, Dimmesdale apparently has made his peace with the natural order and with himself. But he still feels estranged from God and from the community because of his sins of adultery and hypocrisy. His confession on the scaffold, therefore, is necessary as penance for both these sins, and its dual character Dimmesdale himself makes clear:

"God knows; and He is merciful; He hath proved his mercy, most of all, in my afflictions. By giving me this burning torture to bear upon my breast! By sending yonder dark and terrible old man, to keep the torture always at red heat! By bringing me hither, to die this death of triumphant ignominy before the people! Had either of these agonies been wanting, I had been lost forever! Praised be his name! His will be done! Farewell!"

In such a manner does Dimmesdale perform true penance and emerge finally at the moment of his death into a true[53] relation with all the elements against which he has sinned. It is vain for him to hope for "an everlasting and pure reunion," but he has made himself worthy of whatever reunion God grants to those who repent.[54]

. . . .

FROM "Form and Content in *The Scarlet Letter*," *New England Quarterly*, XVII (March, 1944), 25-55. Reprinted by permission of the author and the *New England Quarterly*.

THREE EPIC QUESTS

Hugh N. Maclean

. . . .

Hawthorne knew very well that he was dealing with a theme "not less but more heroic" than anything which had yet appeared in American fiction. Consciously or not, he clothed his fable in epic machinery. The tale begins *in medias res;* it develops in twenty-four books, of which the first twelve lead outward and "downward"; the concluding twelve home to the heart and to salvation—for Dimmesdale, at least. At the halfway mark Chillingworth seems to be triumphant; Pearl has been described in terms almost exclusively of uncontrolled, chaotic passion. A number of "solutions," political, theological, even necromantic, have been tried (or suggested) and found wanting. Dimmesdale allows himself to be led away by the[13] leech. But in the concluding twelve chapters all is reversed. Chillingworth steadily declines in power. Pearl's character, though rudderless for a time, is now considered in terms of its potential intelligence and active fiber. The one true solution to "the dark problem" resolves the bewildered despair of the protagonists on a supernatural plane, to which they can be raised only by supernatural aid. This is "epic machinery" without a self-starter. Only God can provide the vital spark.

There are three epic "quests" in the novel. Dimmesdale's search for salvation is a conscious, if largely involuntary quest, which is one long *agon,* pierced (in Chapter XII), by the *pathos* or apparent "death" of his soul, but concluded by the final triumph (really God's triumph) of the struggling "hero." Two other quests turn on the outcome of this central struggle. Chillingworth, the agent of evil, undertakes a conscious and voluntary quest, with the soul of Dimmesdale as object; this mission, appropriately, is perverted in pattern, and ends (after an apparent victory in Chapter XII) in the destruction of the physician. Pearl, who represents man's hopeful future as Chillingworth recalls his bitter and diseased past, has her quest too. It is first announced by Hester: "My child must seek a heavenly Father; she shall never know an earthly one." This quest, which is unconscious and involuntary, appears doomed for a time. As Dimmesdale falls under Chillingworth's spell, Pearl seeks knowledge, not of any "heavenly Father," but of "the Black Man." At length, of course, she finds her "heavenly Father." After the kiss on the scaffold, Pearl, reconciled to the conditions of life, will not "forever do battle with the world, but be a woman in it."

These quests, however, take place on different levels. Although they are closely interdependent, they differ in kind. The quest and career of Dimmesdale (as of Hester) is carried on in society and in nature. Granting all their passion and determination, it remains a fact that both these figures are ineffectual. Dimmesdale accomplishes nothing positive until the eve preceding the "Election Sermon." Hester's frenetic activity is thoroughly futile. To be sure, this is the level of humanity, on which the story of the novel unfolds. But although we call the events on this level "real" and its characters "central," events and characters both are signs and symbols of the eternal battle being waged by forces altogether outside its limits.[14] Chillingworth, cold and determined, and Pearl, whose heavenly Father waits in the wings, remind us of this struggle. Throughout the action Hester and Dimmesdale, first separately, then together, come under the influence of Chillingworth; and their reactions affect Pearl. Indeed, the actions of Hester and the minister are a kind of "mirror" through which Chillingworth, once he is actively launched on his way of revenge, moves freely into the Pearl-world. Only at the close of the novel does this mirror become opaque, closing Chillingworth out from the New Jerusalem and reflecting merely his own self-destructive image.

The quests of Pearl and the leech, therefore, are in a sense more "real" than those of the two "central" characters. But Hawthorne was careful not to assign a scene to Pearl and Chillingworth alone, as he assigned at least one to every other pair of characters. The child and the physician meet only in the presence of others, and they exchange no word. Hawthorne knew that the past and the future meet only in the present, and that the effect of the one and the hope of the other have meaning for man only in consequence of the thought and action of present time. In *The Scarlet Letter* the level of actuality on which Hester, Dimmesdale, and society move is related both to a threatening symbolic level, acting as it were from below, and also to a hopeful symbolic level, promising more than this world offers. As God knows the necessary outcome, the fate of Chillingworth and Pearl does not literally *depend* on the actions of Hester and Dimmesdale; rather, the manner in which the lives of these four figures turn on each other demonstrates the nature of the divine plan.

The structure of *The Scarlet Letter,* accordingly, is complex; but its complexity is unified by the central theme of God's saving power and man's futility, to which each part of the book directs its readers' attention. The structure is thoroughly balanced and ordered. Professor Gerber finds a four-part progressive division to be the distinguishing principle of the novel's pattern; and it seems to be true that first society at large, then, successively, Chillingworth, Hester, and Dimmesdale take the center of Hawthorne's stage. Yet the parts of the novel *interact* more closely than this interpretation would allow. Chillingworth's quest is the subject of Chapters IV and XIV; Pearl's quest (or "fate") is central first in VI through[15] VIII, later in XV and XVI; Dimmesdale's quest (that of all men) is considered especially in IX through XI and again in XVII through XX. The reactions and attitudes of society are discussed, especially as they affect Hester, in Chapters V, XIII, and XXI-XXII. At regular intervals, finally, those "key" chapters centered on the scaffold sum up and comment on the action. In each of them the fearful symbol appears in a different form. The scarlet letter on Hester's breast in Chapter II reminds us of sin in woman; Dimmesdale's revelation in Chapter XXIII confirms the presence of sin in man; the cloudy yet fiery "A" in the heavens, described in Chapter XII, points to the importance of sin in the universal plan. These groupings are enclosed by Chapters I and XXIV, which symbolically anticipate and confirm the theme of the novel.[16]

. . . .

FROM "Hawthorne's *Scarlet Letter:* 'The Dark Problem of this Life,' " *American Literature,* XXVII (March, 1955), 12-24. Reprinted by permission of the author and the editors of *American Literature.*

FALL AND EXPULSION: THE JOURNEY-MOTIF

Rudolphe von Abele

. . . .

The Scarlet Letter . . . is, like all successful fictions, a book with multiple levels. What can, in one vocabulary, be talked about as the problem of "guilt and expiation," which Hester and Dimmesdale solve each in a different way, can, in another, be figured in terms of "Fall and expulsion." The postulate on which the book is erected is a latter-day version of Original Sin: Hester, who has eaten forbidden fruit, seduces Dimmesdale into doing the same—dragging him out[219] of the paradise of his innocence and sending him into as veritable an exile as Adam ever knew. "Phall if you but will, rise you must," says Joyce in *Finnegans Wake,* exposing the pun inherent in the notion of the Fall of Man; and Dimmesdale's adultery with Hester is but another version, rather more muted, of the same ambiguity. And, if the book takes the Fall for granted, as a piece of "scenery," it is almost entirely concerned with the subsequent "exile" of its Adam and Eve, with their efforts to come to terms with the harsh facts of expulsion, of which Hester's is that of embittered resignation and Dimmesdale's that of submissive acquiescence. The expulsion is here not merely from the innocence of their respective youths but from the City of Man as well, since Hester, palpably, and Dimmesdale, covertly, are fugitives from human society. His closet where the bloody scourge hangs, is after all as far from the marketplace as is her cottage on the headland. Exile is the theme of *The Scarlet Letter;* exile ended after seven years for Dimmesdale, but for Hester, never. The story has affiliations with the underworld journeys of Aeneas and Dante; and its temper is in many ways akin to that of John of the Cross's *Dark Night of the Soul,* and even to that of "The Ancient Mariner."

The journey-motif recurs with striking frequency throughout the book: it is ingrained with its texture so deeply as to be inseparable from it. The book opens with a ritual journey (Hester's) from the town prison to its scaffold, and closes with another (Dimmesdale's) from the governor's palace to the meeting-house. Hester's public ordeal, it is interesting to see, culminates in her elimination from society, while Dimmesdale's secret one leads to his reunion with society—yet another instance of the contrapuntal symmetry so firmly maintained by Hawthorne in the development of the novel. Between these two crucial symbolic journeys there are many others: Hester's walks through the town as she peddles her needlework; the rambles taken along the sea and in the forest by Dimmesdale and Chillingworth; the walk Hester takes with Pearl to the governor's palace; the walk she takes with Chillingworth by the seaside; the forest walk in which she confronts Dimmesdale, who has gone on a journey into the frontier to visit the "apostle Eliot" among the Indians (a symbolic excursion into the wilderness preparatory to his encounter with Hester, who almost leads him into a yet wilder country); the minister's return to the town after the forest scene. And there is that central chapter, XII, in which Dimmesdale takes a mock-penitential walk at midnight to the scaffold— a chapter in which the *paths* of all protagonists[220] (including Chillingworth as such) *meet* and *cross.* They are paths of exile too: Dimmesdale skulking in the night, afraid to be seen by old John Wilson, who has been attending Governor Winthrop's deathbed; and Hester, like the White Old Maid and Edward Fane's brown Rosebud, tolerated as a harbinger of death and a maker of shrouds,—while under the gray cap her hair continues secretly to ripen, a repudiated Isis. Finally, there is the journey that is never taken, the voyage to Bristol or which Hester contracts, which, by a brilliant insight he for once does not spoil by emphasizing, Hawthorne shows as to be taken aboard a *buccaneering,* that is to say, an *outlaw*, ship. The extended treatment given to the crew and especially the captain of that ship figures the kind of life to which Hester is about to commit herself—libertarian, "beyond the pale," sensual to the point of sybaritism. The one significant difference is that the buccaneers, for economic reasons, were indulged in their lawlessness, even in their flouting of Puritan blue-laws; whereas Hester and Dimmesdale, as Chillingworth's accompaniment of them like so much baggage shows, were one step beyond them, over the line into exile absolute and unredeemable.

Nor is this casting of the novel in terms of the symbolic journey restricted to structural aspects alone: the journey as a metaphor occurs a number of times. Hester's life is a "track along which she had been treading since her early infancy"; the scene of her guilt is "the pathway that had been so fatal"; and her conduct leads the populace to suppose that she has returned to the "paths" of virtue. Dimmesdale, child that he is, is "at a loss in the pathway of human existence"; is "a poor pilgrim, on his dreary and desert path"; his mind "impelled itself powerfully along the track of a creed," and "kept an accustomed pathway in the range of thoughts familiar to it." When he and Hester meet in the forest it is "the point whither their pathway had so long been tending," and when she has revived his "torpid" spirits he speaks of the proposed escape from Massachusetts as "the path to a better life." Pearl, considered as a possible demon-child, is said to be a "stumbling-block" in Hester's "path"; and we are told too that Chillingworth's intellect "had now a sufficiently plain path before it." More than this, the journey itself is several times figured as a "wandering" in a labyrinth or maze—an impression which the actual wanderings of these tortured people round and round the same small portion of the world, to whose center, the scaffold, Dimmesdale does not penetrate until the very end, serve to heighten. Hester is "in a labyrinth[221] of doubt," wandering "in the dark labyrinth of mind"; she herself speaks of the course of her life, and Dimmesdale's, as a "wandering in this gloomy maze of evil, and stumbling, at every step, over the guilt wherewith we have strewn our path." The scene in which her unregeneracy reasserts itself and infects even Dimmesdale takes place not in the *town* but in the *forest*, and we are explicitly told that Hester is more accustomed to this kind of "scene" than he, having "wandered, without rule or guidance, in a moral wilderness." And at the close, "in the midst of their path," stands the figure of Chillingworth, image of guilt, blocking their way out of "their labyrinth of misery." To speak of human life as a journey, and of a life tormented with conscience as a labyrinth is scarcely a very original thing; yet perhaps the commonplace character of the metaphor is an asset to its effectiveness rather than the contrary—in that it makes possible the organization of the entire novel around the sensuous counterpart of a moral state with perfect consistency and logicality. The novel, that is, is *at every point* engaged in the objectification of its fundamental theme, so that the theme itself can only factitiously be dislodged from its incarnation in the flesh and blood of textural detail.[222]

. . . .

FROM *"The Scarlet Letter:* A Reading," *Accent,* XI (Autumn, 1951), 211-227. Reprinted by permission of the author and *Accent.*

PART THREE

TOPICS AND QUESTIONS FOR DISCUSSION AND STUDENT PAPERS

*Those who do not read criticism will rarely merit
to be criticized.*—ISAAC D'ISRAELI

TOPICS AND QUESTIONS

I. Theme

A. Woodberry's assertion that *The Scarlet Letter* is pure "shadow" would seem to be contradicted by Hawthorne's carefully tentative comment in Chapter 1 that the rose "may serve, let us hope, to symbolize some sweet moral blossom, that may be found along the track, or relieve the darkening close of a tale of human frailty and sorrow." Defend or attack Woodberry's position.

B. Roper categorizes the three main characters according to heart, mind, and soul. Does this seem like a valid method for getting at the meaning of the novel? If it does, elaborate. If it does not, show where the theory breaks down.

C. The relationship between individual and society is obviously one of the important themes of the novel. Do the critics who deal with this problem see it in fundamentally similar terms? If so, show how the different approaches, while in essential agreement, offer their own special insights into this facet of the novel. Or does one critic seem to have more nearly approached the heart of the matter? Defend your choice.

D. Various of the critics suggest that the novel is a tragedy. Determine just what each critic seems to mean by that term. Which one seems most convincing and why?

E. If, on the other hand, you feel that the novel is not a tragedy, show why not. You may want to begin with one of the famous or important definitions (your instructor can suggest some) and work with the novel from that starting point.

F. Most of the critics touch upon the Puritanism in the novel. How does it function in terms of the theme (or themes) of the novel? (Suggested further reading: Barriss Mills, "Hawthorne and Puritanism," *New England Quarterly,* XXI [March, 1948], 78-102; Herbert W. Schneider, *The Puritan Mind* [New York, 1930], pp. 256-264.)

G. Von Abele's discussion of the relationship between art, religion, science, and nature is, as he admits, "a highly tentative hypothesis." Is the discussion merely eccentric, or can it be related to one or more of the other interpretations of the novel so as to deepen or broaden the thematic implications of the novel? (You may wish to read, in this connection, the section on "Intention" in *Dictionary of World Literature,* Joseph T. Shipley, ed. [New Rev. Ed., New York, 1953], pp. 229-232.)

H. The adultery occurs before the novel begins. How does this help us to determine Hawthorne's thematic intention? (Consult the discussion of Hawthorne's fiction before *The Scarlet Letter* in Part One of this volume for some suggestions.)

I. Is *The Scarlet Letter* a religious novel or a novel about religion? Neither? (Two books which may help you to clarify the terms of your argument are Martin Jarrett-Kerr, *Studies in Literature and Belief* [London, n.d.], and M.H. Abrams, ed., *Literature and Belief* [New York, 1957]. Your instructor can suggest other relevant essays and books.)

II. Characters

A. *Method*

1. Do you agree with Short that the setting of the novel "is singularly substantial and precise"? If you do, try to determine whether these details of setting are used to anchor the "unearthly significance" in historical verisimilitude, or whether they are selected with an eye to their relevance to the "unearthly significance." Analyze several different kinds of historical detail to make your point.

2. Do you agree that Hawthorne strips his characters of all but a few human characteristics? Is this true of all the characters? In equal degree? Can you account for the differences?

3. Are Hawthorne's characters plausible?

4. Short and Bewley take different views of Hawthorne's method of creating characters. Which one seems to you to be more convincing? Or do you feel that the truth resides in a harmony of both views? Defend your choice.

5. Can you defend Bewley's contention that it is the "inner sphere of feeling that Hawthorne's art regularly inhabits, or deals with"?

B. *Hester*

1. Some of the critics see Hester as a romantic and others see her as a moral idealist (or Transcendentalist). Try to determine from the selections just what is meant by these terms. Which of the terms seems a more just description of Hester? If neither, explain.

2. Someone once remarked that people either love Hester or are afraid of her. On the basis of the criticism included in this section of the anthology, does this seem like a fair statement?

3. There is a wider divergence of critical opinion about Hester than about any other aspect of the novel. Why should this be so? That is, what are the difficulties that confront the reader's critical evaluation of her?

4. Defend or attack the following statement: "Hester as a character offers no difficulties; critical confusion results when we try to decide what Hawthorne's attitude toward her was."

5. Munger, Van Doren, and Stein conceive of Hester as saint, tragic heroine, and devil. Analyze the evidence that each critic uses to arrive at his evaluation. Choose one as being the strongest argument and defend your choice.

6. Bewley sees certain similarities between Hester and Ethan Brand and the woman in "The Hollow of the Three Hills." On the basis of your reading of these two stories, defend or attack Bewley's contention.

7. Hester's religious position is the subject of much critical comment. Does Hester accept any relationship between human action and a suprahuman value, or is her code strictly naturalistic?

8. How does Hester conceive of her adultery? Is her attitude toward it essentially fixed? Does it evolve? Or is it confused in the sense that it is always subject to certain emotional pressures of her situation?

9. What are some of the complexities involved in trying to assess the effect of isolation on Hester?

10. What are some of the complexities involved in trying to assess Hester's attitude towards her society?

C. *Dimmesdale*

1. The three critical discussions included in this section of the anthology are based on three different assumptions. What are they? On the basis of your reading of the novel which one seems most valid? Why?

2. What role does God play in Dimmesdale's life? Do you feel that the relationship between Dimmesdale and his religion is an essentially simple and straightforward one that has become complicated by his sin, or is it actually a complex one?

3. What keeps Dimmesdale from confession for so long? What makes him confess when he does?

4. Defend or attack this statement: "Dimmesdale is half in love with death."

5. Does Hawthorne mean for Dimmesdale to be a sympathetic character? Explain.

D. *Chillingworth*

1. On what points do Abel and Stein agree in their analyses of Chillingworth's character? Disagree? Which one of the two essays seems more convincing? Why?

2. Does Hawthorne give a sympathetic dimension to his portrait of Chillingworth, or does he wish him to function purely on the level of demonic evil? Defend your choice.

3. Is Chillingworth's demonism psychologically credible or can it only be comprehended on the level of moral allegory?

4. Trace the evolution of Chillingworth's relationship to Dimmesdale.

5. Chillingworth has been compared to Rappaccini and Ethan Brand. On the basis of your reading of the two stories, determine the validity of such a comparison.

E. *Pearl*

1. Several of the critics discuss Pearl as an amoral child. Do they see this trait in fundamentally similar terms? Do they see it as having the same consequences? If you feel they do not, choose the one that seems to you to be the most valid and defend your choice.

2. Wherein do the difficulties lie when we try to come to terms with Pearl as a child of nature (or a natural child)?

3. Some critics feel that Pearl is not a real child at all, that she is only an animated symbol; others feel that although she does have a symbolic function she is also, nevertheless, a psychologically credible portrait of a child brought up in unnatural circumstances. With which position do you agree? Defend your choice.

4. Discuss Pearl's symbolic function in the novel.

5. Several of the critical selections allude to earlier Hawthorne stories in which children appear. ("Ethan Brand" and "Feathertop," although published after *The Scarlet Letter,* were written earlier.) Do these stories, in your opinion, throw any light on the character of Pearl?

F. *Further Questions on Hawthorne's Characters*

1. In "Endicott and the Red Cross" (1838), Hawthorne described one of the recipients of Puritan punishment as "a young woman, with no mean share of beauty, whose doom it was to wear the letter *A* on the breast of her gown, in the eyes of all the world and her own children. And even her own children knew what that initial signified. Sporting with

her infamy, the lost and desperate creature had embroidered the fatal token in scarlet cloth, with golden thread and the nicest of needlework; so that the capital *A* might have been thought to mean Admirable, or anything rather than Adulteress." How much of this description (and its tone) manifests itself in Hawthorne's portrait of Hester? If you feel that there are differences, try to account for them.

2. Using the criticism contained in this section of the anthology as a model, discuss the function of the minor characters in the novel.

3. One critic has called *The Scarlet Letter* "pure allegory." To what extent can the figures in the novel be interpreted as representations of different aspects of the moral or religious life?

4. Defend or attack this statement: "Hawthorne takes sides with *neither* Hester nor Dimmesdale: he is concerned with their lives, not their morality."

5. There has been critical disagreement on who is the central character in the novel. Do you feel it is Hester or Dimmesdale? Defend your choice.

III. Symbolism

A. Precisely what is the nature of James' objection to Hawthorne's symbolism? If, on the whole, you agree with him, choose other examples of Hawthorne's use of symbolism to substantiate James' contention. If you do not agree with James, show how he is mistaken in his evaluation.

B. Are there other examples in *The Scarlet Letter* of what Matthiessen calls "the device of multiple choice" in addition to those he uses for illustration? Do they seem to operate as Matthiessen indicates?

C. Read "Young Goodman Brown" and "The Snow Image" and compare and contrast the use of "multiple choice" in the stories with the use of it in *The Scarlet Letter*.

D. Defend or attack Hawthorne's use of supernaturalism in the novel. (Prosser H. Frye's "Hawthorne's Supernaturalism," *Literary Reviews and Criticisms* [New York, 1908], pp. 114-129, may serve as a starting point.)

E. In what ways does Hawthorne's use of symbolism enable him to render his theme with greater clarity and complexity? Try to be specific.

F. Discuss Hawthorne's symbolism as a method of characterization. Try to determine where it is most effective (and ineffective) and why.

G. Analyze the symbolic function of nature in *The Scarlet Letter.*

H. Read Hawthorne's "Egotism" and "The Antique Ring." Why is the symbolism so much more effective in *The Scarlet Letter* than in these two stories?

I. Using the essays included in this section of the anthology as models, analyze any additional patterns of symbolism and imagery that you find in the novel. (Some of the most interesting discussions of symbolism in Hawthorne's fiction include Walter Blair, "Color, Light and Shadow in Hawthorne's Fiction," *New England Quarterly,* XV [March, 1942], 74-95; John W. Shroeder, "That Inward Sphere: Notes on Hawthorne's Heart Imagery and Symbolism," *PMLA,* LXV [March, 1950], 106-119; Malcolm Cowley, "Hawthorne in the Looking Glass," *Sewanee Review,* LVI [Autumn, 1948], 545-563; Norris Yates, "Ritual and Reality: Mask and Dance Motifs in Hawthorne's Fiction," *Philological Quarterly,* XXXIV [1955], 56-70.)

IV. Structure

A. On the basis of the essays included in this section of the anthology, is the editor justified in dividing the discussions of structure into "architectural and symbolic"? What distinguishes the two kinds of approach?

B. From the point of view of structure, defend or attack Hawthorne's inclusion of the last chapter, "Conclusion." (For the purposes of this discussion, you may ignore the fact that such a "roundup" was characteristic of many nineteenth-century novels.)

C. Analyze closely the three scaffold scenes for the purpose of extending Schubert's contention that the scaffold is the primary structural device.

D. In what ways do the discussions of structure shed light on the thematic intentions of the novel?

E. Comment on the following statement: "The forest scene is the structural center of the book: everything leads either to or away from it."

V. Further Questions on *The Scarlet Letter* for Extended Discussion

A. In the preface to *The House of the Seven Gables,* Hawthorne distinguishes his own kind of fiction (the romance) from another kind (the novel) as follows:

When a writer calls his work a Romance, it need hardly be observed that he wishes to claim a certain latitude, both as to its fashion and material, which he would not have felt himself entitled to assume had he professed to be writing a Novel. The latter form of composition is presumed to aim at a very minute fidelity, not merely to the possible, but to the probable and ordinary course of man's experience. The former—while it is a work of art, it must rigidly subject itself to laws, and while it sins unpardonably so far as it may swerve aside from the truth of the human heart—has fairly a right to present that truth under circumstances, to a great extent, of the writer's own choosing or creation. If he think fit, also, he may so manage his atmospherical medium as to bring out or mellow the lights and deepen and enrich the shadows of the picture. He will be wise, no doubt, to make a very moderate use of the privileges here stated, and, especially, to mingle the Marvellous rather as a slight, delicate, and evanescent flavor, than as any portion of the actual substance of the dish offered to the public. He can hardly be said, however, to commit a literary crime even if he disregard this caution.

Determine as exactly as you can the terms of Hawthorne's definition, and then discuss *The Scarlet Letter* as a "Romance."

B. Discuss *The Scarlet Letter* as a dramatic exploration of the problem of sin. (Helpful studies, in this connection, include Austin Warren, ed., *Nathaniel Hawthorne: Representative Selections* [New York, 1934], pp. xxxiv-xl; Neal F. Doubleday, "Hawthorne's Inferno," *College English*, I [Nov., 1940], 658-670; Carlos Kiling, "Hawthorne's View of Sin," *Personalist*, XIII [April, 1932], 119-130; Henry G. Fairbanks, "Sin, Free Will, and 'Pessimism' in Hawthorne," *PMLA*, LXXI [Dec., 1956], 975-989; Leonard J. Fick, *The Light Beyond: A Study of Hawthorne's Theology* [Westminster, Md., 1955].)

C. Discuss *The Scarlet Letter* as a dramatic exploration of the problem of isolation. (The student may wish to compare the treatment of this theme in the novel with earlier treatments in the short stories; he might also wish to consult Darrel Abel, "The Theme of Isolation in Hawthorne," *Personalist*, XXXII [Jan., 1951], 182-190.)

D. As this anthology of criticism indicates, there are various ways of getting at the meaning of *The Scarlet Letter;* or, more accurately, there are various levels on which the novel can be approached. Try to define these levels and then attempt to assess their relative significance.

E. Adkins, Levi, and Von Abele (all listed in the annotated bibliography), as well as O. L. Zangwill, "A Case of Paramnesia in Nathaniel Hawthorne," *Character and Personality*, 13 (March-June, 1945), 246-260, all discuss *The Scarlet Letter* from a psychoanalytic point of view. Read these articles, and then, on the basis of your own reading of the novel, write a critique of this kind of approach.

F. Flaubert's *Madame Bovary*, published six years after Hawthorne's novel, has occasionally been compared to *The Scarlet Letter*. On the basis of your reading of both novels, compare and contrast them. (Your instructor may suggest other novels which will bear fruitful comparative analysis.)

PART FOUR
A SELECTED BIBLIOGRAPHY OF
SCARLET LETTER CRITICISM

*Doubtless the meaning of any work of art that plumbs the mysteries of human life will be subject to endless debate.—*Roy R. Male

BIBLIOGRAPHY

NOTE: *The entries preceded by an asterisk (*) are excerpted in this book and therefore carry no annotation. Page references are to discussions of* The Scarlet Letter.

Abbott, Anne W. "Hawthorne's *Scarlet Letter*," *North American Review,* LXXI (July, 1850), 135-148. The first reviewer to cast doubt on the morality of the novel, Miss Abbott appreciates Hawthorne's style, but wonders why he did not "choose a less revolting subject." She is disturbed by Hawthorne's speculation about love and hate being perhaps the same thing at bottom, and irritated by the fact that Hester's suffering and (seeming) humility do not turn out to be Christian at all.

*Abel, Darrel. "Hawthorne's Dimmesdale: Fugitive from Wrath," *Nineteenth-Century Fiction,* XI (Sept., 1956), 81-105.

*Abel, Darrel. "Hawthorne's Hester," *College English,* XIII (March, 1952), 303-309.

*Abel, Darrel. "Hawthorne's Pearl: Symbol and Character," *ELH, A Journal of English Literary History,* XVIII (March, 1951), 50-66.

*Abel, Darrel. "The Devil in Boston," *Philological Quarterly,* XXXII (Oct., 1953), 366-381.

Adkins, Lois. "Psychological Symbolism of Guilt and Isolation in Hawthorne," *American Imago,* XI (Winter, 1954), 417-425. A psychoanalytic interpretation of the novel. "Dimmesdale, Hester, and Pearl may be viewed as aspects of the Freudian complex." Pearl represents the id (the unsocialized aspect of the personality); Dimmesdale the superego (the conscience); and Hester the ego (the rational aspect of the personality which is capable of mediating between the individual and society by acting as a moderator between the id and the superego).

Arvin, Newton. *Hawthorne* (Boston, 1929), pp. 187-191, 200-209. "What makes the outcome of its events so pitiful and terrible is not simply that a great sin has had its retribution, but that the harmony of several related lives has been fatally jangled, that they have been set at odds with the general purposes of life about them, that all fair potentialities of personal development have miscarried grievously and come to nothing."

Arvin, Newton. "Introduction," *The Scarlet Letter* (New York: Harper's Modern Classics, 1950), pp. v-xiii. Briefly extends scaffold structure to cover contrasts of day-night, town-forest, society-solitude; relates these contrasts to the theme of purity and innocence.

*Bewley, Marius. "Hawthorne and 'The Deeper Psychology,'" *Mandrake*, II (1956), 366-373.

*Bewley, Marius. *The Eccentric Design* (New York, 1959), pp. 161-174.

Bier, Jesse. "Hawthorne on the Romance: His Prefaces Related and Examined," *Modern Philology*, LIII (Aug., 1955), 17-24. A study of Hawthorne's attitude towards fiction. Most relevant to the study of *The Scarlet Letter* is the analysis of the moonlit room passage in "The Custom House," which is Hawthorne's "image for the process of the imagination itself."

*Bonham, Sister M. Hilda. "Hawthorne's Symbols *Sotto Voce*," *College English*, XX (Jan., 1959), 184-186.

Brant, Robert L. "Hawthorne and Marvell," *American Literature*, XXX (Nov., 1958), 366. The source for the last line of *The Scarlet Letter* is in Andrew Marvell's "The Unfortunate Lover"—"In a Field Sable, a Lover Gules." The source would seem to imply "a redeeming light in the beauty of the tragedy."

Brownell, W.C. *American Prose Masters* (New York, 1909), pp. 116-123. The novel "is essentially a story neither of sin nor of the situation of illicit love—presents neither its psychology nor its social effects; neither excuses nor condemns, nor even depicts, from this specific point of view. The love of Hester and Dimmesdale is a postulate, not a presentment. . . . the book is a story of the concealment of sin amid circumstances that make a sin of concealment itself."

Brownson, Orestes. *"The Scarlet Letter," Brownson's Review*, VII (Oct., 1850), 528-532. Attacks the novel as "genius perverted," dangerous to the "moral and religious" health of the community. Objects to the fact that neither of the protagonists repents the adultery; Hester suffers only regret, and Dimmesdale's repentance is for hypocrisy. Also finds Hawthorne's treatment of the Puritans unfair: "Their treatment of the adulterers was far more Christian than his ridicule of it."

*Carpenter, F.I. "Scarlet A Minus," *American Literature and the Dream* (New York, 1955), pp. 63-72. This essay originally appeared in *College English*, V (Jan., 1944), 173-180.

Chorley, Henry F. *"The Scarlet Letter," Athenaeum* (June 5, 1850), 634. First English review of the novel. Doubts adultery as a legitimate subject for fiction, but does acknowledge Hawthorne's elevated treatment of it.

Conway, Moncure D. *Life of Nathaniel Hawthorne* (London, 1890), pp. 123-131. Finds the book daring in its disregard of ethical platitudes; this is surprising because Hawthorne was a purist in the matter of sexual morals. Hester shines like a star beside "stolid Respectability, and priestcraft cruel and cowardly." Feels that Hester may be more of a morally free soul than Hawthorne intended, and that when he came to revise the novel he inserted qualifying statements.

Cowie, Alexander. *The Rise of the American Novel* (New York, 1948), pp. 335-339. The formidable lesson of the novel is "inescapable . . . but not simple": society will punish violations of the moral law, but concealment will be utterly corrosive and personal vengeance dehumanizing.

Cowley, Malcolm. "Five Acts of *The Scarlet Letter,*" *College English,* XIX (Oct., 1957), 11-16. This essay first appeared in shorter form as "100 Years Ago: Hawthorne Set a Great New Pattern," *New York Herald Tribune Book Review* (Aug. 6, 1950), 1, 13. It has also been reprinted in somewhat longer form in *Twelve Original Essays on Great American Novels,* Charles Shapiro, ed. (Detroit, 1958), pp. 23-43. The essay shows how Hawthorne's novel naturally breaks down into dramatic acts and scenes.

Coxe, Arthur Cleveland. "The Writings of Hawthorne," *Church Review,* III (Jan., 1851), 489-511. Sees the novel as an American imitation of George Sand; "a running undercurrent of filth has become as requisite to a romance, as death in the fifth act of a tragedy." Finds the novel morally deleterious because it argues for a new commandment to supersede the seventh.

Cronin, M. "Hawthorne on Romantic Love and the Status of Woman," *PMLA,* LXIX (March, 1954), 89-98. Hawthorne does not approve of Hester's romantic justification of her adultery; his seeming approval stems from his critical portrayal of the Puritans and his appealing portrait of her. "One experiences Hester as one does not experience Hawthorne's moralizing. But the effect was unintentional."

Doubleday, Neal F. "Hawthorne's Hester and Feminism," *PMLA,* LIV (Sept., 1939), 825-828. Hawthorne's characterization of Hester is, in part, an attack on the feminism of his day; as such, it gives further proof that Hester's "consecration" speech in the forest does not indicate the moral bias of the novel.

Duychinck, Evert A. *"The Scarlet Letter,"* *Literary World,* VI (March 30, 1850), 323-325. First review of the novel, which he calls a psychological romance. Praises Hawthorne's depiction of Puritanism and the delicate handling of the adultery. "We hardly know another writer . . . who would have handled this delicate subject without an infusion of George Sand."

*Eisinger, Chester E. "Pearl and the Puritan Heritage," *College English,* XII (March, 1951), 323-329.

Erskine, John. "Hawthorne," *Cambridge History of American Literature* (New York, 1933), Vol. I, pp. 26-28. Analyzes the novel in terms of Transcendentalism. Hester shows self-reliance "in a way that some Emersonians may have found not altogether comfortable." Chillingworth's revenge is a form of "compensation." The optimism of Emerson's "Circles" is to be seen in Hester's sin having led her to a "fuller life."

*Feidelson, Charles, Jr. *Symbolism and American Literature* (Chicago, 1953), pp. 9-12.

*Fogle, Richard H. *Hawthorne's Fiction: The Light and the Dark* (Norman, 1952), pp. 104-121.

*Garlitz, Barbara. "Pearl: 1850-1955," *PMLA,* LXXII (Sept., 1957), 689-699.

*Gerber, John C. "Form and Content in *The Scarlet Letter,*" *New England Quarterly,* XVII (March, 1944), 25-55.

Gerber, John C. "Introduction," *The Scarlet Letter* (New York: Modern

Library College Editions, 1950), pp. vii-xxxi. Discusses Hawthorne's distinction between novel and romance; most of the introduction is a shorter version of his "Form and Content" article. See previous item.

Gleckner, Robert F. "James' *Madame de Mauves* and Hawthorne's *Scarlet Letter*," *Modern Language Notes*, LXXII (Dec., 1958), 580-586. Interesting parallels between the two novels; most interesting is the discussion of James' criticism of Hawthorne's method in the forest scene by means of his own method in a comparable scene.

Gorman, Herbert. *Hawthorne: A Study in Solitude* (New York, 1927), pp. 83-90. Whereas Chillingworth's problem is insolvable, Hester and Dimmesdale regain the world through suffering and confession. "The air of unreality about the book is the result of careful esthetic selectivity"—almost Elizabethan in design.

Hall, Lawrence S. *Hawthorne, Critic of Society* (New Haven, 1944), pp. 163-173. Sees theme of novel as concerned with isolation of individual from society. Hester by acknowledging her guilt can face society; Dimmesdale rejects the true relationship to society that would have saved him; Pearl stands for Hester's obligation to society; and Chillingworth represents those forces which were originally designed to make harmonious life possible, but which have become so devoid of humanity that they are destructive forces instead.

Hart, John E. "*The Scarlet Letter*: One Hundred Years After," *New England Quarterly*, XXIII (Sept., 1950), 381-395. "As a way of reexamining *The Scarlet Letter*, we might read it as a symbolic action and say . . . . the attitudes and actions of the characters . . . represent different sides of [Hawthorne's] own personality." Through the characters Hawthorne explores the relationship of art to his guilt feelings about the past. To avenge his feelings by the intellect is to decay like Chillingworth; to disguise them in religion is to become hypocritical like Dimmesdale; to to rely wholly on art is to become isolated like Hester. Only by showing heart and mind freely to the world, like Pearl, can he gain release from the past.

Haugh, Robert F. "The Second Secret in *The Scarlet Letter*," *College English*, XVII (Feb., 1956), 269-271. Discusses Hester's acceptance of Chillingworth's command not to disclose his identity as a motivating and structural force in the novel.

*Hawthorne, Julian. "Problems of *The Scarlet Letter*," *Atlantic Monthly*, LVII (April, 1886), 471-485.

Hawthorne, Julian. "The Making of *The Scarlet Letter*," *Bookman*, LXXIV (Dec., 1931), 401-411. Interesting biographical information about Hawthorne during the writing of the novel. For example, Hawthorne's first child, Una, served as a model for Pearl, and the death of Hawthorne's mother cast a shadow over the writing of the novel.

Hoeltje, Hubert H. "The Writing of *The Scarlet Letter*," *New England Quarterly*, XXVII (Sept., 1954), 326-346. The fullest, most reliable account of Hawthorne's dismissal from the Salem Custom House and its effect on the novel.

Howe, Irving. "Hawthorne and American Fiction," *American Mercury*, LXVIII (March, 1949), 367-374. "In *The Scarlet Letter* Hawthorne comes into closest relationship with that center of experience he always sought. Despite all the formal disavowals with which Hawthorne surrounds her, Hester Prynne is a living creature superior to all moral codes, just as life is superior to all theories about it."

Howells, William Dean. "Hawthorne's Hester Prynne," *Heroines of Fiction* (New York, 1901), Vol. I, pp. 161-174. Hester's "transgression does not qualify her, as transgression never does unless it becomes habit. She remains exterior and superior to it. . . . what she did has become a question between her and her Maker, who apparently does not deal with it like a Puritan."

*James, Henry. *Hawthorne* (New York, 1879), pp. 102-118.

Johnson, W. Stacey. "Sin and Salvation in Hawthorne," *Hibbert Journal*, L (Oct., 1951), 39-47. Hester and Dimmesdale are degraded by their sin until they can confess it in humble honesty. Human love is redeemed when the illicit passion is no longer a barrier to human communion. There is final salvation for Dimmesdale on the scaffold, and a "regenerative experience of salvation's way for Pearl and Hester."

Lathrop, George Parsons. *A Study of Hawthorne* (Boston, 1876), pp. 210-225. Sees the novel as a "massive argument" for repentance, which is "the flinging aside of concealment." In the Puritan mode of dealing with sin, and in their belief in visible symbols, Hawthorne found the whole problem of repentance and confession bodied forth in a startlingly dramatic form.

Lawrence, D.H. "Nathaniel Hawthorne and *The Scarlet Letter*," *Studies in Classic American Literature* (New York, 1923), pp. 121-147. The novel is a disguised exploration of the demonism that lies beneath the surface of American innocence. Hester is the destructive female principle that delights in making of Dimmesdale a fallen saint ("that was her life work"). And the devil in Hester brought forth an even "purer devil in Pearl," who, having married an Italian count, will bring forth "a new brood of vipers."

Lawton, William C. *The New England Poets* (New York, 1898), pp. 82-88. Evil in the novel is not a demoniacal power, but the distortion or misuse of powers not in themselves evil; therefore, atonement is possible. Hester and Dimmesdale's love is never destroyed, only purified.

Jones, Llewellyn. "Mr. Hawthorne's *Scarlet Letter*," *Bookman*, LVIII (Jan., 1924), 622-625. Finds main strands of the novel to be psychological analysis; a Puritan disapproval of earlier Puritanism, mixed with admiration for it; and a playing with Gothic romanticism. Feels Hawthorne's moral interpolations are "unhealthily Puritan and bigoted."

Leavis, Q.D. "Hawthorne as Poet," *Sewanee Review*, LIX (Summer, 1951), 429-440. Contains many illuminating insights into Hawthorne's symbolic use of language in the novel and points out relationships between the novel and earlier stories.

Levi, Joseph. "Hawthorne's *The Scarlet Letter*: A Psychoanalytic Interpretation," *American Imago*, X (Winter, 1953), 291-306. The "plot of

The Scarlet Letter deals with the Oedipal theme. It describes the struggle of two men—one older, one younger—for the love of a woman." The novel is, moreover, a projection of Hawthorne's own Oedipus complex: Dimmesdale represents Hawthorne's own weak ego; Chillingworth his cruel superego; Pearl his id. Hester is Hawthorne's mother-ideal, a substitute for his own lack of mother love in real life.

Levin, Harry. *The Power of Blackness: Hawthorne, Poe, Melville* (New York, 1958), pp. 73-78. "Among the possible morals, the one Hawthorne selects is: 'Be true. . . .'" Dimmesdale atones for his sin with his life, Hester by her life, but Chillingworth, whose sin is intellectual pride, is beyond redemption.

*Lewis, R.W.B. *The American Adam* (Chicago, 1955), pp. 111-114.

Loring, George B. "Hawthorne's *Scarlet Letter*," *Massachusetts Quarterly Review*, III (Sept., 1850), 484-500. Puritan dogma and the society it gave rise to are the culprits in the novel. Dimmesdale, because he struggles within Calvinistic belief, struggles almost hopelessly—no good comes of his spiritual travail. But Hester, because she is cast out of the Puritan world, achieves "moral and religious excellence."

*Maclean, Hugh N. "Hawthorne's *Scarlet Letter:* 'The Dark Problem of This Life,'" *American Literature*, XXVII (March, 1955), 12-24.

*McNamara, Anne Marie. "The Character of Flame: The Function of Pearl in *The Scarlet Letter*," *American Literature*, XXVII (Jan., 1956), 537-553.

*Male, Roy R. "'From the Innermost Germ,' the Organic Principle in Hawthorne's Fiction," *ELH, A Journal of English Literary History*, XX (Sept., 1953), 218-236.

*Male, Roy R. *Hawthorne's Tragic Vision* (Austin, 1957), pp. 90-118.

Marx, Leo. "Foreword," *The Scarlet Letter* (New York: Signet Classics, 1959), pp. vii-xii. *The Scarlet Letter* "is the most economical, the most thoroughly composed and unified of our great novels." Discusses symbolic contrasts in the novel (town-forest, red-black, iron-wild) to point up the essential conflict between "restraint, order and institutional control" and "the impulsive, passional and spontaneous." But Hawthorne commits himself to neither contrast completely: "Neither Hester nor Dimmesdale has the answer. Without the other each is incomplete. . . . Hawthorne finally would have us see that as a principle the wild rose is no more adequate than iron."

*Mathews, James W. "Hawthorne and the Chain of Being," *Modern Language Quarterly*, XVIII (Dec., 1957), 282-294.

*Matthiessen, F.O. *American Renaissance* (New York, 1941), pp. 275-282.

Michaud, Regis. "How Hawthorne Exorcized Hester Prynne," *The American Novel Today* (Boston, 1928), pp. 25-46. Hawthorne's imagination, despite the conventional ending of the novel, was pagan—he really approved of the adultery. Hester and Dimmesdale "begin in anguish through the suppression of their desires, and end in happiness through their abandonment to the freed libido."

*Munger, Theodore T. "Notes on *The Scarlet Letter,*" *Atlantic Monthly,* XCIII (April, 1904), 521-535.

Pearce, Roy Harvey. "Introduction," *The Scarlet Letter* (London: Everyman's Library, 1957), pp. v-x. *The Scarlet Letter* is Hawthorne's most complex and full treatment of his major subject: the individual's discovery of his authentic self through sin, the isolation which is a consequence of that sin, and the struggle to endure which is the consequence of that isolation. Public acknowledgment of private sin is the requisite condition for survival. "Hester, Dimmesdale, Chillingworth—each can at once be understood and judged as he or she is able to measure up to this prescription. Correspondingly, the sin of each can be at once understood and judged as it constitutes a violation of the private and true self of another. The terrible irony is perhaps that the necessity of the first rises out of the inevitability of the second."

Pearson, Norman Holmes. "Introduction," *The Complete Novels and Selected Tales of Nathaniel Hawthorne* (New York: Modern Library, 1937), pp. xi-xii. The moral of the novel lies in Pearl's rebuke to her father that he was not true. Chillingworth's hidden persecution, not his desire for revenge, ruins him. Dimmesdale suffers not because he sinned, but because he confuses his conscience. Even Hester is not wholly "true," for she kept the identity of Chillingworth secret.

Rahv, Philip. "The Dark Lady of Salem," *Partisan Review,* VIII (Sept.-Oct., 1941), 362-381. Reprinted in his *Image and Idea* (Norfolk, 1949), pp. 22-41. A valuable discussion of Hawthorne's "dark ladies": Hester, Beatrice ("Rappaccini's Daughter"), Zenobia (*The Blithedale Romance*), and Miriam (*The Marble Faun*). These women are "one heroine," who dominates all the other characters because she alone personifies the "contrary values that her author attached to experience."

Reid, Alfred S. "A Note on the Date of *The Scarlet Letter,*" *Furman University Bulletin,* IV (Winter, 1957), 30-39. Hawthorne began writing the novel in October or November, 1849, rather than on June 8, 1849, as Hawthorne's son Julian asserted.

Reid, Alfred S. *The Yellow Ruff and The Scarlet Letter: A Source of Hawthorne's Novel* (Gainesville, 1955). The source is the murder of Sir Thomas Overbury in 1613. Book contains detailed analyses of parallels in plot, character, setting, and style between the novel and the printed accounts of the murder.

Reid, Alfred S., ed. *Sir Thomas Overbury's Vision (1616) by Richard Nicolls and Other English Sources of Nathaniel Hawthorne's "The Scarlet Letter"* (Gainesville, 1957). Reprints the primary documents Hawthorne used.

Ringe, Donald. "Hawthorne's Psychology of the Head and Heart," *PMLA,* LXV (March, 1950), 124-130. Puritan society is evil because "head" (thought or reason) has been separated from "heart" (passion or emotion). All of the characters, though Chillingworth least so, represent the head and heart in conflict.

Ripley, George. "*The Scarlet Letter,*" *New York Daily Tribune* (April 1, 1850), 2. Reprinted in *Littel's Living Age,* XXV (May 4, 1850), 203-207.

Discusses Hawthorne's supernatural effects, which he finds more convincing than Poe's because of Hawthorne's insight into the springs of humanity.

*Roper, Gordon. "Introduction," *The Scarlet Letter and Selected Prose Works* (New York: Hendricks House, 1949), pp. vii-xlvi.

Roper, Gordon. "The Originality of Hawthorne's *The Scarlet Letter,*" *Dalhousie Review,* XXX (April, 1950), 62-79. Hawthorne's morality "was not Calvinistic, nor was it a conventional Christian view of his Salem; it was an examination and acceptance of the darker ambiguities of life." The three main characters can best be understood as representing facets of Hawthorne's contemporary psychology; that is, Hester is heart (the quest for fulfilment through love and the family); Dimmesdale is soul (the quest for Grace); and Chillingworth is mind (the quest for intellectual truth).

Ross, E.C. "A Note on *The Scarlet Letter,*" *Modern Language Notes,* XXXVII (Jan., 1922), 58-59. Points out use of number seven in the novel. The action of the novel covers seven years to harmonize with the violation of the seventh commandment. The phrase, "seven years," occurs seventeen times in Chapters XII-XXIII.

Sampson, Edward C. "Motivation in *The Scarlet Letter,*" *American Literature,* XXVIII (Jan., 1957), 511-513. Argues against Anne Marie McNamara's assertion that Pearl is primary motivation in Dimmesdale's confession. Finds sufficient motivation in Dimmesdale's ethical sense and in his agony. Moreover, it is Hester, not Pearl, to whom he turns when he has made his decision.

*Schubert, Leland. *Hawthorne the Artist* (Chapel Hill, 1944), pp. 136-161.

*Schwartz, Joseph. "God and Man in New England," in Harold C. Gardiner, ed., *American Classics Reconsidered: A Christian Appraisal* (New York, 1958), pp. 131-133.

*Sherman, Stuart P. *Americans* (New York, 1922), pp. 122-152.

*Short, Raymond W. "Introduction," *Four Great Novels* (New York, 1946), pp. xxi-xxviii.

Stanton, Robert. "Hawthorne, Bunyan, and the American Romances," *PMLA,* LXXI (March, 1956), 155-165. Includes a discussion of the parallels between Chapters XVI-XX (the forest scene and Dimmesdale's return to town) and a section of *Pilgrim's Progress.*

*Stein, William Bysshe. *Hawthorne's Faust: A Study of the Devil's Archetype* (Gainesville, 1953), pp. 104-122.

Stewart, Randall. "The Vision of Evil in Hawthorne and Melville," in Nathan A. Scott, Jr., ed., *The Tragic Vision and the Christian Faith* (New York, 1957), pp. 245-250. The chief tension in the novel is between Romantic and Puritan impulses. Shows how this tension is rendered symbolically in the forest scene.

Stocking, David M. "An Embroidery on Dimmesdale's Scarlet Letter," *College English,* XIII (March, 1952), 336-337. Discusses the four alternatives that Hawthorne gives us for the *A* on Dimmesdale's breast. Finds that as the four explanations descend in order of probability they ascend in order of relevance to the moral issues concerned.

Stone, Edward. "The Antique Gentility of Hester Prynne," *Philological Quarterly*, XXXVI (Jan., 1957), 90-96. Discusses the theme of Old World gentility fighting a losing battle against the temper of the New World. In Hester, forgiveness, humility, and prayer struggle unsuccessfully with aristocratic stubbornness. Only in her epitaph does Hester recover her aristocratic birthright.

Trollope, Anthony. "The Genius of Nathaniel Hawthorne," *North American Review*, CXXIX (Sept., 1879), 208-213. The story is one of love and jealousy, but love is given little scope; full scope is given to the hatred that can spring from injured love. Although Dimmesdale is the greater sufferer, it is Hester who evokes our sympathy.

Van Doren, Carl. *The American Novel* (New York, 1940), pp. 65-71. Although Hawthorne begins with a Puritan conception of adultery, the broader implications of the novel transcend Puritan doctrine. Hester becomes the type "of the moving principle of life which different societies in different ways may constrain but which itself irresistibly endures."

*Van Doren, Mark. *Nathaniel Hawthorne* (New York, 1949), pp. 114-166.

Von Abele, Rudolphe. *The Death of the Artist: A Study of Hawthorne's Disintegration* (The Hague, 1955), pp. 45-57. A psychological analysis. Dimmesdale's secret guilt is related to Hawthorne's feelings about his writing. Hester's maternalism "may be a depiction of what Hawthorne did not get from his mother." "*The Scarlet Letter* can be seen . . . as a compendium of Hawthorne's problems about art, sex and society projected in terms of an historical fable."

*Von Abele, Rudolphe. "*The Scarlet Letter:* A Reading," *Accent*, XI (Autumn, 1951), 211-227.

*Waggoner, Hyatt H. *Hawthorne: A Critical Study* (Cambridge, Mass., 1955), pp. 118-150.

Waggoner, Hyatt H. "Nathaniel Hawthorne: The Cemetery, the Prison, and the Rose," *University of Kansas City Review*, XIV (Spring, 1948), 184-190. Puritan society shares Hester's guilt, but exactly how, Hawthorne does not say. In distributing his sympathies—Chillingworth is the worst sinner, Dimmesdale next, and Hester least—Hawthorne implies agreement with Catholic not Puritan doctrine. But his conclusion is only "Be true," which seems to indicate that though Hawthorne was more enlightened than the Puritans, he was unable to recapture traditional Christian values, except in the most general way.

Walcutt, Charles C. "*The Scarlet Letter* and its Modern Critics," *Nineteenth-Century Fiction*, VII (March, 1953), 251-264. Summarizes the ways in which the novel has been read: romantic, fortunate fall, orthodox, Transcendental, relativist. Finds causes for lack of critical agreement in (1) Hawthorne's symbols convey different meanings from his expository statements; (2) although orthodox by impulse, Hawthorne writes with such tenderness of Hester that it seems like justification; and (3) "although Hawthorne firmly believes sin to be permanently warping, he does not in his heart like the Providence which ordains it thus."

Warren, Austin. "Introduction," *The Scarlet Letter* (New York: Rinehart Editions, 1947), pp. v-ix. Includes some seventeenth-century analogues to the situation in the novel. In reconstructing the genesis of the novel one "can add to social and literary history conjectures concerning the psychological and speculative motives that impelled the writing." These are a sense of indirect responsibility for the death of a friend, guilt for his ancestors' persecution of Quakers and witches, and his own temptation to withdrawal—the sin of pride.

Whipple, Edwin Percy. "*The Scarlet Letter,*" *Graham's Magazine,* XXXVI (May, 1850), 345-346. An early laudatory review. Feels that the novel would have a salutary effect on any libertine that would read it. "[Hawthorne] has made the guilty parties end, not as his own fancy, or his benevolent sympathies might dictate, but as spiritual laws, lying back of all persons, dictated."

Williams, Stanley T. "Nathaniel Hawthorne," *Literary History of the United States* (Rev. Ed., New York, 1953), pp. 425-431. The novel is less a narrative than a problem discussed and rediscussed by the grouping and regrouping of characters. We are not given three characters caught in a fantastic theology, but three high minds facing universal dilemmas.

Winters, Yvor. "Maule's Curse, or Hawthorne and the Problem of Allegory," *In Defense of Reason* (New York, 1947), pp. 164-175. The novel is "pure allegory." Hester represents the repentant sinner, Dimmesdale the half-repentant sinner, and Chillingworth the unrepentant sinner.

*Woodberry, George E. *Nathaniel Hawthorne* (Boston, 1902), pp. 159-205.

Ziff, Larzer. "The Ethical Dimension of 'The Custom House,'" *Modern Language Notes,* LXXIII (May, 1958), 338-344. The fullest discussion of Hawthorne's Introduction. "The ethical formula . . . is one which characterizes the good life as a life which blends the reveries of the past with the actions of the present, which combines morality with materiality. Just as a good romance strikes a balance between the actual and the imaginary, so the man of good character strikes a balance between his inner state and the materiality of the world."